SOCIAL SCIENCE, LAW, AND PUBLIC POLICY

STUART S. NAGEL

WITH

LISA A. BIEVENUE

UNIVERSITY OF ILLINOIS

UNIVERSITY
PRESS OF
AMERICA

LANHAM • NEW YORK • LONDON

Library of Congress Cataloging-in-Publication Data
Nagel, Stuart S., 1934-
Social science, law, and public policy / Stuart S.
Nagel with Lisa A. Bievenue.
p. cm.
1. Justice, Administration of.   2. Public policy (Law)
3. Judicial process.   4. Social sciences—Methodology.
5. Decision-making—Data processing.   6. Policy sciences.
I. Bievenue, Lisa A.   II. Title.
K2100.N335   1992   300—dc20   91-27808 CIP

ISBN 0-8191-8428-4 (cloth, alk. paper)
ISBN 0-8191-8429-2 (pbk., alk. paper)

 The paper used in this publication meets the minimum requirements of
American National Standard for Information Sciences—Permanence
of Paper for Printed Library Materials, ANSI Z39.48–1984.

Dedicated to Joyce Nagel
for her perseverance through
the behavioralism of the 60s,
the policy relevance of the 70s,
the software revolution of the 80s,
and whatever the future brings

ABSTRACT OF THE BOOK ON
SOCIAL SCIENCE, LAW AND PUBLIC POLICY

This book provides a grand sweep of the relations among social science, law, and public policy over the past 30 years. The emphasis is on three stages in social science development. They include establishing relationships, optimizing of decisions, and multi-criteria decision-making with decision-aiding software. The applications are in law, public policy, and other substantive aspects of social science. The book provides an integration of the behavioralism of the 60s, the policy relevance of the 70s, and the software revolution of the 80s.

For each time period there were important methodology and substantive developments in the integration of law, policy, and social science.

1. In the 1960s, methods moved from being highly verbal to being highly quantitative. Substance moved from describing the legal system and government structures to evaluating ways of improving the legal and political process.
2. In the 1970s, methods moved from the quantitative correlation of variables to the quantitative optimization of objective functions. Substance moved from evaluating the process to evaluating the outputs.
3. In the 1980s, methods moved from deducing predictions and prescriptions from facts and values to subjecting such deductions to more what-if analysis with a great multiplicity of goals and alternatives. Substance moved from liberalism versus conservatism to a greater concern for pluralism, pragmatism, and mutually beneficial solutions.

Some of the underlying goals beneath those developments include obtaining (1) knowledge from empirical sources, (2) useful knowledge, (3) causal explanations, (4) improved quality of life, (5) technological innovation, (6) encouragement of socially desired behavior, and (7) still higher goals.

SUMMARY TABLE OF CONTENTS

PREFACE

This book provides a grand sweep of the relations among social science, law, and public policy over the past 30 years. The emphasis is on three stages in social science development. They include establishing relationships, optimizing of decisions, and multi-criteria decision-making with decision-aiding software. The applications are in law, public policy, and other substantive aspects of social science. The book provides an integration of the behavioralism of the 60s, the policy relevance of the 70s, and the software revolution of the 80s.

THE CHRONOLOGICAL DEVELOPMENT

The *1960s* were revolutionary years in American and world social science, especially political science. *Methodology* moved from being highly verbal (with an emphasis on philosophy, history, and journalism) to being highly quantitative (with an emphasis on statistics, mathematics, and economic analysis). The most relevant research tools changed from the card catalog at the library to the cross-tabulation table, the regression equation, and survey research.

The *substance* emphasis was on explaining variance, especially in why people have different behaviors, decisions, and attitudes. The most relevant decisions for political scientists were those of voters, legislators, administrators, and judges. The latter half of the 1960s began to see a concern for applying such methods to improving the political and legal process. That concern was partly prompted by the Vietnam War, the war on poverty, the civil rights struggles, women's liberation, the environmental movement, and other concerns for public policy problems. The studies then began to talk in terms of how to improve scientifically the decision-making processes of voters, legislators, administrators, and judges.

In the *1970s*, the *methods* and the substance again changed. On quantitative methodology, social scientists who were concerned with improving institutions began to look toward methodologies that related to prescription and evaluation, as well as prediction and explanation. The new tools related to concepts like benefit-cost analysis, payoff matrices, decision trees, calculus optimization, linear programming, and time optimization models. There was increased talk about optimum choice, public choice, allocation logic, and related subjects.

The *substance* changes began looking more at the substance of public policy, rather than just describing or improving the process. Substance meant economic, social, technological, political, and legal policy problems. The approach, however, was not speculative philosophy, descriptive history, or legalistic analysis, but rather an approach that talked in terms of which policies could most achieve given goals.

In the *1980s*, microcomputers and spreadsheet software greatly changed the *methodology* of social science designed to improve law and public policy. The microcomputer stimulated creativity by allowing users to experiment with varieties of what-if analysis which mainframe computers could not handle so easily. At the same time, there was a movement away from the methods associated with single objective functions toward methods associated with multiple criteria decision-making. Such methods worked well with the new spreadsheet software. Lots of goals could be shown on the columns, alternatives available for achieving them on the rows, relation scores in the cells, overall totals for each alternative at the far right, and an ability to determine what it would take to bring a second-place or other-place alternative up to first place.

In the late 1980s, there was also a shift in policy *substance* away from the traditional liberal versus conservative dichotomy. The move was toward the creative development of alternatives that might be simultaneously capable of achieving liberal and conservative goals more so than the original liberal and conservative alternatives. This new orientation was bipartisan in including supply-side economics, industrial policy. and a variety of expanded-pie thinkers. There was an increasing emphasis on pluralism in political matters, pragmatism in economic matters, and the use of positive incentives to encourage socially desired behavior.

Looking into *the 90s* to see where we might be going, some policy analysts are predicting and advocating the idea of super-optimum solutions, where all sides in traditional policy and legal conflicts can come out ahead of their original best expectations. An example is the American national debt. Traditional conservatives argue the need to cut domestic spending. Traditional liberals argue the need to cut defense spending. They may reluctantly compromise by cutting both, and even by raising some taxes. The new expansionist thinkers look for multiple ways to increase the gross national product so there can be increased revenue even with a constant tax rate and without cutting needed expenditures. The future looks good for creative thinkers, systematic policy analysts, and insightful futures researchers.

SOME UNDERLYING PRINCIPLES

Beneath these developments are certain underlying principles such as:

1. Knowledge can be best obtained by observing reality, consulting other people's observations, or deducing from observations, as contrasted to knowledge through intuition, revelation, or other non-empirical or non-scientific sources.
2. Knowledge should be useful, rather than knowledge for knowledge's sake, and one of the highest forms of usefulness is in improving public policy.
3. It is important to be able to explain cause-and-effect relations, especially where causes are alternative public policies, and the effects are societal goals or social indicators.
4. It is important to think positively about the potential of innovative ideas for dealing with policy problems, but only in the sense that hard work will pay off in developing and implementing those ideas, rather than in the sense that progress is inevitable.
5. Technological innovation and diffusion is especially important for increasing the quality of life. Such developments, however, can be substantially facilitated by appropriate public policy incentives.
6. The essence of public policy may be to encourage socially desired behavior in all fields of activity. Law is especially important in that regard by clarifying the kind of behaviors that are considered socially desired, and clarifying the rewards for complying and the penalties for not complying.
7. It is desirable to seek higher goals including making public policy more effective, efficient, equitable, participatory, predictable, procedurally fair, and constitutionally, politically, and administratively feasible. Those are the three E's associated with economics, the three P's associated with political science, and the three F's associated with law, politics, and public administration.

BASIC CONCEPTS

The title of this book contains three basic concepts. "Social science" substance refers to knowledge about the interaction of human beings, especially in the context of political, economic, social, and other institutions. Social science methods traditionally refer to developing hypotheses about relations between variables that deal with social science substance, and then testing the hypotheses on an appropriate sample of persons, places, or things using reasonably objective, empirical measures.

"Law" substance refers to knowledge about prescriptions of human behavior that come from governmental institutions and that are backed by positive or negative sanctions. Law methods traditionally refer to inductive reasoning from cases to legal generalizations, or deductive reasoning from legal rules and facts to predicted judicial decisions.

"Policy" substance refers to knowledge about why laws or other governmental decisions get adopted, what effects they have, and what laws or other governmental decisions should be adopted in order to achieve given effects. Policy evaluation methods refer to processing a set of goals to be achieved, alternatives available for achieving them, and relations between goals and alternatives in order to arrive at the best alternative, combination, allocation, or predictive decision-rule.

PREVIOUS BOOKS

This book builds on a number of previous books by the same author mainly including the following:

1. On establishing relations in legal matters, see *Causation, Prediction, and Legal Analysis* (Greenwood-Quorum, 1986).
2. On optimizing in legal matters, see *Law, Policy, and Optimizing Analysis* (Greenwood-Quorum, 1986).
3. On MCDM applied to law, see *Decision-Aiding Software and Legal Decision-Making* (Greenwood-Quorum, 1989).
4. On establishing relations in public policy matters, see *Policy Analysis: In Social Science Research* (Sage, 1979, and University Press of America, 19881.
5. On optimizing in public policy matters, see *Policy Evaluation: Making Optimum Decisions* (Praeger, 1982).
6. On MCDM applied to public policy, see *Super-Optimum Decisions in*

Public Controversies (Forthcoming).

The present book differs from the previous books mainly by integrating the previous ideas into a coherent whole. It also differs from each book individually by emphasizing the more general principles, rather than the case studies. The present book is especially concerned with seeing the big picture regarding relations among social science, law, and public policy, both in terms of methods and substance. It primarily emphasizes methods since they tend to have broader applicability than the more time-bound aspects of the substance of law and public policy.

ACKNOWLEDGEMENTS

There are many acknowledgments appropriate to this book since the book combines the *behavioralism of the 60s*, the policy relevance of the 70s, and the software revolution of the 80s. The individuals who have had the most influence in stimulating my involvement in behavioral methods applied to law and public policy especially include members of the behaviorally-oriented faculty in the graduate political science program at Northwestern University. They include Richard Snyder, Harold Guetzkow, and Victor Rosenblum. Also deserving mention are such relevant people in my early years of teaching at the University of Illinois as Charles Hagen and Jack Peltason, and such funding sources as the Social Science Research Council, American Council of Learned Societies, Center for Advanced Study in the Behavioral Sciences, and the Russell Sage Foundation.

My involvement in *policy-relevant activities of the 70s* owes considerable credit to the people who provided me with opportunities to become involved in applied political science. That includes people associated with hiring and task assignments within the United States Senate Judiciary Committee, the Legal Services Corporation, and the National Institute of Justice. Special credit is owed to those who helped found the Policy Studies Organization including Robert Lane, Thomas Dye, Duncan MacRae, David Easton, and others. Credit should also be given to Marion Neef for co-authoring a number of policy-relevant books and articles in the 1970's. Also such funding sources as the Ford Foundation, the National Science Foundation, and numerous government agencies who supported PSO-related research. Also such book publishers as Dorsey Press, Sage Publications, and Lexington Books.

As for the *software revolution of the 1980s*, I owe a debt of gratitude to the insightful software skills of David Garson of North Carolina State University and John Long of the University of Illinois. I am also grateful to the American Law Institute and the American Society for Public Administration for providing opportunities to present decision-aiding software as part of their training programs. Credit should also be given to Miriam Mills for co-authoring a number of software relevant books and articles in the 1980s. Also such book publishers as JAI Press, Greenwood-Praeger-Quorum Press, and Macmillan Press.

There have been two sets of people to whom acknowledgements are owed who cut *across all three time periods*. One set relates to the University of Illinois as an inspirational employer. That includes chairs of the Political Science Department, beginning with Charlie Hagen in the early 1960s and continuing through Murray Edelman, Neil Garvey, Victor Thompson, Phil Moneypenny, Ed Kolodziej, Dick Merritt, Roger Kanet, and George Yu. The other set relates to inspirational relatives including my mother, father, daughter Brenda, son Robert, and wife Joyce. My parents have been instrumental in my development prior to the 1960s. My wife and children have been especially involved in our family enterprise of applying social science to the understanding and development of law and public policy.

DETAILED TABLE OF CONTENTS

LIST OF TABLES

PART ONE:

THE SOCIAL SCIENCE OF ESTABLISHING RELATIONS

SECTION A:

THE LEGAL PROCESS FROM A BEHAVIORAL PERSPECTIVE

1

A CONCEPTUAL SCHEME OF
THE LEGAL PROCESS

Systematic conceptual schemes have been devised for analyzing psychological,[1] sociological,[2] and political[3] phenomena. These schemes reveal gaps in the literature and thereby generate hypotheses as did Mendelyev's periodic table of chemical elements. They also provide categories for integrating empirically tested propositions. It is the purpose of this short chapter to present a modest conceptual scheme of the legal process.

THE SCHEME

Legal policies represent the heart of the legal process. Such policies may be made by judicial, legislative, or administrative policymakers. They may

---

[1]*Handbook of Social Psychology*, 257-58 (G. Lindzey, ed., 1954). Some of the citations in the footnotes to this book do not show the name of the publisher, or sometimes they do not show the city of publication. See the Bibliography at the end of this book for the complete citations to all the books and articles cited.

[2]*Theories of Society* (T. Parsons, et al., eds., 1961).

[3]*Approaches to the Study of Politics* (R. Young, ed., 1958).

involve substance or procedure and any field of public law (government-to-citizenship and government-to-government relations) or private law (citizen-to-citizen relations). They may represent a response to prior stimuli, or they may represent stimuli to subsequent responses.

LEGAL POLICIES AS RESPONSES

The prior stimuli that bring about legal policies consist of normative standards of right and wrong and of empirical facts. The normative standards consist of legal norms promulgated by governmental bodies and nonlegal norms that are not so promulgated. The legal norms are embodied in constitutions, statutes, administrative regulations, judge-made law, and administrative adjudications depending on the nature of the promulgating governmental body. The nonlegal norms are embodied in customs of the populace, in scholarly commentaries, and in recorded notions of justice and social utility.

The empirical facts, which also serve as stimuli to legal-policy responses, consist of evidentiary facts (which according to the norms can or should be considered in reaching decisions) and nonevidentiary facts (which the norms do not deem relevant but which do empirically correlate with differential outcomes). The evidentiary facts consist of admissible testimony by laymen and experts, and admissible physical evidence. The nonevidentiary facts (some of which may be evidentiary in some instances) consist of the time when the policymaking occurs, the place where it occurs, and the status and other normatively irrelevant characteristics of the parties (both formal parties and behind-the-scene parties) and their pleaders (court counsel and legislative lobbyists).

The normative standards and empirical facts are filtered through the policymakers before policy response results. The policymakers thus correspond to the organisms in stimulus-response theory. Two aspects of the policymakers are particularly relevant in determining how the standards and facts will be perceived and weighed. One is the characteristics of the individual policymakers, and the other is the interaction among the policymakers. Relevant individual characteristics have to do with recruitment (e.g., elected, appointed), education (e.g., preschool socialization, college training), group affiliations (e.g., political party, ethnic), demographic statuses (e.g., age, birthplace), and acquired attitudes (e.g., liberalism, dogmatism). Relevant forms of interaction have to do with relations of attraction-repulsion (e.g., friendship, respect) and relations of leadership-followship (e.g., formal, informal).

6

The stimuli being channeled through the policymakers lead to a policy, but the policy can also have a feedback effect on the stimuli, since the new policy is likely to become part of the growing, changing body of normative standards for future policymaking.

LEGAL POLICIES AS STIMULI

The policy so made also becomes (along with other reinforcing and conflicting policies) a stimulus toward subsequent compliance responses. Degrees of compliance and noncompliance are stimulated not only by the policy and related policies but also by various facilitating and inhibiting factors. These factors may be natural or social. The natural factors relate to physical phenomena such as geological changes (which might affect land ownership) and to biological phenomena such as sexual drives (which might affect compliance to family or criminal laws). The social factors relate to economic, political, religious, educational, familial, linguistic (including communication media), and aesthetic phenomena, each one of which can in some instances influence the impact of legal policies.

The policy and these factors feed through a set of policy appliers and policy recipients. The policy appliers generally consist of administrators and judges, but they may also consist of legislators writing statutes designed to implement a broader policy. Administrators, like judges, in some circumstances also may be important policymakers whose policies are applied by other administrators. The policy recipients consist of the total public, or some segment within it that is ultimately affected by the policy. The characteristics and interaction of the policy appliers and recipients (like those of the policymakers) affect their differential response.

The policy effects represent the response to the stimulus provided by the policy, the facilitating and inhibiting factors, and the filtering of the policy appliers and recipients. The policy effects may manifest themselves in behavioral or attitudinal change, or in lack of change. Sometimes, one can infer attitudes from observed or recorded behavior, but frequently it is necessary to question the attitude holders themselves. The behavioral and attitudinal effects may relate to the goals expressed in the policy or to side effects.

Thus, if the policy is "no admissibility of illegally seized evidence" then the most relevant policy appliers would be police, prosecutors, and trial court judges, while criminals and law-abiding citizens would be the main policy recipients. The desired goals of such a policy would probably be a decrease in illegal searches (a behavioral effect) and thus an increase in public attitudes of security from arbitrary search (an attitudinal effect), without substantially increasing criminality (a behavioral effect) or lowering police morale (an attitudinal effect). Possible side effect (not likely to be mentioned as part of the goals of the policy) might include the simplification of search warrant procedures, the broadening of the concept of legal search, and perhaps increased friction between prosecutors and police over police tactics.

Like the response of the policymakers, the response of the policy appliers and the policy recipients has a feedback effect. It feeds back on the policy in that noncompliance or adverse effects may result in changing the policy, while high compliance and beneficial effects may result in broadening the policy. The policy effects also lead back on the facilitating or inhibiting factors in such a way as to strengthen or weaken them, depending on the circumstances involved.

This scheme can be made clearer with the aid of conceptual boxes, connective horizontal lines, subordinate vertical lines, and causal arrows (see Table 1-1). What is especially needed in legal research are more empirically tested propositions to provide details on the more specific nature of the interrelations shown by the arrows running along and through the primary concepts. A perusal of legal research literature reveals a particular lack of propositions with regard to the relation between (1) the presence or absence of various nonevidentiary facts and (2) alternative policy outcomes, and also between (1) the presence or absence of alternative policies and (2) differential attitudes and behaviors of policy recipients. In addition to empirical testing, there is need for more hard thinking about the meaning and elaboration of the categories and subcategories which belong in such a conceptual scheme.

AN APPLICATION

To illustrate the scheme presented, one may very briefly try to apply it to the legal policy of school desegregation enunciated in Brown v. Board of Education, 347 U.S. 483 (1954). This policy represented a response to certain normative standards and empirical facts being filtered through the Supreme Court policymakers. The normative standards of a legal nature include the relevant precedents which ordered desegregation on narrower grounds such as Missouri ex rel. *Gaines v. Canada*, 305 U.S. 337 (1938) (equal protection violated by subsidizing blacks to attend out-of-state schools), and *Sweatt v. Painter*, 339 U.S. 629 (195) (equal protection violated by the intangible

TABLE 1-1. A CONCEPTUAL SCHEME OF THE LEGAL PROCESS

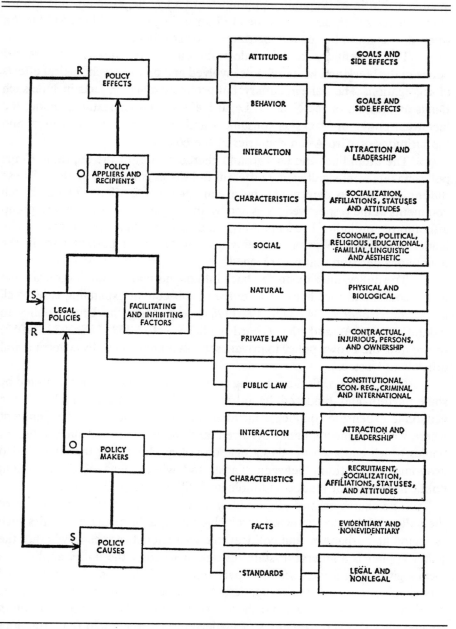

NOTE: See the text for concepts beneath the thrid level of subordination.

differences between black and white law schools). The nonlegal norms include a shift in white public opinion toward a less negative attitude toward blacks than was present at the time of *Plessy v. Ferguson*, 163 U.S. 537 (1896), when the separate but equal doctrine was established.

The evidentiary facts include testimony on the physical differences between the black and white schools involved and on the psychological effects of segregation. The nonevidentiary, but probably relevant, facts include such things as the role of the NAACP Legal Defense and Educational Fund, the increased power of blacks as consumers and as Northern-urban voters, and the attitudes of Afro-Asian countries in the cold war.

The attitudinal and background characteristics of the Supreme Court policymakers were significantly different in 1954 as compared to 1896. These differences can be determined by a content analysis of the off-the-bench comments of the respective judges and by an analysis of their respective group affiliations, prejudicial occupations, and presidential appointers. The leadership of Earl Warren probably also played an important part in the unanimous decision that was reached.

The policy, once made, fed back into the normative standards available to the courts and thus became a source of subsequent expanding cases such as *Bolling v. Sharpe*, 347 U.S. 497 (1954) (expanding the Brown policy to federal territory), and the Girard College case, 353 U.S. 922 (1957) (expanding the Brown policy to private schools administered by governmental officials as trustees).

Compliance with the resulting constitutional policies was facilitated by some factors and hindered by others. Facilitating factors included the economic expense of duplicate facilities, the loss of industrial development where violent noncompliance occurred, and the influence of many religious bodies which endorsed the desegregation policy. Inhibiting factors included economic competition between blacks and whites, fear of the potential political strength of blacks, and biological differences in skin color.

The characteristics of the policy appliers have affected the impact of the policy. Relevant characteristics include geographical characteristics such as region and urbanism, and political role characteristics such as whether the policy applier is a federal or state official, or whether the policy applier is a local legislator or a local school superintendent. Relations of attraction and repulsion among the policy appliers have affected implementation (e.g., relations between certain northern congressmen and certain southern congressmen), as have relations of leadership and followship (e.g., relations between Senator Byrd and the state officials in the Virginia government.

Likewise, the characteristic of the policy recipients have partially determined the differential impact of the policy on them. Characteristics like race, region, urbanism, age, and class account for some people's having been effected differently than other people by the desegregation policy.

The policy enunciated in *Brown v. Board of Education* has had many effects. The behavioral goal of the policy was to remove race as a consideration in determining which public school a schoolchild could attend. The degree to which this goal has been achieved and measured by determining the percent of school districts that are integrated, using as a percentage base only those school districts that have some schoolage black children and some schoolage white children. The degree of this type of goal achievement can also be measured by determining the percent of black school children who attend schools with whites and the percent of white schoolchildren who attend schools with blacks, again using only school districts that have biracial populations. Other behavioral side effects that may be attributed to the Brown decision include the partial breakdown of the practice of segregation in non-education activities, such as housing and employment, and the anti-segregation demonstrations that Brown has indirectly inspired.

The attitudinal goal of the school desegregation policy was to lessen the feelings of black inferiority, which common sense and social science evidence tended to indicate was partially a result of school segregation. Psychological depth studies of black schoolchildren could be made before and after various communities desegregate their schools, using similar non-desegregating communities as a control group. One may hypothesize that, in the desegregating communities, one will find an increase in optimism and possibly ambition on the part of both the blacks who go to the white schools and also the blacks who remain in the black schools. Other attitudinal side effects include the changed attitudes one may find on the part of whites toward blacks and on the part of Afro-Asians toward American foreign policy.

The effects of the desegregation policy have already had some feedback effects on related policies and on the facilitating and inhibiting factors. Related policies that have been partially stimulated by the effects include the Civil Rights Act of 1957 and 1960, and such court precedents as *Cooner v. Aaron*. 358 U.S. 1 (1958) (reaction to the Little Rock violence), and *Watson v. City of Memphis*, 373 U.S. 526 (1963) (reaction to the slowness of desegregation). Facilitating factors that have been strengthened by the effects include the attitude of the Catholic church and other religious bodies, and inhibiting factors that have been weakened include the resistance of lower federal court judges and other political officials.

The above application could have been elaborated in more detail. As mentioned above, however, what seems to be needed in applying the conceptual scheme to a legal policy or a set of legal policies or decisions is not only further hypothesizing but also systematic empirical testing (through questionnaires, content analysis, and statistical techniques) of the explicit and implicit hypotheses that the conceptual scheme may lead one to formulate.[4]

---

[4]Recent books dealing with conceptual schemes of reality, society, government, and law include Jacques Richardson (ed.), *Models of Reality: Shaping Thought and Action* (Lomond Books, 1984); Arthur Stinchcombe, *Constructing Social Theories* (Harcourt, 1968); David Easton, *The Analysis of Political Structure* (Routledge, 1990); William Evan, *Social Structure and Law: Theoretical and Empirical Perspectives* (Sage, 1990); Gordon Tullock, *Trials on Trial: The Pure Theory of Legal Procedure* (Columbia University Press, 1980); and Don Gottfredson and Michael Tonry (eds.), *Prediction and Classification: Criminal Justice Decision Making* (University of Chicago Press, 1987).

2

TESTING EMPIRICAL GENERALIZATIONS IN LEGAL RESEARCH

Social scientists for many years have been testing empirical generalizations in their respective disciplines.[1] Some of their techniques are beginning to trickle into the legal journals at an increasing rate.[2] The legal research that has thus far used such techniques, however, has largely been done by social scientists rather than by legal scholars.[3] It is the purpose of this chapter to describe briefly some of the techniques involved in systematically testing empirical generalizations, in the hope that increased understanding will

---

[1] The standard textbooks on general social science methodology include W. Goode & P. Hatt, *Methods in Social Research* (1952); C. Selltiz et al., *Research Methods in Social Relations* (1959); T. McCormick & R. Francis, *Methods of Research in the Behavioral Sciences* (1958); and G. Lindzey (ed.), *Handbook of Social Psychology* 259-561 (1954). These textbooks elaborate many of the points made in this paper.

[2] See, e.g., Tanenhaus, "Supreme Court Attitudes toward Federal Administrative Agencies: Application of Social Science Methods to the Study of the Judicial Process," 14 *Vanderbilt Law Review* 473 (1961); Zeisel, Kalven, & Bucholz, "Is the Trial Bar a Cause of Delay?" 43 *J. Am. Jud. Soc'y* 17 (1959); Ulmer, "An Empirical Analysis of Selected Aspects of Lawmaking of the United States Supreme Court," 8 *J. Pub. L.* 414 (1959); Barton & Medlovitz, "The Experience of Injustice as a Research Problem," 13 *J. Legal Ed.* 24 (1960); and Nagel, "Judicial Backgrounds and Criminal Cases," 53 *J. Crim. L., C. & P.S.* 333 (1962) (Chap. 18, infra).

[3] See Jones, "Some Current Trends in Legal Research," 15 *J. Legal Ed.* 121 (1962).

stimulate more law school schools to apply them.[4]

Basically, the steps involved in empirically testing generalizations are approximately as follows: (1) decide on a general topic; (2) review the relevant prior literature; (3) decide which hypotheses to test; (4) decide on the research design to make the tests; (5) compile the data in accordance with the research design; (6) draw conclusions from the data in accordance with the research design; and (7) offer explanations for one's findings. One can, however, reconsult the relevant literature or reformulate the hypotheses or research design out of the sequence presented.

The most technical step is the research design. It involves determining the sample of entitles on which to test the hypotheses, determining the method of measuring the relevant variables, and especially determining what analysis of the data will be used to indicate whether the hypotheses have been confirmed or refuted. In order to clarify what is involved each of the testing steps and each of the aspects of the research design need to be discussed in more detail and with legal research examples.

THE STEPS

CHOOSING THE TOPIC AND REVIEWING THE LITERATURE

Between alternative topics for research, the better topic is the one that has the greater social or legislative benefit, or at least the greater theoretical significance. Topics that are more likely to lead to findings that will generate other studies are more worthwhile than topics that have less heuristic value. The better topic, of course, is also the one that is more controversial and that has been less adequately researched previously. It is also the one that is more easily researched, given the limited time, expertise, interests, funds, and other resources of the researcher. Ease of research, however, should not be a significant consideration unless the other criteria of social utility, heuristic value, and prior inadequacy are also met.

---

[4]For a defense of the desirability of applying the general scientific method to legal research (as contrasted to a clarification of some of the techniques involved) see Loevinger, "Jurimetrics: Science and Prediction in the Field of Law," 46 *Minn. L. Rev.* 255 (1961); H. Cairns, *The Theory of Legal Science* (1941); and Cohen, "Transcendental Nonsense and the Functional Approach," 35 *Colum. L. Rev.* 809 (1935).

After a topic has been chosen, one should make an extensive search of the relevant literature in order to avoid wasteful duplication and in order to obtain useful ideas for the hypotheses and the research design. In addition to consulting the traditional legal indexing tools (such as the Index to Legal Periodicals and the various tools for finding relevant cases), a search should also be made of the indexes likely to reveal relevant social science material, such as the International Index to Periodical Literature and the Cumulative Book Index.

FORMULATING THE HYPOTHESES

After deciding on a general topic and reviewing the literature, at least one hypothesis or tentative conclusion should be formulated. The most interesting kind of hypothesis are those that indicate a relationship between the two or more variables. A one-variable hypothesis merely indicates the degree to which one variable is present among a set of entities (e.g., the percent of contested wills among the wills probated before a given court in a given year). A two-variable hypothesis says, in effect, "If I know X is present, then I can generally predict that Y will be present. In this context, X is called the independent variable (the thing used to predict), and Y is called the dependent variable (the thing predicted). One usually cannot substitute "always" for "generally", in social science research because, unlike the chemist and physicist, the socials scientist cannot consistently eliminate or control other variables that may interfere with the relation. Unless the hypothesis specifies otherwise, no causal relationships are assumed between the variables, although frequently the independent variable is a cause (or something related to a cause) of the dependent variable.

The independent variable of a hypothesis may refer to an element in an adjudication (e.g., an element relating to the evidence, the personnel, the place, or the time period, and the dependent variable may refer to a case outcome (e.g., decision for the defendant, decision within a short time from initiation of the case, or amount of damages awarded). The independent variable may also refer to a type of law (e.g., one that provides for relatively easy divorce, one that provides for a state income tax, or one that provides for capital punishment), and the dependent variable may refer to a characteristic of a geographical area (e.g., the number of divorces per 1,000 population, the state's gross economic product, of the number of murders per 1,000 population). In fact, the variables can refer to almost anything, although in order to keep the hypothesis within the field of law, at least one of the variables must refer to some legal phenomenon.

A meaningful empirical hypothesis is one that is potentially capable of being proved or disproved through observation or through the examination of someone else's observations (e.g., the observations of a court reporter who records judicial voting behavior).   A hypothesis that is true or false by definition is not an empirical hypothesis (e.g., "If a society uses the interrogatory system of adjudication, then its judges will take an active part in the trial process.").   Likewise, a hypothesis is nonempirical if it is normative or policy-oriented without providing reasonably objective criteria of the goals sought (e.g., "Where X law has been adopted, the results have been good."). If such criteria are provided, however, the hypothesis may be empirically testable (e.g., "Where X law or analogous laws have been adopted, the amount of disparity in sentences for similar crimes from judge to judge has been reduced.").

SAMPLING THE ENTITIES

After a hypothesis has been formulated, one must decide which entities to sample in order to test the hypothesis.   The nature of the hypothesis will, in part, indicate the entities to be used.   The entities may consist all the northern states that have or have not adopted certain legislation, all the cases heard by the Supreme Court in 1958, or all the justices of the peace serving in Ohio between 1930 and 1935.   They may also consist of time periods before and after an event, lawyers, courts, votes, legislators, occurrences, pressure groups, countries, or any other entities relevant to the hypothesis.

In addition to relevancy, the type of entity chosen should be a type on which data is accessible.   The study, however, should address itself to how the findings might have differed if a different type of relevant entity were used. This may involve reasoning from analogy or from small unrepresentative samples of alternative entities.   Thus, a hypothesis about American judges may be meaningfully tested mainly on appellate judges if one is rationally capable of indicating whether the relations observed between the variables should be stronger, weaker, or about the same with trial court judges, given the relevant differences between trial and appellate court judges.

After the type of entity has been decided, the specific entities on which data will be compiled must be determined.   One can sometimes compile data on all the entities within the type.   If this number is too large to be manageable, however, and there is no meaningful way to limit the entities to a narrower time period, geographic region, or the like, then random sampling may be used to limit the size of the sample. Random sampling involves giving a numerical designation to all the entities that potentially could come into the sample. For instance, one number might be assigned to each case in a set of 1,000 cases; or each case might be given a number in terms of the page, column, and number of inches from the top of the page on which the case appears if the names are already in some form of a list, such as the cases in one of the decennial digests of the American Digest system. Then one can draw as many random numbers out of a list of random numbers as one needs to fill his sample quota. Lists of random numbers can be found in many textbooks on statistical techniques.[5]

MEASURING THE VARIABLES

The next step in the research design is to determine how the variables are to be measured or, in other words, how the entities are to be positioned on each of the variables. For example, if one has a hypothesis dealing with the political party affiliation of judges, this step will involve deciding whether certain minor parties should be grouped with the Democrats, the Republicans, or neither. It will also involve determining what sources will be consulted to find the party affiliation of the judges.

If one has a hypothesis about the effect of a statute (e.g., a statute establishing a public-defender system) or a judge-made law (e.g., the exclusionary rule as applied to illegally seized evidence), the measurement step may involve preparing a meaningful questionnaire or observation checkoff list and deciding how it is going to be administered. Questions can sometimes be used from standardized questionnaires to determine certain background characteristics, attitudes, and abilities, but most of the questions will probably have to be original. The items can be structured so that the respondent must check off or otherwise choose between the alternative responses that are provided (e.g., agree or disagree); or they can be open-ended, where one seeks more extended answers or descriptions. The questionnaire can be administered by mail or by competent interviewers. Mailing is less costly, but it generally brings a lower response (although sometimes a more frank response) than personal interviews do. Mailed questionnaires are most effective when accompanied by an explanatory letter

---

[5]For an example of a random numbers table and a description of how to use one in drawing samples, see H. Walker & J. Lev, *Statistical Inference* 126, 171-173, 484 (1953).

and a return envelope, and followed by a reminder letter.[7]

Sometimes, a controlled behavioral index can be used in order to position the entities on a variable instead of, or in addition to, analyzing the subjective views of the participants. For instance, in order to determine how states's rights-oriented various Supreme Court judges are relative to one another, one might give each judge a score representing the difference between (1) the percentage of state statutes he upheld that expanded economic regulation, and (2) the percentage of federal statutes he upheld that also expanded economic regulation. Likewise, one might determine how powerful various pressure groups are before the Supreme Court by giving each pressure group a score that represents the difference between (1) the group when it provided counsel or an amicus curiae brief, and (2) the percentage of victories for the pressure groups position in similar cases in which it did not participate, provided there were at least a few of both types of cases. In a similar manner, one could possibly measure the amount of courtroom discrimination against blacks from one period to another by giving each period a group of scores, each of which would represent the difference between (1) the average sentence received by black defendants, and (2) the average sentence received by white defendants committing a similar type of crime, with a different such score for each type of crime.[8]

PLANNING THE ANALYSIS

The research design should systematically plan how the data compiled will be analyzed to determine whether or not the hypothesis has been confirmed. A basic social science tool for analyzing data relevant to a two-variable hypothesis is the fourfold table. A fourfold table has the form shown in Table 2-1. The cell labeled a should show the number of entities that have a negative position on the independent variable and a positive position on the dependent variable. Likewise, cell b should show the number of entities that have a negative position on the dependent variable. And so on with cells c and d. If neither of the positions on a variable are negative (less affirmative)

---

[7]For further details on conducting a survey, see M. Parten, *Surveys, Polls, and Samples: Practical Procedures* (1950).

[8]For more complex aspects of measuring variables (including factor analysis and Thurstone, Guttman, and Likert scales), some of which may occasionally be applicable to testing empirical relationships in legal research, see J. Guilford, *Psychometric Methods* (1954).

TABLE 2-1.   A FOURFOLD TABLE

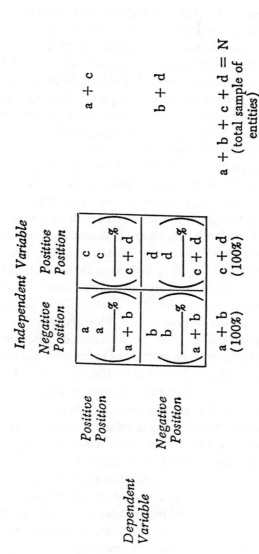

or positive (more affirmative), then the positions should be placed in such a way that a concentration of entities in cells b and c confirm rather than refute the hypothesis being tested. Cell a should also show the percentile of entities in the negative group on the independent variable that were in the positive group on the dependent variable, and so on with cells b, c, and d. The percentages in cells a and b add down to 100 per cent, as do the percentages in cells c and d. Decimal points should be eliminated from these percentages, since they are unnecessary and confusing in this context.

If the percentage in cell c is greater than the percentage in cell a, then there is a direct or positive correlation between the independent variable and the dependent variable. If the percentage in cell c is the same as the percentage in cell a, then there is a zero correlation. On the other hand, if the percentage in cell c is less than the percentage in cell a, then there is an inverse or negative correlation between the two variables.

A fourfold table provides only two positions for each variable--for example, being high or low on a self-restraint variable, or relatively effective or relatively ineffective on an effectiveness variable. For most empirical legal research, two positions on each variable are adequate. If, however, one of the variables provides for three positions, then one could use a three-by-two or a two-by-three table, with six cells, rather than a two-by-two table, with four cells. In other words, the number of cells in an expanded fourfold table equals the number of positions or intervals provided for on the independent variable times the number of positions or intervals provided for on the dependent variable. The method of calculating percentages downward is still the same as in the basic fourfold table; and just as in the fourfold table, one compares the percentages toward the right side of the larger table with those toward the left side to determine the direction of the correlation. If the percentages on the far left are relatively low, however, and the percentages in the middle are high, and the percentages on the right are also low (or vice versa), then a curvilinear correlation is present.

One can plan to compile the data on index cards, and then sort and count the cards to fill in the cells of the fourfold table. If the number of entities or the number of interrelated variables becomes large, however, this method of transcribing the data from the source material to the fourfold or comparable tables becomes extremely cumbersome. In such circumstances, it is advisable to compile the data on IBM cards. Each IBM card corresponds to a different entity (unless the quantity of 10 numbers (0 through 9) corresponds to a variable (unless more than 10 positions are provided for on a variable). Thus, a punch in position 1 on column 57 might indicate that the criminal case represented by the card was decided in favor of the prosecution; and a punch in position 2 on column 57 might indicate that the case was decided in favor of the defense.

In using IBM cards to process data, one has to devise a coding key that describes which column corresponds to each variable and which hole on the column corresponds to each position on the variable. One should then transcribe the source data (e.g., scratch notes) onto the coding sheets in light of the coding key. The coding sheets consist simply of a pile of sheets with 80 short lines on each sheet corresponding to the 80 columns available on each IBM card. After the transcribing or coding is complete, one then takes the coding sheets to an IBM key punch and punches a set of IBM cards from the coding sheets as if he were typing from the coding sheets. The next step in using IBM equipment is to feed the set of punched cards into an electric counter-sorter or an electronic computer in order to get the numbers for the cells in the fourfold or comparable tables.[9]

After the fourfold tables have been filled in, one may want to determine the degree of correlation between the variables not just whether there is a positive, zero, or negative direction. The difference between the percentage in cell c and the percentage in cell a gives a rough measure of the degree of correlation. This difference can be any number from plus 100 percentage points (perfect positive correlation) to 0 per percentage points (no correlation) to minus 100 percentage points (perfect inverse correlation). If one wants a more precise measure of the degree of correlation or a measure of correlation in a six-cell or greater table, one can make use of the correlation coefficients described in the standard textbooks on statistical techniques.[10]

---

[9]For greater detail concerning the key punch, the sorter-counter, and other basic IBM equipment, see B. Friedman, *Punched Card Primer* (1965); and IBM Corp., *IBM Operators' Guide* (1959). For more recent microcomputer hardware, see Larry Goldstein, *Microcomputer Applications: A Hands-On Approach to Problem Solving* (Addison-Wesley, 1987); Blaine Brownell, *Using Microcomputers: A Guidebook for Writers, Teachers, and Researchers in the Social Sciences* (Sage, 1985); and Joan Lasselle and Carol Ramsay, *The ABC's of the IBM PC* (Sybex, 1984).

[10]On statistical techniques in general, see J. Guilford, *Fundamental Statistics in Psychology and Education* (1956); and Walker & Lev. op. cit. supra note 5. On statistical techniques especially designed for use with the crude kind of measurement frequently necessary in legal research, see S. Siegal, *Non-Parametric Statistics for the Behavioral Sciences* (1956). For a simplified step-by-step approach to statistics, see H. Yuker, *A Guide to Statistical Calculations* (1958).

In addition to determining the degree of correlation, one might want to determine the probability of arriving at the observed correlation purely by chance, given the sample size involved. A rough way to calculate this chance probability is simply to multiply the sample size for the fourfold table by the square of the difference between the percentage in cell c and the percentage in cell a. One then takes this product to the first row of any chi-square probability table and reads off half the chance probability immediately above the place where the product appears in the table. The probability is not halved if one merely hypothesizes that there will be a difference between the two groups or positions on the independent variable without specifying the direction of the difference. Chi-square tables, as well as more complex ways of calculating chance probabilities, can be found in statistical textbooks.[11] If a correlation could occur purely by chance less than 5 times in 100 (i.e., contrary to 19-to-1 odds), then it is conventional among social scientists to say that the correlation was not owing to chance coincidence but, rather, to the presence of a real relationship between the variables.

In planning the analysis, it is productive of useful insights to apply the plan of analysis to a few select hypotheses on a small sample from the total sample before making the full study. Such a pilot study or microcosm of the full study usually proves time-saving in the long run because of the unanticipated defects it tends to reveal in the research design. Pilot studies are also helpful for generating hypotheses.

COMPILING THE DATA AND DRAWING A CONCLUSION

In accordance with the sampling techniques, the measurement techniques, and the plan of analysis developed in the research design, data should now be compiled for the purpose of testing the hypothesis or hypotheses. The data may be obtained from library materials, interviews, mailed questionnaires, observation, contrived experiments, court records, or from any other relevant sources. This step can be extremely time consuming, and therefore techniques should be devised to minimize the time involved and to delegate much of the work to competent research assistants.

After the data is compiled and placed in the relevant tables, one should observe the tables and make whatever calculations are needed to

---

[11]See note 10 supra. For a more detailed explanation and justification of the statistical estimation methods given in this paper, see Nagel, "Estimation of Correlation and Statistical Significance in Fourfold Tables," a mimeographed paper, available from the writer on request.

determine if the data confirms or fails to confirm the hypothesis.[12] Depending on one's purposes, one might decide to conclude that the hypothesis is confirmed if the correlation goes in the direction hypothesized (1) beyond both a certain intensity and a certain chance probability, (2) merely beyond a certain intensity where one does not seek to generalize beyond the sample involved, or (3) merely beyond a certain chance probability where one does not seek a high-intensity relation. A hypothesis is further confirmed if it is consistent with other known relationships and if a repetition of the research design reveals similar findings.

EXPLAINING THE CONCLUSION

The testing of empirical generalizations is not complete until a tested or untested explanation is offered for *why* the relationship found exists, or for why the relation hypothesized hut not found does not exist. One should attempt to account for not only why the relation went in the direction it did, but also why it was not a stronger relationship. For example, the initial hypothesis may have been that a greater percentage of Democratic members rather than Republican members of the independent regulatory agencies are above the average liberalism score of their respective agencies. In positioning the commissioners on the liberalism variable, each commissioner can be given a score equal to the proportion of times he decided in favor of what might be considered the liberal rather than the conservative side in those adjudications where this variable is applicable. If a +.30 correlation were present, one might hypothesize that it was *not weaker* partly because a greater percentage of Democratic commissioners rather than Republican commissioners come from urban areas (a testable hypothesis) and urban commissioners tend to vote more liberally than rural commissioners of the same agency (also a testable hypothesis). Likewise, one might hypothesize that the correlation was *not stronger* because a greater percentage of the Democratic commissioners rather than the Republican commissioners come from the South (a testable hypothesis) and southern commissioners tend to vote more conservatively than northern commissioners of the same agency (also a testable hypothesis).

---

[12]To simplify the mechanical work involved in making the calculations, see W. Varner, *Computing with Desk Calculators* (1957); and H. Borko, *Computer Applications in the Behavioral Sciences*, 1-171 (1962). For more recent microcomputer statistical software, see Philip Schrodt, *Microcomputer Methods for Social Scientists* (Sage, 1984); Thomas Madron, Neal Tate, and Robert Brookshire, *Using Microcomputers in Research* (Sage, 1985); and Bryan Pfaffenberger, *Microcomputer Applications in Qualitative Research* (Sage, 1988).

If an explanation is tested and shown to be true, one might go further and attempt to explain why the explanation is true. For instance, one might attempt to explain why southerners tend to be Democrats in terms of historical reasons and why southerners tend to be conservatives in terms of lack of industrialization. Once the chain of explanations leaves the realm of social science and enters into the realm of natural science, however, the explanation process should end. Thus, one need not go on to indicate that the lack of industrialization in the South may be attributable to its warmer climate, which, in turn, is attributable to the tilt of the earth's axis, which, in turn, is attributable to certain gravitational factors.

In general, there are four basic kinds of explanations to account for a correlation between an independent and a dependent variable: (1) the independent may be a cause or the cause of the dependent variable, or vice versa: (2) the independent and dependent variables may be coeffects of an explanatory variable or set of explanatory variables: (3) the independent may be the cause of an explanatory variable or variables, which, in turn, may be the cause of the dependent variable: or (4) there may be a combination of the above three kinds of explanations operating simultaneously.

Basically, there are two ways of testing an explanatory variable - a positive method and a negative method. The positive method recognizes that if the explanatory variable is responsible for the relation, then when the explanatory variable is present or increased, the relation should generally be present or increased. The negative method recognizes that if the explanatory variable is absent or decreased, the relation should generally be absent or decreased. For example, one might suspect that part of the reason for the liberal voting behavior of Democratic commissioners is that they have liberal attitudes as measured by a liberalism questionnaire. In accordance with the positive method, one would test (1) to see if Democratic commissioners scored higher on the liberalism questionnaire than Republican commissioners, and also (2) to see if high questionnaire scorers tended to vote more liberally than low questionnaire scorers. In accordance with the negative method, one would test (1) to see if liberal Democrats (high questionnaire scorers) distributed themselves on the voting dependent variable about the same as liberal Republicans, and also (2) to see a conservative Democrats (low questionnaire scores) distributed themselves on the voting dependent-variable about the same as conservative Republicans. This fractionation of the sample into a Liberal fourfold and a separate conservative fourfold in effect holds constant the liberalism-conservatism variable, while allowing political party and voting behavior to fluctuate freely. Fractionation of a sample is comparable to chemist using a vacuum in order to hold constant the wind resistance that might interfere with the testing of a hypothesis concerning falling objects.

To feel more confident that a *causal* relation is present, one should not only satisfy the positive and negative methods of explanation testing, but one should also find that an increase in the alleged cause is generally followed in time by an increase in the alleged effect. Some would further say that one should also find that an increase in the alleged effect is generally preceded by an increase in the alleged cause, although such a requirement overemphasizes single causes at the expense of multiple causes.

Explaining the conclusion may also involve pointing out conditioning or catalytic variables, which, unlike explanatory variables, do not in themselves cause an increase or decrease in the independent or dependent variables. Instead, a conditioning variable, when it accompanies an independent variable, tends to increase the relation between the independent and dependent variables. Thus, American history seems to show that having substantial difference (the conditioning variable) in the political party affiliations of the Supreme Court and Congress will not in itself bring on court-curbing bills (the dependent variable), but such party differences may be an important or even necessary condition to facilitating court-curbing bills when intense judicial activism (the independent variable) is present. Complete explanations may also point out the relevance of unique variables that may be responsible for another matter. Thus, having a close relative who was a murder victim may make a juror prosecution-oriented, but few prosecution oriented jurors are so oriented for that reason.

In explaining why complex relations exist, it is sometimes helpful to draw a diagram with the variables in boxes or circles connected by arrows to indicate causal direction and dotted lines to indicate non-causal connections.[13]

AN APPLICATION

In order to clarify further the concepts and techniques that have been presented, it may be helpful to go through one application from the topic step through the explanation step.

---

[13]For further detail on causal explanations, see R. MacIver, *Social Causation* (1942).

An interesting topic that potentially could have social or theoretical significance is the broad topic of variables that influence the outcome of litigation. The topic may be narrowed to deal just with variables concerning the attraction and repulsion that certain courts seem to have for each other as sources of authority in certain types of cases. Approached from a different point of view, the topic may be narrowed to deal just with labor law litigation.

A review of the prior literature would reveal little concerning the phenomenon of favorable or unfavorable attitudes among American courts toward each other. A review of the literature would, however, reveal many studies of factors influencing labor litigation. Nearly all of these studies, however, are merely designed to describe and evaluate the rulings laid down in the relevant precedents. Few of them empirically test the extent to which the presence of variables mentioned in the rulings and variables not mentioned in the rulings correlate with whether the union interest wins or loses in a sample of labor law cases.

A pair of hypotheses that the topic and the literature might suggest is that the Supreme Court is more likely to reverse antiunion decisions from southern courts than from northern courts, but is more likely to affirm prounion decisions from southern courts than from northern courts.

These hypotheses logically indicate that the relevant entities are Supreme Court opinions (or cases) involving labor law disputes. Professor Harold Spaeth, of the University of Detroit, has compiled for a different purpose a list of 91 such opinions from the 1953 through 1959 terms of the Supreme Court.[14] Labor law disputes in this context refer to formal opinions dealing with the kind of subjects covered in such statutes as the Taft-Hartley Act,[15] the Fair Labor Standards Act,[16] the Railway Labor Act,[17] the Norris-LaGuardia Act,[18] and analogous state statutes, but not workmen's compensation or antitrust statutes. In light of the hypotheses, cases involving disputes between two unions are excluded from the sample, although they are

---

[14]Spaeth, "An Analysis of Judicial Attitudes in the Labor Relations Decisions of the Warren Court," 25 *J. Pol.* 290 (1963).

[15]61 Stat. 136 (1947), 29 U.S.C. §§ 141-44, 151-67, 171-82, 185-87 (1958).

[16]52 Stat. 1060 (1938), 29 U.S.C. §§ 201-19 (1958).

[17]44 Stat. 577 (1926), 45 U.S.C. §§ 151-63. 181-88 (1958).

[18]47 Stat. 70 (1932), 29 U.S.C. §§ 101-15 (1958).

included in Spaeth's list. Two or more cases decided under the same opinion are treated as separate cases if the separate cases differed with regard to the decision of the Supreme Court, the decision of the initial court, or the region of the initial court. In light of these considerations, the original 91 opinions become 94 cases. If the hypothesis is confirmed with this sample of cases, one might try to test on a broader sample of cases whether appellate courts in general in economic regulation cases tend (1) to reverse conservative decisions from relatively conservative lower courts more than those from liberal lower courts while tending (2) to affirm liberal decisions from relatively conservative lower courts more than those from liberal lower courts.

There are three variables involved in the pair of hypotheses. The independent variable relates to region. A southern court can be meaningfully defined as a state or federal court located in one of the states that had legalized slavery as of 1860. A northern court can be defined as any other state or federal court. The federal courts of appeals from the third, sixth, eighth, and tenth circuits cover some southern states and some northern states, but they are classified as northern courts because a check of *Who's Who in America* indicates that more of the judges on each of these courts were appointed from northern rather than southern states. For the same reason, the courts of the District of Columbia are classified as northern courts, although many of their judges are natives of the District of Columbia. The dependent variable simply involves determining whether the Supreme Court affirmed or reversed the initial court's decision. The third variable (called an intervening or constant variable) relates to whether the initial court's decision was favorable or unfavorable to the union interests involved. In his work with these cases, Spaeth sometimes attempts to determine whether the decisions were favorable or unfavorable to the workers' interests, which is a more subjective variable to measure. By initial court in this context is meant the first court in the judicial hierarchy that heard the case. The initial court is used rather than the court immediately prior to the Supreme Court in order to have more cases decided by southern courts, and because predictions tend to be more interesting if they are based on data further away from the event being predicted.

Any case that cannot be clearly positioned on all three variables are excluded from the analysis (e.g., an affirmance in part and reversal in part), thereby decreasing the sample of 94 cases to a sample of 91 cases. The finding would probably be strengthened if only those cases are used in which a prounion decision also means a proworker, antimanagement decision (and vice versa with an antiunion decision), but purifying the sample in this manner might unduly decrease the sample size. All three variables are measured dichotomously (i.e., with two positions per variable). There seems to be little purpose in talking about the degree southernness (border versus deep), the degree of anti- or prounion impact (based on the extent each case is cited in certain labor law treatises), or the degree of affirmance (nine to zero, five to four, zero to nine, and so on), although these kinds of measurement could be used later if they subsequently appeared fruitful.

The plan of analysis calls for positioning each case on each of the three variables in order to obtain the information necessary to fill Table 1-2. Either index-type cards alone or index cards transcribed to IBM cards can be used to record the necessary information from the cases prior to sorting and counting. The pair of hypotheses will be considered confirmed if there is at least a 20 percentage point difference in the direction hypothesized between the affirmance rate of the North and the South for each of the two hypotheses, and if the relevant differences observed could not have occurred more than 5 times out of 100 purely by chance. As of the 1980's, one can more easily hold constant a third variable by using microcomputer software for doing statistical analysis. The reasoning is the same, but microcomputers are more user friendly, and much faster from the time the data is submitted to the time one obtains the results. Mainframes can do more calculations per minute, but it may be days before one can pick up the results from the batch processing window. The results may also be meaningless because the user failed to do something trivial like leaving out a right parenthesis. Microcomputers have revolutionized the ability to test causal hypotheses and experiment with variations.

Table 2-2 contains the data compiled. Any set of two or more fourfold tables with a common independent or dependent variable, like those in Table 2-2, can be converted for easier reading into a table like Table 2-3, which contains all the essential data from Table 2-2. As indicated in rows one and two of Table 2-3, there is more than a 20 percentage point difference in the direction hypothesized between the affirmance rate of the North and the South for only the first of the two hypotheses. Given the group sizes of 17 and 40, the difference of 25 percentage points in Table 2-3 could have occurred purely by chance only 4 times out of 100, which meets the predetermined standard of confirmation. On the other hand, given the groups sizes of 9 and 25, the other difference of 19 percentage points could have occurred purely by chance as many as 15 times out of 100, which does not meet the predetermined standard of confirmation. In view of the interlocking nature of the hypotheses, however, the really important difference is not the

TABLE 2-2

THE RELATION BETWEEN INITIAL COURT REGION AND SUPREME COURT DECISION
IN LABOR LITIGATION (Detailed Presentaion)

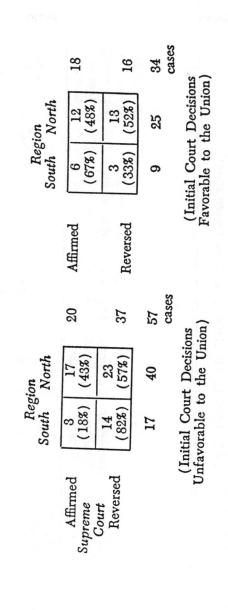

	Region		
	South	North	
Affirmed	3 (18%)	17 (43%)	20
Reversed	14 (82%)	23 (57%)	37
	17	40	57 cases

(Initial Court Decisions Unfavorable to the Union)

	Region		
	South	North	
Affirmed	6 (67%)	12 (48%)	18
Reversed	3 (33%)	13 (52%)	16
	9	25	34 cases

(Initial Court Decisions Favorable to the Union)

TABLE 2-3

THE RELATION BETWEEN INITIAL COURT REGION AND SUPREME COURT DECISION
IN LABOR LITIGATION (Simplified Presentation)

Initial Court Decision	Number of Southern Cases	Number of Northern Cases	Percentage of Southern Cases Affirmed	Percentage of Northern Cases Affirmed	Difference	Probability of Difference Being Due to Chance
Unfavorable to Union	17	40	18	43	+25	about 4/100
Favorable to Union	9	25	67	48	−19	about 15/100

isolated difference between 18 percent and 43 percent or the one between 67 percent and 48 percent, but rather the overall difference between +25 and -19. This difference of 44 percentage points, given the relevant group sizes of 57 and 34, could not have occurred purely by chance more than about once in 100 times.[19]

A tentative explanation that one might offer to account for the basic phenomenon observed in the difference column of Table 2-3 is that southern courts have a reputation for having a more antiunion bias relative to thenorthern courts (a testable hypothesis using questionnaires applied to lawyers), and this reputation is valid in light of southern court behavior (a hypothesis testable on a random sample of southern and northern labor cases). Therefore, when a southern court hands down an antiunion decision, the Supreme Court is more likely to be suspicious (not so testable, given the reluctance of Supreme Court justices to answer questions about things like this), and the southern court decision is more likely to be erroneous (not so testable, given the subjectivity of the concept of "erroneous," although questionnaires presenting hypothetical cases to lawyers might be feasible), and therefore the southern court decision is more likely to be reversed. On the other hand, for reasons converse to the above explanation, if the southern court decides in favor of a union the southern court is more likely to be upheld than is a northern court similarly deciding in favor of a union. The relations were not stronger because Supreme Court affirmance or reversal in labor union cases obviously is dependent on more variables than just region and the decision of the initial court. Other relevant variables may relate to the law involved, the evidence introduced, the group interests at stake, and the historical context of each case.

Incidentally, the practicing lawyer (who is usually more interested in bread-and-butter predictions than in theoretical hypotheses) may observe that Table 2-2 indicates that by predicting an affirmance when the Supreme Court takes on a prounion decision and a reversal when the Supreme Court takes on an antiunion decision, he would have predicted accurately 55 times (18 plus 37) and inaccurately only 36 times (16 plus 20). The numbers in parentheses, in effect, represent the entries from a fourfold table deductible from Tables 2-2 and 2-3, in which the independent variable is the initial court's decision and the dependent variable is the Supreme Court's decision.

---

[19]This combined chance probability was calculated simply by multiplying 4/100 by 15/100. The chance probabilities were calculated by the estimation method described in note 11 supra and the accompanying text.

From the data given in Tables 2-2 and 2-3, one can deduce other interesting tables. For example, if the independent variable is the decider (initial courts versus the U.S. Supreme Court) and the dependent variable is the decision (favorable to the union versus unfavorable to the union), the one finds that 60 percent of the 91 Supreme Court decisions were favorable to the union, whereas only 37 percent of the initial court decisions were favorable to the union. This difference of 23 percentage points in the direction hypothesized with a sample of 182 decisions could occur purely by chance less than 1 in 1,000 times. This table clearly refutes Glendon Schubert's conclusion from the same data that "the evidence is so slight that on the basis of this sample, there is little ground for such an inference...that the union bias (i.e., decisional orientation) is opposite to the bias of the trial (i.e., initial) courts."[20]

Findings like those of Tables 2-2 or 2-3 could conceivably have some value to legislators who write labor legislation, to persons responsible for staffing the relevant courts, to judges who want to know their biases better in order to control them better, as well as to the practitioner who seeks additional information about whether to appeal and about what to emphasize or include in an appellate brief.

CONCLUSION

In the last few hundred years, the systematic empirical testing of generalizations has become more and more important in one field of knowledge after another. First, it was the physical sciences, including astronomy, physics, chemistry, and geology. Then, the scientific method enveloped the biological sciences. The 20th century has been witnessing a methodological revolution in the social sciences. Psychology, which is partly a biological science, was the first social science affected. Then sociology succumbed. Then economics. Since the end of World War II, political science has been undergoing a methodological rejuvenation. Its close neighbor, the field of law, seems next in line.

Legal scholars have long been concerned almost exclusively with individual case studies, chronologies of precedent development, armchair speculation, statements of author preferences, individual biographies, and

---

[20]G. Schubert, *Judicial Behavior: A Reader in Theory and Research* 459 (1964).

especially descriptions of the holdings in sets of judicial opinions. In order to further aid the legislator, administrator, judge, and practitioner, it seems time to supplement traditional scholarship with more testing of empirical generalizations in legal research.[21]

---

[21]Recent books dealing with testing empirical generalizations in social, political, and legal research include David Nachmias and Chava Nachmias, *Research Methods in the Social Sciences* (St. Martin's, 1981); William Matlack, *Statistics for Public Policy and Management* (Duxbury, 1980); Susette Talarico (ed.), *Criminal Justice Research: Approaches, Problems, and Policy* (Anderson, 1980); Noreen Channels, *Social Science Methods in the Legal Process* (Rowman and Allanheld, 1985); Donald Vinson and Philip Anthony, *Social Science Research Methods for Litigation* (Michie, 1985); and David Barnes, *Statistics as Proof: Fundamentals of Quantitative Evidence* (Little, Brown, 1983).

3

THE UTILITY OF THE CONCEPTS
AND THE METHODS

It is the purpose of this chapter to offer some tentative answers to the question, "What can social science contribute to law?" It seems logical to answer this question from the point of view of the three main types of personnel within the legal profession: the practicing lawyer, the legal policymaker, and the legal scholar. The specific examples given in the footnotes represent a sampling of the relevant literature.[1]

THE PRACTICING LAWYER

Social Science methodology and substance can be useful to the practicing lawyer mainly by providing him with some materials that he might be able to introduce into evidence to win specific cases or points.[2] With regard to

---

[1] For further discussion of the relations between social science and law, see *Law and Sociology* (Evan, ed., 1962); Davis et al., *Society and the Law: New Meanings for an Old Profession* (1962); and "Frontiers of Legal Research," 7 *American Behavioral Science* 1 (December, 1963).

[2] Greenberg, "Social Scientists Take the Stand: A Review and Appraisal of Their Testimony in Litigation," 54 *Michigan Law Review* 953 (1956).

methodology, polling techniques may be valuable in resolving such issues as trademark infringement,[3] change of venue,[4] or community standards of fitness for citizenship.[5] Systematic statistical analysis may be relevant to show that an alleged favoritism or discrimination is not readily attributable to chance.[6] Systematic observation or content analysis of documents may reveal patterns of behavior relevant to determining what constitutes reasonable care in a negligence case or common usage in a contract dispute.[7]

With regard to substance, psychological information may be crucial in civil or criminal insanity cases[8] or in any case involving the perceptive powers of witnesses.[9] Economic information may be crucial in antitrust, labor-management, or commercial disputes.[10] Information gathered from historical[11] or political science[12] sources may be relevant to interpreting a statute or other legal document; it may also be relevant to a constitutional or administrative law issue. Sociological knowledge may be important in the sentencing aspects of a criminal case or the disposition of a family law

---

[3]Zeisel, "The Uniqueness of Survey Evidence," 45 *Cornell Law Quarterly* 322 (1960).

[4] Sherman, "Use of Public Opinion Polls in Continuance and Venue Hearings," 50 *American Bar Association Journal* 357 (1964).

[5]Repouille v. United States, 165 F. 2d (1947). especially Jerome Frank's dissent.

[6]Ulmer, "Supreme Court Behavior in Racial Exclusion Cases," 56 *American Political Science Review* 325 (1962).

[7]Sellitz, et al., *Research Methods in Social Relations* 199-234 and 315-42 (1962).

[8]Lassen, "The Psychologist as an Expert Witness in Assessing Mental Disease or Defect," 50 *American Bar Association Journal* 239 (1964).

[9]McCarty, *Legal and Criminal Psychology* (1961).

[10]"Economics in Antitrust Policy and Practice," 20 *American Bar Association Antitrust Section* (1962).

[11]Kelly, "The Fourteenth Amendment Reconsidered," 54 *Michigan Law Review* 1049 (1959).

[12]*Reynolds v. Sims*, 377 U.S. 533 (1964), cites numerous political scientists on various aspects of the reapportionment controversies.

case.[13]

Social science methodology and substance, in addition to being of value to the practicing lawyer with regard to the presentation of evidence in specific cases, can also help to improve his or her techniques as a lawyer in general.

As to trial techniques, social science methods are capable of testing a variety of hypotheses concerning the relative effectiveness of alternative techniques. Professors Kalven and Zeisel of the University of Chicago jury project, for instance, have played tape recordings of trials to many actual juries in order to determine how the juries would react to slight variations in the trials. Among other things, they found that if the plaintiff's lawyer mentions that the defendant has insurance and the defendant's lawyer successfully objects, then the juries will tend to award higher damages to the plaintiff than if the defendant's lawyer did not object at all. They also found that working-class jurors in personal injury cases are more likely to find liability but are less likely to award higher damages than upper-class jurors. This is a bit of information helpful in picking juries after one has assessed the probability that liability will be found.[14]

Social science potentially can contribute to the skillful handling of clients in one's office. The Jury Verdict Research Corporation of Cleveland, Ohio, for instance, publishes a loose-leaf service indicating the percentage of a wide variety of cases that have been decided in favor of the plaintiff and the average damages awarded. This kind of information, systematically gathered from across the country, can be helpful in advising a client on an out-of-court settlement.[15] A number of social psychologists have made systematic studies of elements affecting bargaining and negotiation. These would also be of value in developing out-of-court settlement techniques.[16]

Linguistic analysis, which is becoming an increasingly important part of social science, can be of value to lawyers interested in drafting legal

---

[13]Rose, "The Social Scientist as an Expert Witness," 40 *Minnesota Law Review* 205, 209 (1956).

[14]Broader, "University of Chicago Jury Project," 38 *Nebraska Law Review* 744 (1959).

[15]Nagel, "Statistical Prediction of Verdicts and Awards," 63 *Modern Uses of Logic and Law* 135 (1963).

[16]Sacks, "Human Relations Training for Law Students and Lawyers," 11 *Journal of Legal Education* 316 (1959).

instruments that are more meaningful and precise.[17]   Content analysis by computer, which is being developed by social scientists, shows promise of becoming a useful aid in legal research.[18]

THE LEGAL POLICYMAKER

By legal policymaker in this context is meant a legislator, appellate court judge, or upper level administrator. Social science can possibly contribute to improving both the procedure of the policymaker and the substantive materials available to him.

With regard to procedure, social science studies have tested systematically a number of proposals to reduce delay in the courts, such as splitting the liability and damages decision,[19] providing for nonjudicial auditors,[20] and a variety of other techniques.[21] Other procedural reforms have also been subjected to social science analysis, such as providing neutral medical testimony,[22] appointing rather than electing the judiciary,[23] using blue-ribbon juries,[24] providing counsel to the indigent,[25] and releasing

---

[17]Allen, "Some Uses of Symbolic Logic in Law Practice," 8 *Practical Lawyer* 51 (1962).

[18]Gurr & Panofsky (eds.), "Information Retrieval in the Social Sciences: Problems, Programs, and Proposals, 7 *American Behavioral Science* 1 (June, 1964).

[19]Zeisel & Callahan, "Split Trials and Time Saving: A Statistical Analysis," 76 *Harvard Law Review* 1606 (1963).

[20]Rosenberg, "Auditors in Massachusetts as Antidotes for Delayed Civil Courts," 110 *University of Pennsylvania Law Review* 27 (1961).

[21]Zeisel, Kalven, & Bucholz, *Delay in the Court* (1959).

[22]Assoc. Bar. N.Y.C., *Impartial Medical Testimony* (1956).

[23]Nagel, "Political Party Affiliation and Judicial Decisions," 55 *American Political Science Review* 848 (1961) (partly included in Chap. 15 infra).

[24]Fay v. New York, 332 U.S. 261 (1947).

[25]Silverstein, *Defense of the Poor in Criminal Cases in American State Courts: A Preliminary Summary* (1964). This study, made possible by the American Bar Foundation, was presented to the House of Delegates of the American Bar Association in August of 1964. The House of Delegates adopted recommendations for standards of representation of the indigent accused. 50 *American Bar Association Journal* 969 (1964).

indigent criminal defendants without bail pending trial.[26] The last study, for example, showed that a careful screening and notifying of defendants released without any bond produced a higher percentage of court appearances than the traditional bail bond system.

As to substantive developments in the law, social science has been helpful in many fields. A revealing study was made, for instance, on the effects of replacing the contributory negligence rule with the comparative negligence rule.[27] The effects of capital punishment have also been subjected to social science scrutiny,[28] as have the effects of income taxes on incentives to work[29] and the minimum wage on the labor market.[30] Of course, the effects of segregation and desegregation have been studied extensively.[31] There has recently been a call for more social science research aimed at improving compliance with international law[32] and into the effects of prayers and Bible reading in the public schools.[33] At a more down-to-earth level is the perceptive questionnaire study that was made to determine the extent to which inheritance laws conform to the intent of people who die without wills.[34]

---

[26]Ares, Rankin, & Sturz, "Manhattan Bail Project," 38 *New York University Law Review* 67 (1963).

[27]Rosenberg, "Comparative Negligence in Arkansas: A Before and After Survey," 13 *Arkansas Law Review* 89 (1959).

[28]Sellin, *The Death Penalty* (1959) (a report for the Model Penal Code project).

[29]Break, "Income Taxes and Incentives to Work: An Empirical Study," 47 *American Economics Review* 529 (1957).

[30]Douty, "Some Effects of the $1.00 Minimum Wage in the U.S.," 27 *Economica* 137 (1960).

[31]Myrdal, *An American Dilemma* (1944).

[32]Larson, *International Rule of Law* (1961).

[33]Abington Township School District v. Schempp, 374 U.S. 203, 190, 319 (1963).

[34]Dunham, "Method, Process, and Frequency of Wealth Transmission at Death," 30 *University of Chicago Law Review* 1 (1963).

THE LEGAL SCHOLAR

Legal scholars in this context refers to law professors and to practicing lawyers and policymakers who are interested in the theoretical aspects of the legal process. Social science can probably make its greatest contribution to legal theory by investigating the causal forces behind judicial, legislative, and administrative decision-making and by probing the general effects of such decisions.

With regard to the causal forces behind the lawmaking and law-applying processes, the anthropologists[35] and historians[36] especially can broaden the legal scholar's perspective of the cultural roots beneath his legal field. The impact of public opinion on some aspects of the legal system also has been scrutinized systematically.[37] Likewise, the interactions between governmental bodies as a factor in determining decisional outcomes has been studied,[38] as has the role of pressure groups[39] and political parties.[40] Witnesses,[41] lawyers,[42] and litigants[43] have all been the subject of systematic social science study. Studies have also been made of the relation between the backgrounds and attitudes of judges[44] and legislators[45] and

---

[35]Hoebel, *Law of Primitive Man* (1954).

[36]Kempin, *Legal History: Law and Social Change* (1963).

[37]Rose and Press, "Does the Punishment Fit the Crime: A Study in Social Valuation," 61 *Am. J. Soc.* 247 (1955).

[38]Murphy, "Lower Court Checks on Supreme Court Power, 53 *American Political Science Review* 1017 (1959).

[39]Vose, "Litigation as a Form of Pressure Group Activity," 319 *Annals* 20 (1958).

[40]Sayre & Kaufman, *Governing New York* (1960).

[41]Fishman & Morris (eds.), "Witnesses and Testimony at Trials and Hearings," 13 *Am. J. Soc. Issues* 1 (1957).

[42]Ladinsky, "Careers of Lawyers, Law Practice, and Legal Institutions," 28 *Am. Soc. Rev.* 47 (1963).

[43]Hunting & Neuwirth, *Who Sues in New York City* (1962).

[44]Nagel, "Judicial Backgrounds and Criminal Cases," 53 *Journal of Criminal Law, Criminology, and Police Science* 333 (1962) (Chap. 18 infra).

their decisional behavior.

As to the general impact of broad fields of law contrasted to specific laws, a number of studies have been and are under way. One sociologist has been studying the relation of legal impact to informal and formal controls[46] and to negative and positive appeals.[47] Other social scientists have contributed theory and data to the analysis of sanctions and legal compliance in general,[48] in public law[49] and in private law.[50] Using extensive interviewing techniques, one legal scholar analyzed the impact of contract law on business practice.[51] The role of such factors as the mass media, which facilitate or inhibit the impact of the law, has also been studied.[52]

Although this chapter has dealt only with what social science can contribute to law, it should be noted that no social scientist can really understand the American or any other society unless he or she has a reasonable understanding of its legal system. Nevertheless, there is much that lawyers can learn from social scientists. What is probably needed is a greater awareness by lawyers of the research of interest to them that social scientists and lawyers oriented to social science are doing.[53]

---

[45]Wahlke, et al., *The Legislative System: Explorations in Legislative Behavior* (1962).

[46]Schwartz, "Social Factors in the Development of Legal Control," 63 *Yale Law Journal* 471 (1954).

[47]Schwartz, "Field Experimentation in Socio-legal Research," 13 *Journal of Legal Education* 401 (1961).

[48]Arens & Lasswell, *In Defense of the Public Order: The Emerging Field of Sanction Law* (1961).

[49]Ball, "Social Structure and Rent Control Violations," 65 *Am. J. Soc.* 598 (1960).

[50]Litwak, "Three Ways in Which Law Acts as a Means of Social Control: Punishment, Therapy, and Education--Divorce as a Case in Point," 34 *Social Forces* 217 (1956).

[51]Macaulay, "Non-Contractual Relations in Business, 28 *Am. Soc. Rev.* 55 (1963).

[52]Newland, "Press Coverage of the U.S. Supreme Court," 17 *W. Pol. Q.* 15 (1964).

[53]Recent books dealing with the utilization of social science in society, government, and law include Edward Glaser, Harold Abelson, and Kathalee Garrison, *Putting Knowledge to Use: Facilitating the Diffusion of Knowledge and the Implementation of Planned Change* (Jossey-Bass, 1983); Richard Nathan, *Social Science in Government: Uses and Misuses* (Basic Books, 1988); Carol Weiss (ed.), *Using Social Research in Public Policy Making* (Lexington-Heath, 1977); Leon Lipson and Stanton Wheeler (eds.), *Law and the Social Sciences* (Russell Sage Foundation,

1986); Wallace Loh (ed.), *Social Research in the Judicial Process: Cases, Readings, and Text* (Russell Sage Foundation, 1984); Burton Wright et al., *Criminal Justice and the Social Sciences* (Saunders, 1978); and Martin Kaplan (ed.), *The Impact of Social Psychology on Procedural Justice* (Charles Thomas, 1986).

SECTION B:

IMPROVING THE LEGAL PROCESS

4

CHOOSING AMONG ALTERNATIVE PUBLIC POLICIES

The purpose of this chapter is to provide an introduction to a basic methodology which is used throughout this book for testing the effects of alternative legal or public policies. The testing methodology depends mainly on whether the legal policies involve (1) making legal or illegal some activity like capital punishment or (2) deciding how to allocate governmental funds to alternative activities like subsidizing low-rent public housing versus home ownership for the poor.

Other examples of controversial legal policies involving the issue of whether something should be made legal or illegal include legalizing marijuana, prohibiting malapportioned legislatures, legalizing medical abortions, or providing for elected rather than appointed judges. Other examples of controversial legal policies involving the allocation of scarce governmental resources include allocating funds between busing versus compensatory education in improving educational opportunities for poor children, between antipollution water enforcement programs versus water clean-up facilities, and allocating funds between fair employment enforcement activities versus manpower training to provide better employment opportunities to minorities.[1]

CHOOSING AMONG NON-EXPENDITURE POLICIES

THE GENERAL PROBLEM AND THE ILLUSTRATIVE DATA

Table 4-1 summarizes the decision rules involved for adopting or preferring non-expenditure policies. Each row in the table illustrates a different problem situation. The first situation involves one policy and one goal, and the problem is to decide whether or not to adopt the policy in light of its relation to the one goal. The second situation involves two policies and one goal, and the problem is to decide which policy to prefer if they both cannot be adopted. Situation three involves one policy and two goals, and the problem (like the first problem) is to decide whether or not to adopt the policy in light of its relation to the two goals. Situation four involves two policies and two goals, and the problem there (like the second problem) is to decide which policy to prefer if they both cannot be adopted.

In order to better understand the decision rules, it is helpful to have a concrete example. One concrete example that can be used is the problem situation of deciding what to do to decrease the occurrence of illegal searches by the police. One alternative that the courts have adopted is to exclude or throw out illegally obtained evidence from courtroom proceedings in criminal cases on the theory that doing so will deter the police from using illegal methods to obtain evidence. Prior 1961 the United States Supreme Court in the case of *Mapp v. Ohio* declared that the fourth amendment required that illegally seized evidence be inadmissible in all American criminal cases, at least when objected to by defense counsel.

In 1963 a mailed-questionnaire survey was made of one randomly selected police chief, prosecuting attorney, judge, defense attorney, and ACLU

---

[1]The distinction between legalization policies and expenditure policies made in this article is closely related to the distinction between regulatory and distributive policies made by Theodore Lowi, "American Business, Public Policy, Case Studies, and Political Theory," 16 *World Politics* 677-715 (1964) and the distinction between legal and economic policies made by Peter Szanton, "Public Policy, Public Good, and the Law," *Journal of Antitrust Law and Economics* (1973). This distinction is also partly one between policies that are primarily dichotomous versus those that are measured on a continuous interval scale.

TABLE 4-1

DECISION RULES FOR ADOPTING OR PREFERRING NON-EXPENDITURE POLICIES

Problem Situation	Policies or Means (X's)	Goals or Ends (Y's)	Adopt X_1 (where there is only one policy under consideration) if:	Prefer X_1 over X_2 if:
One	X_1	Y_a	$R_{X1Ya} \cdot z$ is greater than zero	
Two	X_1 and X_2	Y_a		$R_{X1Yz} \cdot z$ is greater than $R_{X2Ya} \cdot z$
Three	X_1	Y_a and Y_b	$[(R_{X1Ya} \cdot z$ times $W_{Ya})$ plus $(R_{X1Yb} \cdot z$ times $W_{Yb})]$ is greater than zero.	
Four	X_1 and X_2	Y_a and Y_b		U_{X1} is greater than U_{X2} where U_{X1} = the expression in brackets under situation three.

Meaning of Symbols:

$R_{X1Ya} \cdot z$ = the correlation or slope between X_1 and Y_a holding constant intervening variables Z.

W_{Ya} = the value weight of goal a.

U_{X1} = the rank-order utility of policy 1.

X, Y, and Z can be dichotomous attributes or interval-measured variables.

X, Y, and Z can be static (i.e., one point in time) or dynamic (i.e., ΔX, ΔY, and ΔZ, where Δ = change in).

Numbered subscripts differentiate policies, and alphabetic subscripts differentiate goals.

official in each of the fifty states to determine among other things their perceptions of changes in police behavior before and after *Mapp v. Ohio*. The experiment was aided by virtue of the fact that twenty-four of the fifty states had already adopted the exclusionary rule before *Mapp v. Ohio*, and respondents from those states could thus serve as a control group; twenty-three were newly forced to adopt the rule at that time, and respondents from those states could thus serve as an experimental group; and three states which were not used in the analysis had partially adopted it.

Table 4-2 shows that 57 percent of the respondents from the control group of states reported an increase in police adherence to legality in making searches since 1961; whereas 75 percent of the respondents from the experimental group of newly-adopting states reported an increase. This 18 percentage points difference (or, roughly speaking, a correlation of +.18) cannot be readily attributed to a chance fluke in the sample of respondents since there is less than a five out of 100 probability that one could distribute 104 respondents over the six cells in Table 4-2 purely by chance and come out with a +.18 correlation. This +.18 correlation is also not readily attributable to a misperception of the reality on the part of the respondents since there was such a high correlation among the different kinds of respondents from the same state or type of states on the empirical question of police adherence to legality, even though there was great disagreement on the normative question of the desirability of the exclusionary rule.

The +.18 correlation between newly adopting the exclusionary rule and increased police adherence to legality in searches seems to be largely attributable to the fact that the states that newly adopted the exclusionary rule also disproportionately reported an increase in programs designed to educate the police as to search and seizure law, which in turn correlates highly with increased police adherence to legality.   States that already had the exclusionary rule also often underwent an increase in police adherence to legality possibly because of the stimulus of the publicity given in *Mapp v. Ohio*, and because of long-term public opinion trends demanding higher standards of police behavior.[2]

---

[2]For further discussion of the problem of increasing police adherence to legality in making searches, see Dallin Oaks, "Studying the Exclusionary Rule in Search and Seizure," 37 *University of Chicago Law Review* 665-757 (1970); Wayne LeFave, "Improving Police Performance Through the Exclusionary Rule," 30 *Missouri Law Review* 391 (1965); and Stuart Nagel, "Testing the Effects of Excluding Illegally Seized Evidence," *Wisconsin Law Review*, 283-310 (1965). reproduced as Chapter 23 in Nagel, *The Legal Process from a Behavioral Perspective* (Dorsey, 1969).

TABLE 4-2

THE RELATION BETWEEN ADOPTING THE EXCLUSIONARY RULE AND
INCREASED POLICE ADHERENCE TO LEGALITY IN MAKING SEARCHES

Exclusionary Rule

Police Adherence to Legality	*Had All Along (Control Group)*	*Newly Adopted (Experimental Group)*	
Increase since 1961	57%	75%	+18 percentage points difference
No change	34%	21%	
Decrease	9%	4%	
Number of Respondents	48	56	104

THE FOUR DECISION SITUATIONS

Table 4-3 shows the relation between alternative policies and alternative goals involved in the problem of increasing police adherence to legality in making searches, and can be nicely used to illustrate the decision rules in Table 4-1. The top part of Table 4-3 shows that the exclusionary rule (X_1) should be adopted (in light of the decision rule for problem situation one) if increased police adherence to legality (Y_a) is one's only goal since there is a positive correlation between X_1 and Y_a.

Many judges and others (including Felix Frankfurter in his dissenting opinion in *Mapp v. Ohio*) have argued that tort or criminal actions against the police are far more effective than adopting the exclusionary rule as a means of increasing police adherence to legality. The questionnaire asked the respondents how often tort or criminal actions had occurred against the police in their communities for making illegal searches. If one divides the respondents into those relatively few who said there had been at least one such action in recent years versus those who said there had been none, then there is only an $+.05$ correlation between the occurrence of such actions and increased police adherence to police legality. The low correlation and the low occurrence of such actions may be attributable to the fact that prosecutors are reluctant to prosecute the police who have been aiding them and searched individuals are reluctant to sue because of the time, cost, embarrassment, unsympathetic juries, police discretion, and difficulty of assessing collectible damages. Thus, the exclusionary rule (X_1) should be preferred (in light of the decision rule for problem situations two) over tort or criminal actions (X_2) if increased adherence to legality (Y_a) is one's only goal (and the decisionmaker cannot adopt both policies) since there is a greater positive correlation between X_1 and Y_a than there is between X_2 and Y_a.

An additional goal one might have in dealing with the problem of increasing police adherence to legality in making searches is the goal of simultaneously increasing police morale, or at least not decreasing it. The mailed questionnaire asked the respondents about changes in police morale before and after *Mapp v. Ohio*. The correlation between being a respondent from a state that had newly adopted the exclusionary rule (X_1) and reporting increased police morale (Y_b) in making searches was a -37. The negative correlation which may be attributable to the fact that when evidence is thrown out which the police have worked hard to obtain through what they may have considered a lawful search, this is demoralizing to their enthusiasm for making future searches. If the correlation between X_1 and Y_b had been positive like

TABLE 4-3. ALTERNATIVE POLICIES AND GOALS
INVOLVED IN INCREASING POLICE ADHERENCE
TO LEGALITY IN MAKING SEARCHES

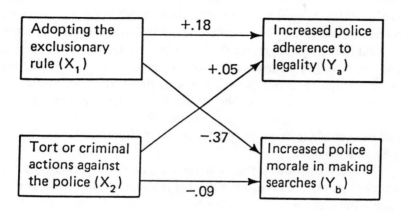

the correlation between X_1 and Y_a then it would be easy to decide in favor of adopting X_1. However, since the correlation between X_1 and Y_b is negative, one must decide whether that negative correlation is enough to offset the positive correlation between X_1 and Y_a. The matter is not resolved simply by noting that the X_1 and Y_b correlation is greater than the X_1 and Y_a correlation. This is so because it is unlikely that one would weight the Y_a and Y_b equally. If the Y_a goal has a weight 3 times or more the Y_b goal, then the -.37 correlation would not be enough to offset the +.18 correlation in view of the fact that 3 times .18 is greater than 1 times -.37. On the other hand, if the Y_a goal has a weight 2 times or less the Y_b goal, then the .-37 correlation would be enough to offset the +.18 correlation. In other words, if the correlation of X_1 and Y_a (times the weight of Y_a) plus the correlation of X_1 and Y_b (times the weight of Y_b) is greater than zero, then X_1 should be adopted in light of the decision rule for problem situation three if Y_a and Y_b are one's only goals.[3]

The most complicated problem situation involves both multiple policies and multiple goals, but even this situation is simple to resolve conceptually after going through the first three problem situations. Suppose the weight of Y_a is 3 times greater than the weight of Y_b as determined by a scientific psychological survey of public, legislative, or judicial opinions. Note also that the correlation between the occasional occurrence of tort or criminal actions against the police and increased police morale was a negative -.09. Thus the exclusionary rule (X_1) should be preferred (in light of the decision rule for problem situation four) over tort or criminal actions (X_2) if increased adherence to legality (Y_a) and increased police morale (Y_b) are one's only goals (and the decisionmaker cannot adopt both policies) since in Table 4-3: +.18 x 3 plus -.37 x 1 is greater than +.05 x 3 plus -.09 x 1. In other words, .54 plus -.37 is greater than .15 plus .09.

VARIATIONS AND ALTERNATIVES TO THE BASIC RULES

Instead of using the correlation coefficients between the variables shown in Table 4-3 in order to make the policy choices shown in Table 4-1, one could use the regression slopes between the policy and goal variables when a line is fitted to the dots on a graph of the variables. The dots are generated by

---

[3]On the methodology of weighting goals, see J. P. Guilford, *Psychometric Methods* (McGraw-Hill, 1954), 154-301; and Churchman, Ackoff, and Arnoff, *Introduction to Operations Research* (Wiley, 1957), 136-154.

plotting the positions of the communities of the respondents. Whether regression or correlation measures are more meaningful is a somewhat disputed issue among social scientists.[4] Correlation coefficients are simpler and not influenced by the units of measurement used, but unlike regression coefficients they are not capable of being used to predict how many additional units of Y can be obtained by an increase in units of X. Correlation coefficients should be favored in this decision-making contest because each one can be used to indicate the amount of variation on Y_a and Y_b accounted for by X_1 and X_2 respectively. Regression weights cannot be used in this comparative context because they can be increased or decreased by changing the units of measurement (e.g., from dollars to pennies) without changing how closely the variables vary together.[5]

The decision rules in Table 4-1 can be logically extended to cover more policies. For example, three or more policies and one goal is analogous to situation two. One policy and three or more goals is analogous to situation three. Likewise, analogous to situation four is (1) two policies and three or more goals, (2) three or more policies and two goals, or (3) three or more policies and three or more goals. Additional policies concerning the problem of illegal police searches might relate to police training and police selection practice. Additional goals might relate to decreasing the crime rate and decreasing the unsuccessful prosecution rate.

The methodology can also be extended to other areas of controversy like marijuana, malapportionment, abortion, and judicial selection, provided that one can obtain data on the relations between adoption of the controversial policy (and alternative policies) and the goals (on which there are some mutual agreement). In the American federal system where states

---

[4]Hubert Blalock, *Causal Models in the Social Sciences* (Aldine, 1972), 73152; and Hubert Blalock, *Causal Inferences in Non-experimental Research* (U. of North Carolina Press, 1964), 50-52.

[5]Hubert Blalock, *Social Statistics* (McGraw-Hill), 1973, 361-385, especially 383-385. Unstandardized regression weights statistically hold constant the influence of other variables, but so do partial correlation coefficients and standardized regression weights. *Ibid*, 429-458. The difference between the two upper percentages in table 1-2 is closer to the regression weight of X (as the independent variable) and Y (as the dependent variable) in the table, than the correlation coefficient of X and Y. *Ibid*, 294, 385. The correlation coefficient equals the regression weight if both variables have the same spread or dispersion. *Ibid*, 384. The closer the standard deviations of the two variables, the more useful the correlation is for predicting Y from X, but not the correlation squared although it more accurately indicates the percent of variation on Y accounted for by X. Mueller, et al., *Statistical Reasoning in Sociology* (Houghton Mifflin, 1970), 315-319.

and cities do experiment with alternative approaches to given social problems, these kind of data can often be obtained provided one has (1) some financial support and (2) some cooperation from knowledgeable persons. Even if solid data cannot always be fully obtained, use of the conceptual approach outlines can often be helpful in clarifying and making more effective governmental policy analysis.[6]

The correlation approach just presented is closely related to benefit-cost analysis in that for each situation, benefit-cost analysis says make the following decisions:[7]

Situation one.   Adopt X_1 if the benefits of X_1 are greater than the costs of X_1.

Situation two.   Prefer X_1 if the B-C of X_1 is greater than the B-C of X_2.

Situation three.   Adopt X_1 if B of X_1 is greater than C of X_1 where B = B_{Ya} + B_{Yb} and C = C_{X1} + C_{X2}.

Situation four.   Prefer X_1 if the B-C of X_1 is greater than the B-C of X_2, where B and C are figured as in situation three.

Determining such benefit minus cost differences is often less meaningful than the correlation approach for three reasons. First, the B-C approach does not consider the correlation or probability that X will achieve Y, unless one resorts to a complicated system of probability calculations.[8] Second, the B-C approach does not measure X in interval units but just as present or absent, unless one resorts to a complicated system of marginal analysis. Third, the B-C approach requires B and C to be measured in the

---

[6]For another more concrete, less abstract example of the use of the correlation approach in making non-expenditure policy choices, see Stuart Nagel, *Comparing Elected and Appointed Judicial Systems* (Sage Publications Series on American Politics, 1973).

[7]Wherever the equations use B - C, one can substitute B/C if the benefit and costs are not measured in the same units. The B - C calculation, however, is more meaningful if the same units are used since one is more interested in maximizing total profits (i.e., B - C) than in maximizing the profit rate (i.e., B/C). See Roland McKean, *Efficiency in Government Through Systems Analysis* (Wiley, 1966), p. 35-37, 46-47.

[8]The correlation coefficients or regression weights can be treated roughly as probabilities as in decision theory under risk. In the regression approach, Y = a + bX where a linear relation is present, and Log Y = Log a + bLogX where a nonlinear relation is present. In the probability approach, EU or expected utility equals the probability of the occurrence (or non-occurrence) of some crucial intervening Z event times the +X payoff (or -X payoff). EU is like Y, probability like b, and the X payoff is like X.

same units, unless one resorts to a complicated system of exponent weights.[9]

The correlation approach can also be distinguished from the matrix decision theory approach for choosing among non-expenditure policies. In the matrix decision approach to the problem of increasing police adherence to legality, there is one state or nature or Z variable, unless one wants to distinguish between rural and urban police or some other possibly significant intervening variable. There are four alternative policies since there are two positions on X_1 and two positions on X_2. There are nine possible payoff alternatives since there are three positions on Y_a and three positions on Y_b. This yields a matrix with one column and four rows. In each cell of the matrix, one shows the average payoff score (with ranks from 1 to 91 for each of the four alternative strategies. The strategy to choose using this approach is simply one with the highest payoff score.[10]

This matrix decision approach, however, won't work relative to the correlation approach if one X or means variable is measured on a continuum, rather than broken into a few discrete sub-positions. If an X variable is continuous, then theoretically there are an infinity of alternatives. If the X variables yields a manageable 10 to 15 alternative strategies, then the drawback exists that the strategy with the highest payoff may be one that exists in only a few communities; but by small-sample coincidence, those few communities may have undergone an increase in both police adherence and police morale. In other words, the decision matrix approach can lead to faulty decisions if the sample size is not substantial for the empirical occurrences of each alternative strategy, whereas the correlation approach mainly requires

---

[9]For further discussion of benefit-cost analysis, see A. R. Prest and R. Turvey. "Cost-Benefit Analysis: A Survey." 75 *The Economic Journal* 683-735 (1965); Guy Black, *The Application of Systems Analysis to Government Operations* (Praeger, 1968), 37-118; and David Miller and Martin Starr, *Executive Decisions and Operations Research* (Prentice-Hall, 1960), 33-102.

[10]In situation 1, our decision choices are to choose $+X_1$ or $-X_1$. If the percentage of $+X_1$ places which are $+Y_a$ is greater than the percentage of $-X_1$ places which are $+Y_a$, then choose $+X_1$. Those percentages stated as decimals can be considered the payoffs. In situation 2, the choices are $+X_1 +X_2$; $+X_1 -X_2$; $-X_1 +X_2$; and $-X_1 -X_2$. Choose whichever one of those four choices gives the highest percentage of $+Y_a$. Alternative one, however, is impossible if we cannot have both X_1 and X_2. Alternative two says prefer X_1, and alternative three says prefer X_2. In situation 3 we have to choose between $+X_1$ and $-X_1$ as in situation 1. Choose $+X_1$ if the $+X_1$ places have a higher $W_a \cdot Y_a \cdot W_b \cdot Y_b$ or on $Y_a{}^{Wa} \cdot Y_b{}^{Wb}$ than the average score of the $-X_1$ places on those same dependent variable measures. The same payoff approach is used in situation 4 as in situation 3 except the decision choices are the same as those in situation 2.

a substantial sample only for the overall sample size.[11]

One of the goals that can be included (in the correlation analysis) is to keep costs down. However, when trying to decide how to allocate scarce financial resources among diverse policy activities, it may be more meaningful to use a kind of linear programming approach about to be described rather than the correlation approach which we have just presented.[12]

CHOOSING AMONG EXPENDITURE POLICIES

THE GENERAL PROBLEM AND THE ILLUSTRATIVE DATA

To illustrate on a very simple level what is involved in applying linear programming concepts to choosing among alternative expenditure policies, let's take the problem of allocating $10 in campaign expenditure money to media dollars and precinct organization dollars. Suppose we are in a congressional district in which thirty-nine votes are expected to be cast among the two candidates running, which means our candidate needs twenty votes to win.[13]

There may be some combination of media and precinct dollars that will enable us to get our twenty votes while spending substantially less than the $10 we have available. Finding that combination is the cost minimization

---

[11]For further discussion of matrix decision theory, see Samuel Richmond, *Operations Research for Management Decisions* (Ronald Press, 1968), 3-39, 501-560; and David Miller and Martin Starr, *Executive Decisions and Operations Research* (Prentice-Hall, 1960), 55-100.

[12]For further discussion of some important aspects of the correlation approach to making non-expenditure policy choices, see Donald Campbell, "Reforms as Experiments." 24 *American Psychologist* 409-429 (1969); Hubert Blalock, *Causal Inferences in Non-experimental Research* (U. of North Carolina Press, 1964); and Stuart Nagel; "Optimizing Legal Policy." 18 *University of Florida Law Review*, 577-590 (1966), reproduced as Chapter 25 in Nagel, *op. cit.*, note 1. The Nagel article mainly deals with the statistical manipulation of dichotomous policy and goal variables that have been coded 1 for present and 0 for absent.

[13]For further discussion of the problem of rationally allocating campaign expenditures, see Gerald Kramer, "A Decision-Theoretic Analysis of a Problem in Political Campaigning," *Mathematical Applications in Political Science*, (Arnold Foundation, 1966), 137-160; Robert Agranoff, *The New Style in Election Campaigns* (Holbrook Press, 1972); and S. Nagel, *Policy Evaluation: Making Optimum Decisions* (Praeger, 1982), especially Chapter 10 on "Allocating Campaign Funds Across Elections" and Chapter 11 on "Allocating Campaign Funds Across Activities and Places."

problem. Likewise, there may be some combination of media and precinct dollars that will enable us to get as many votes as possible above twenty votes while spending no more than the $10 we have available. This is the benefit maximization problem. Linear programming is an excellent method for determining what combination of expenditures will minimize costs while achieving at least a minimum benefit level or determining what combination will maximize benefits while keeping within a maximum cost level.

Linear programming or optimizing can be defined as a procedure whereby one finds the optimum allocation of funds or some other scarce resource between two or more alternatives in light of a given minimizing or maximizing goal and in light of given constraints or conditions. In order to be linear rather than non-linear programming, the relations between the resources and the goals must be straight-line or constant-return relations rather than curved-line or diminishing-return relations.

Suppose that we have obtained (1) data from the Federal Communications Commission showing how much money was spent by each of the approximately 800 congressional candidates in 1972 on television and radio, (2) data from the General Accounting Office showing how much money was spent in total by each of the candidates, and (3) data from the *Congressional Quarterly* showing how many votes were obtained. If we subtract the FCC media expenditures from the GAO total expenditures, we should have a rough estimate of precinct organization expenditures for each candidate. If we then do a regression analysis with media dollars (M) and precinct dollars (P) as the independent variables and votes obtained as the dependent variable, we should be able to come up with a roughly accurate empirical equation between these variables, which might read something like Votes Obtained = 5 + 2M + 1P. The 5 in this equation indicates the number of votes likely to be obtained without any expenditure of funds. The 2 and the 1 indicate the relative weights of media dollars and precinct dollars in determining the number of votes obtained.[14]

In our illustration there are basically only two constraints. One relates costs to our two activity variables; the other relates benefits to our two activity variables. The first says the sum of media dollars and precinct organization dollars must be less than or equal to $10. This is our maximum cost constraint. The second constraint says 20 Votes = 5 + 2M + 1P. This is our

---

[14]On doing a regression analysis between policy alternatives and goals, see Hubert Blalock, *Social Statistics* (McGraw Hill, 1960), 273-285; and N. R. Draper and H. Smith, *Applied Regression Analysis* (Wiley, 1966).

minimum benefits constraint.

GRAPHING THE SOLUTION

To understand better what is involved in finding optimum expenditure combinations through linear programming, it is helpful to make a graph depicting our constraints. Table 4-4 shows the maximum cost line as a straight line connecting (1) the point at which $0 is spent for precinct organization and $10 is spent for media to (2) the point where $0 is spent for media and $10 is spent for precinct organization. Every point on that line involves a combination of M and P that adds up to $10 which is why it is also called an equal cost line.

Table 4-4 also shows the minimum benefits line as a straight line connecting (1) the point at which $0 is spent for precinct organization and $7.50 therefore has to be spent for media (in order for 5 + 2M + 1P to add up to 20) to (2) the point at which $0 is spent for media and $15 therefore has to be spent for precinct organization (in order for 5 + 2M + 1P to add up to 20). Every point on that line involves a combination of M and P that produces twenty votes, which is why it is also called an equal benefit line or an indifference line.

Regardless of whether we want to minimize costs or maximize benefits, the ideal combination has to be below the maximum cost line. Likewise, it has to be above the minimum benefit line. This means the ideal combination has to be a point somewhere in Table 4-4 within the area marked "feasible region" since that is the only area where both constraints are satisfied simultaneously.

Point A (where M = $7.50, and P = $0) is the point where total cost is minimized while providing at least twenty votes. This is so because that is the point furthest away from the maximum cost line that is still within the feasible region. By only spending $7.50, we save $2.50 for the next election or for other worthwhile causes. Point B (where M = $10 and P = $0) is the point where votes are maximized while not spending more than $10. This is so because that is the point furthest away from the maximum benefit line that is still within the feasible region. At that point, twenty-five votes will be obtained since the number of votes obtained equals 5 + 2M + 1P. One may wish to obtain these extra votes as insurance against miscalculation or in order to claim a mandate for an aggressive political program or for ego

TABLE 4-4
ALLOCATING MEDIA DOLLARS AND PRECINCT DOLLARS
TO MINIMIZE COSTS OR MAXIMIZE VOTES
(With Constant Returns to Dollars Spent)

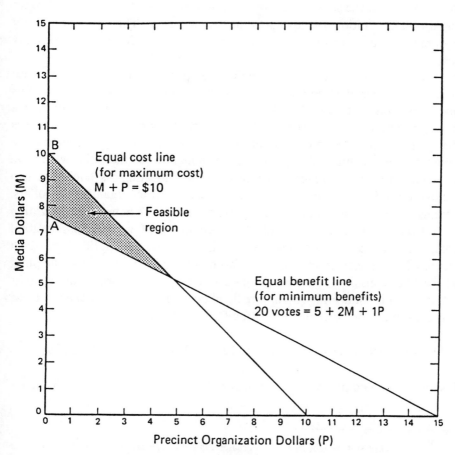

Point A is where total cost is minimized while providing at least 20 votes.
$$M = \$ 7.50 \qquad P = \$0 \qquad TC = \$ 7.50 \qquad Votes = 20$$

Point B is where votes are maximized while not spending more than $10.
$$M = \$10.00 \qquad P = \$0 \qquad TC = \$10.00 \qquad Votes \times 25$$

gratification.[15]

Note that the minimum benefits line represents a binding constraint on cost minimization in the sense that if we did not need to get at least twenty votes, we could save additional money. The money we are not saving by virtue of that constraint can be considered an opportunity cost. Also note that the maximum cost line represents a binding constraint on benefit maximization in the sense that if we did not need to limit ourselves to $10 we could obtain additional votes up to thirty-nine votes. The votes we are not obtaining by virtue of that constraint can also be considered an opportunity cost.

An alternative way of interpreting the optimizing in Table 4-4 is to use concepts from production and consumption economics. With those concepts one recognizes that point A is the cost minimization point because there is a family of parallel equal cost lines for every possible total cost, and point A is the point where the lowest equal cost line is at which just touches the minimum benefit line. This point can be thought of as the point where the producer of votes minimizes his total costs in allocating his budget to two factors of production, namely media dollars and precinct organization dollars, analogous to labor and capital. Likewise, point B is the benefit maximization point because there is a family of equal benefit lines for every possible total vote, and point B is the point where the highest equal benefit line is at which just touches the maximum cost line. This point can be thought of as the point where the consumer purchasing media and precinct organization units maximizes his total utility by optimally allocating his budget between these two consumer goods, analogous to food and clothing.

VARIATIONS AND ALTERNATIVES TO THE BASIC SCHEME

It should be noted that one cannot in our illustration maximize benefits minus

---

[15]If the regression weight of P were greater than the regression weight of M, then the minimum benefits line would intersect the vertical axis above the maximum cost line rather than below it. In other words, the minimum benefits line would be substantially steeper thereby showing just a little change in P is needed to offset a relatively big change in M to hold votes constant. In figure 1-2, however, just a little change in M is needed to offset a relatively big change in P to hold votes constant. The consequences of such a shift in the relative slopes and positions of the linear constraints are to (1) shift the feasible region to the lower portion of the hour glass figure, (2) shift minimization point A to the intersection of the P axis with the minimum benefits line, and (3) shift the benefits maximization point B to the intersection of the P axis with the maximum TC line.

costs. This is so because we do not know how many dollars we or our candidate considers a given vote to be worth. If one vote is worth $1, then point B maximizes benefits minus costs better than point A since 25 votes x $1 (minus $10 in costs) is more than 20 votes x $1 (minus $7.50). If, however, one vote is worth only $0.45, then point B maximizes benefits minus costs <u>worse</u> than point A since 25 votes x $0.45 (minus $10 in costs) is <u>less</u> than 20 votes x $0.45 (minus $7.50 in costs). Unless one can somehow convert a non-monetary benefit like votes into monetary units, one may have to choose between the goals of minimizing total costs or maximizing total benefits rather than trying to combine these two goals together.

Although one cannot (1) simultaneously minimize costs and maximize benefits or (2) maximize benefits minus costs, one can arrive at a compromise position between minimizing costs and maximizing benefits. Thus, with the data from Table 4-4, one can choose an M of $8.75, which is the midpoint between $7.50 (the cost minimization position) and $10.00 (the benefit maximization position). Doing so will mean a midpoint or compromise P of $0, TC of $8.75, and 22.5 votes.

In some linear programming problems, the activity variables cannot be allowed to go as low as $0 as we allowed them to do here. For example, in our problem, perhaps our candidate might insist on a minimum expenditure of $2 for precinct organization in order to preserve the precinct machinery which is needed for liaison work with his constituents between elections. This would mean drawing a vertical line in Table 4-4 up from the $2 precinct organization point to the top of the graph, thereby narrowing the feasible region and shifting it to the right. If such a constraint existed in our problem, then the new cost minimization point would be to spend $2 for precinct organization and $6.50 for media. The $6.50 is needed to bring the total expenditure up high enough to obtain twenty votes in light of the equation 20 votes = 5 + 2M + 1P. Likewise, if such a constraint existed in our problem, the new benefit maximization point would be to spend $2 for precinct organization and $8 for media. Such a combination will mean spending our full $10 in order to obtain twenty-three votes in light of the equation, votes obtained = 5 + 2M + 1P.

An alternative way of expressing the same ideas shown in Table 4-4 (that is more like the non-expenditure correlation analysis model previously presented) is to plot four separate graphs for the two goal variables and the two policy variables.[16] The first graph would show total cost as a goal or dependent variable on the vertical axis and precinct dollars as a policy or independent variable on the horizontal axis. One would then plot the relation TC = 7.5 + .5P, which follows from the fact that TC = M + P and M = (20 - 5 - P)/2. Doing so indicates total cost is at a minimum at $7.50 with twenty votes where P = $0. The second graph would show total cost against media dollars by plotting the relation TC = 15 - M, which follows from TC = M + P and P = 20 - 5 - 2M. Doing so also indicates that total cost is at a minimum at $7.50 where M = $7.50, provided neither P nor M can be negative. The third graph would show total votes against precinct dollars by plotting votes = 25 - P, which follows from votes = 5 + 2M + 1P and M = 10 - P. Doing so indicates that total votes are at a twenty-five-vote maximum when $0 are spent for P which means the whole $10 is being spent for M. The fourth graph would show total votes against media dollars by plotting votes = 15 + M. which follows from votes = 5 + 2M + 1P and P = 10 - M. Doing that also indicates total votes are at a maximum of twenty-five when M = $10.

To make our expenditure allocation problem somewhat more realistic, although somewhat more complicated, we could change the minimum benefit line to reflect the fact that incremental expenditures of either media or precinct organization dollars do not bring equally incremental votes. Instead, additional dollars spent tend to produce additional votes at a decreasing rate by virtue of the fact that additional votes, at least beyond a certain point, become harder to get.[17] A minimum benefit equation reflecting this phenomenon (and at the same time indicating that media dollars are more potent vote getters than precinct organization dollars) would be 20 votes = $5 \cdot \sqrt[2]{M} \cdot \sqrt[3]{P}$.

Table 4-5 shows this new diminishing-returns minimum-benefit line as a straight line because it is drawn on logarithmic interval paper rather than

---

[16]Graphing a goal variable against a policy variable (rather than graphing the policy variables against each other as in linear programming) is what Richmond refers to as a deterministic model. Samuel Richmond, *Operations Research for Management Decisions* (Ronald Press, 1968), pages 87-124. The deterministic approach especially lends itself to the use of differential calculus (where curved line relations are involved) for finding the slope of the goal variable with respect to the policy variable, setting this slope equal to zero, and then algebraically solving to find the optimum position on the policy variable.

[17]For an analysis of some aspects of curvilinear correlation, see Nagel, "Simplified Curvilinear Correlation" (mimeographed paper available from the writer).

TABLE 4-5
ALLOCATING MEDIA DOLLARS AND PRECINCT DOLLARS
TO MINIMIZE COSTS OR MAXIMIZE VOTES
(With Diminishing Returns to Dollars Spent)

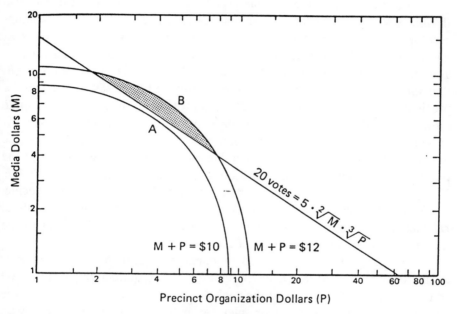

Point A is where total cost is minimized while providing at least 20 votes.

   M = \$6.20   P = \$4.15   TC = \$10.35   Votes = 20

Point B is where votes are maximized while not spending more than \$12.

   M = \$7.23   P = \$4.77   TC = \$12.00   Votes = 23

equal interval paper. The $10 maximum-cost line comes out to be a curved line rather than a straight line on logarithmic interval paper. Logarithmic interval paper is used because it converts the equation $20 = 5 \cdot \sqrt[2]{M} \cdot \sqrt[3]{P}$ into a straight line which makes it much easier to plot. Note that there is no point on the $10 maximum cost line which touches the minimum benefit line, and therefore, there is no combination of M and P adding up to less than $10 which will achieve twenty votes with this new minimum benefit line.

In order to create a feasible region, a $12 maximum cost line is also shown. The feasible region is then logically at or beneath the $12 maximum-cost line and also at or above the twenty-vote minimum benefit line. The cost minimization point A is at the point on the minimum benefit line furthest away from the $12 cost line or closest to the $10 cost line. It just so happens that this is the point where $6.20 is spent for media and $4.15 is spent for precinct organization. This exact allocation was determined by using simple differential calculus, but one can make an accurate enough estimate by carefully examining the graph especially if more one-tailed one-cycle logarithmic graph paper is used. The benefit maximization point B is at the point on the maximum cost line furthest away from the minimum benefit line. This is the point where $7.23 is spent for media and $4.77 is spent for precinct organization. This exact allocation was also determined by using differential calculus, but again, one can make a reasonably accurate estimate from the graph or a more detailed version of it.[18]

To ease the work involved in linear programming, there are now available many canned computer routines that only require a simple statement of the constraints to satisfy and the goals to optimize in order to calculate the optimum allocation points for two or more expenditure alternatives. Unfortunately, such computer routines are not so readily available for the diminishing returns or non-linear programming problem, but it can often be handled either graphically or with the aid of an electronic calculator for doing the calculus arithmetic involved. Computer routines for doing linear and non-linear regression analysis are helpful for determining the benefit constraint

---

[18]To make a calculus determination of M at the cost minimization point, find the slope of the equation $TC = M + P$, with $(20/(5 \cdot \sqrt[2]{M}))^3$ substituted for P. Then set the expression for the slope equal to zero, and solve for M. To make a calculus determination of M at the votes maximization point, find the slope of the equation $V = 5 \cdot \sqrt[2]{M} \cdot \sqrt[3]{P}$, with $10 - M$ substituted for P. Then set the expression for the slope equal to zero, and solve for M. Richmond, *op cit.* note 11, at 40-66 and 577.

equations.[19]

THE NEED FOR REFINEMENTS AND APPLICATIONS

In many expenditure-policy problems, the goal or benefits variable is not as easy to measure as votes are. Nevertheless there are a number of imaginative ways to measure psychological satisfaction or other goal variables.[20] Goal measurement problems are involved in both expenditure and non-expenditure policies. They are generally not as difficult to handle as the broader problem which this chapter has emphasized of relating means or policies to goals in making policy choices.

Many further refinements can be developed on the basic methodological techniques presented here for choosing among non-expenditure and expenditure policies. What is especially needed, however, is not so much additional methodological refinements, but rather the application of these existing methodologies to more public policy controversies by social scientists, policy appliers, and policymakers.

This research is one of a series of policy science studies on measuring and achieving effects of alternative legal policies partly financed by the National Science Foundation grant GS-2875. The writer also thanks Duncan MacRae for his suggestive ideas.[21]

---

[19]For further discussion of the linear programming approach to making expenditure policy choices, see Charles Laidlaw, *Linear Programming for Urban Development Plan Evaluation* (Praeger, 1972); William Baumol, *Economic Theory and Operations Analysis* (Prentice-Hall, 1965), 70-102; and Stuart Nagel, *Minimizing Costs and Maximizing Benefits in Providing Legal Services to the Poor*, (Sage Publications Series on Administrative and Policy Studies, 1973).

[20]On measuring benefits and costs of public policies, see Guy Black, *The Application of Systems Analysis to Government Operations* (Praeger, 1968), 37-89; R. Dorfman, *Measuring Benefits in Government Investments* (Brookings, 1964); David Alberts, *A Plan for Measuring the Performance of Social Programs: The Application of Operations Research Methodology* (Praeger, 1970); and J. P. Guilford, *Psychometric Methods* (McGraw-Hill, 1954), 154-301.

[21]Recent books on choosing among alternative public policies include Edward Quade and Grace Carter, *Analysis for Public Decisions* (North-Holland, 1989); S. Nagel, *Public Policy: Goals, Means, and Methods* (St. Martin's, 1984, and University Press of America, 1991); S. Nagel, John Long, and Miriam Mills, *Evaluation Analysis with Microcomputers* (JAI Press, 1989); Michael White et al., *Managing Public Systems: Analytic Techniques for Public Administration* (Duxbury, 1980); Duncan MacRae and James Wilde, *Policy Analysis for Public Decisions* (Duxbury, 1979); Edith Stokey and Richard Zeckhauser, *A Primer for Policy Analysis and Planning* (Norton, 1978); Carl Patton and David Sawicki, *Basic Methods of Policy Analysis*

and Planning (Prentice Hall, 1986); and Christopher McKenna, *Quantitative Methods for Public Decision Making* (McGraw Hill, 1980).

5

THE NEED FOR JUDICIAL REFORM

There are seven judicial reform problems which tend to be felt in criminal and civil cases: (1) bail reform, (2) legal counsel for the poor in criminal and civil cases, (3) delay in civil and criminal cases, (4) mass media reporting on pending cases, (5) judicial selection, (6) the jury system, and (7) judicial nullification of legislative and administrative acts.

PRETRIAL RELEASE

One of the first stages in criminal proceedings which seems to call for judicial reform is the stage at which a decision is made about an arrested suspect prior to his trial. The basic alternatives involve releasing or not releasing him prior to trial depending on (1) whether he can offer a sufficient money deposit to serve as a guarantee or incentive that he will return for trial, or (2) whether his characteristics are such that he is likely to return for his trial rather than risk being prosecuted as a bail jumper. The first alternative is referred to as the traditional bail bond system, and the second alternative as release on one's own recognizance or the ROR system.

In past years, the bail system was by far the dominant method. This was so partly because of the belief that individuals were economically motivated and partly because the system favored middle class people whose interests tended to dominate legal rulemaking.   The reform trend is increasingly toward a more objective and scientific ROR system for a number of reasons.

Studies by the Vera Institute in New York City have shown that by carefully screening arrested suspects into good risks and bad risks (largely on the basis of their roots in the community and the seriousness of their crimes), one can obtain at least as low a percentage of bail jumpers as one does with the traditional money-deposit system.[1] Trial-day mail or phone reminders also help reduce bail jumping. These studies have further shown that, with the screening and notification system, a far higher percentage of arrested suspects can be released from jail pending their trial than under the money-deposit system. Such release means these good risks can (1) continue their jobs, (2) better prepare their cases to establish their innocence, (3) save the taxpayer money by not occupying jail space, and (4) be less bitter than if they spent time in jail and were then acquitted. The money-deposit system so inherently discriminates against the poor that the United States Supreme Court may someday declare it to be in violation of the equal protection clause of the Constitution.[2]

One objection to the ROR system is that it might result in releasing a number of arrested suspects who will commit crimes while awaiting trial. One response to this objection is that truly dangerous persons should be kept in jail pending a speedy trial regardless of how able they are to offer a large money deposit. Another response is to point out that pretrial crimes are more often due to long delays prior to trial than to poor screening or the lack of a bail bond requirement. The delay problem, however, is a separate area of judicial reform.[3]

---

[1]C. Ares, A. Rankin, and H. Sturz, "The Manhattan Bail Project: An Interim Report on the Use of Pre-Trial Parole," 38 *New York University Law Review* 67-95 (1963)

[2]Bandy v. United States, 364 U.S. 477 (1960)

[3]For further detail on bail reform, see D. Freed and P. Wald, *Bail in the United States* (Washington, D.C.: Government Printing Office, 1964) and R. Goldfarb, *Ransom: A Critique of the American Bail System* (New York: Harper & Row, 1965). See also the article by R. Pious in the July, 1971, *Current History.*

LEGAL COUNSEL FOR THE POOR

In the 1962 case of Gideon v. Wainwright, the Supreme Court declared that criminal defendants who could not afford to hire an attorney to represent them should be provided with a free attorney by the prosecuting government at least for crimes involving more than a possible six-month jail sentence.[4] Prior to 1962, some states already provided counsel to indigent defendants before the Supreme Court required it, although many states felt that free counsel to the poor was too expensive, or socialistic, or unnecessary.

The big problem now is how, not whether, to provide counsel. The basic alternatives are either (1) relying on unpaid or paid volunteer attorneys, (2) having the courts assign attorneys to represent indigent defendants, or (3) using full-time public defenders who receive a salary from the government to which they are attached.

The unpaid volunteer system has the disadvantage that it too often attracts young attorneys who are seeking experience at the possible expense of a client whose liberty might be jeopardized. The paid volunteer system, however, works well at the federal level, where only well qualified attorneys are allowed to volunteer, and where they are fully compensated for their services. In smaller communities, where assigned counsel is often used, clients are frequently represented by reluctant attorneys or by attorneys who have had little or no criminal case experience.

The full-time public defender system is being increasingly used, although many public defender offices are under-financed and under-staffed and thus cannot investigate and defend their cases as vigorously as they otherwise should. To make the public defender applicable to smaller communities, states like Minnesota are beginning to experiment with regional public defenders who cover a number of rural counties.

Although the Supreme Court has not yet required free counsel for the poor in housing eviction, auto repossession, or other civil cases, the federal Office of Economic Opportunity and most local communities have sought to provide some form of civil legal aid. Their efforts are justified on the grounds that legal aid can promote respect for the law, protect the innocent, encourage orderly law reform, and educate the poor to their legal rights and obligations.

The basic alternatives for civil legal aid are similar to those for

---

[4]Gideon v. Wainright, 372 U.S. 335 (1963)

criminal legal aid. The traditional system has involved volunteer attorneys whose availability is generally limited and little known. In recent years, the O.E.O. has provided many cities with full-time civil legal services programs similar to public defender offices. Some attorneys have proposed the judicare system for civil legal aid whereby poor clients go to the attorney of their choice, and the government pays the attorney's fee as in medicare. The judicare system has been criticized as lacking visibility, specialists in poverty law, preventative education, and law reform; it is also criticized for an excess of bookkeeping, potential federal regulation, and expensiveness.

To provide legal service to middle class people, proposals have been made for various kinds of legal insurance and various plans whereby attorneys for unions or other organizations can represent individual members. Such plans have, however, been opposed by bar associations who fear that organization attorneys will lack a close attorney-client relationship and who also fear the economic competition which such a system would represent to traditional law practice. Certain organizational schemes, however, have been declared by the Supreme Court to be protected by the freedom of assembly clause of the Constitution, and will probably increasingly be established.[5]

DELAY IN THE COURT

Increased industrialization and urbanization have indirectly produced undesirable delays in both civil and criminal cases. Automobile accidents mainly explain the long delays in civil cases, often extending to five years in the larger cities. Urbanization and the accompanying increased crime rates have significantly added to criminal court congestion.

In a delayed personal injury case, the injured party may be unable to collect what he is entitled to because of the forgetfulness and loss of witnesses and the pressure to settle for quicker, although reduced, damage payments. Although the delays are shorter in criminal cases, they can be especially harmful if the arrested suspect must wait in jail pending his trial and then receives an acquittal or a sentence shorter than the time he has already waited in jail. Criminal case delays are also harmful if the arrested suspect is released pending trial and commits further crimes during the long waiting

---

[5]For further detail on legal aid programs, see P. Wald, *Law & Poverty* (Washington, D.C.: Government Printing Office, 1965) and L. Silverstein, *Defense of the Poor* (Boston: Little Brown, 1966).

period.

To reduce delay in civil cases, various reforms have been attempted or proposed. Some reforms are designed to encourage out-of-court settlements by providing for impartial medical experts, pretrial settlement conferences, interest charges beginning with the day of the accident, and pretrial proceedings to enable the parties to know where they stand with regard to each other's evidence. Other reforms are designed to remove personal injury cases from the courts by shifting them to administrative agencies, or by providing that injured parties automatically collect from their own insurance company regardless of their negligence as with fire insurance.

The time consumed by the jury trial stage can be reduced by having high jury fees, providing earlier trial for non-jury cases, randomly picking 12 jurors without lengthy selection, and by separating the liability and damage issues (so there is no need to discuss damages if the defendant is found non-liable, and so settlement can be facilitated if liability is established). Reformers have also recommended that delay be reduced by having more judges, making them work more days per year and more hours per day. shifting judges from low to high congestion courts, and decreasing wasted judge-time due to poor scheduling of the same attorney in two different courts.

Reforms designed to reduce delay in criminal cases are similar to those in civil cases. There can be better screening of complaints, more encouragement of guilty pleas where merited, more criminal court personnel, less use of grand jury indictment, more pretrial proceedings to narrow the issues, random jury selection, and release of the defendant within a specified period of time if he is not tried. The Supreme Court has recently made speedy trial in criminal cases a constitutional right at both the state and federal levels.[6]

REPORTING ON PENDING CASES

How to handle the problem of mass media reporting on criminal cases involves an interesting conflict between two civil liberties. On the one side

---

[6]Klopfer v. North Carolina, 386 U.S. 213 (1967). For further detail in court delay, see H. Zeisel, Hans Kalven, and B. Buchholz, *Delay in the Court* (Boston: Little Brown, 1959); and H. Jones, *The Courts, the Public, and the Law Explosion* (Englewood Cliffs, N.J.: Prentice Hall, 1965).

is freedom of speech and freedom of the press which includes the right to report on pending cases. On the other side is the constitutional right to a fair trial which should not be prejudiced by distorted reporting or by reporting evidence that is not admissible in court.

The United States Supreme Court has been more sensitive to the fair trial interest than to the free press interest in cases where the two have conflicted. This was especially so in the 1966 Sam Sheppard case where the Cleveland newspapers published front page editorials demanding Sheppard's conviction, created near chaos outside the courtroom with their numerous photographers, and published unsubstantiated damaging statements by Walter Winchell and the Cleveland police chief that were never testified to at the trial.[7] The Supreme Court declared that in future sensational cases the trial should be held away from the community where the crime was committed; attorneys should be reprimanded for gossiping to reporters; jurors and sometimes witnesses should be kept from seeing newspapers; reporters should be held in contempt for printing gossip while a trial is still in process; and the number of reporters in the courtroom should be severely limited. After many years in prison, Sam Sheppard was eventually retried without prejudicial press publicity, and in that trial he was acquitted.

Since the Sam Sheppard case, many newspapers and newspaper associations have established various rules providing for voluntary press restraints. The American Bar Association has likewise established a set of rules restraining attorneys in criminal cases from communicating prejudicial information to the press. Because these restraints have not been sufficiently effective, some reformers have proposed more use of the British system whereby newspapers are readily held in contempt of court for publishing almost anything other than the barest facts about criminal trials until the trial is completed.[8]

JUDICIAL SELECTION

How should judges be chosen? Basically, they are either (1) appointed by the President, governor, or mayor with or without the approval of a bipartisan

---

[7]Sheppard v. Maxwell, 384 U.S. 333 (1966)

[8]For further detail on pretrial publicity, see A. Friendly and R. Goldfarb, *Crime and Publicity* (New York: Twentieth Century Fund, 1967); and D. M. Gillmore, *Free Press and Fair Trial* (Washington, D.C.: Public Affairs Press, 1966).

nominating commission or legislature, or (2) elected by the general public with partisan or non-partisan election procedures. Originally nearly all United States judges were appointed, but during the period of Jacksonian democracy a shift toward electing state and local judges began. Federal judges have always been appointed as specified in the Constitution. In the last few decades, there has been a shift back to gubernatorial appointment of state and local judges.

Those who argue in favor of elected judges point out that judicial decisionmaking frequently involves subjective value judgments. In a democracy, these values should probably reflect general public opinion. The electoral advocates also point out that elected judges will come closer in their backgrounds to the general public than appointed judges, especially if the nominating commission tends to be dominated by the state bar association. These and other differences in the attitudes and background of elected and appointed judges can be tested[9] by comparing elected judges with judges who have been appointed on appointed courts or on elected courts as interim judges to complete the unexpired terms of dead, retired, or resigned judges.

Those who argue in favor of appointed judges seek to establish that appointed judges are less partisan in their judicial voting behavior. This may, however, be due more to the bipartisan approval that is needed for appointment, to appointment across party lines by some governors, and to the differences in how appointed judges view their roles, rather than directly to the selection process. The advocates of appointment also argue that appointed judges are technically more competent because they tend to come from the better law schools and colleges than elected judges, but the empirical evidence does not support this point.

Closely related to the method of judicial selection is the length of judicial tenure, since judicial reform movements usually advocate both appointive selection and longer judicial terms. Longer terms give a judge more independence from political party pressures. Such terms, however, are likely to make judges less responsive to public opinion although possibly more sensitive to minority rights.

Because of the somewhat evenly divided controversy over elected versus appointed judges, various compromises have developed. Illinois, for instance, has provided for regular elections for vacant judgeships (with

---

[9]H. Jacob, "The Effect of Institutional Differenes in the Recruitment Process: The Case of State Judges," 13 *Journal of Public Law* 104-119 (1964) and S. Nagel, *The Legal Process from a Behavioral Perspective* (Homewood, Ill.: Dorsey Press, 1969), pp. 173-197)

provision for opposition candidates) to be followed periodically by retention elections (whereby each sitting judge runs against his record with the voters being able to vote only yes or no on his retention). Such compromises will probably become increasingly prevalent.[10]

THE JURY SYSTEM

Jurors in medieval England were originally persons from the community who were witnesses to the facts in dispute. Eventually the jury evolved into a group of community representatives who resolved factual disputes in cases, while the judge determined the applicable law. Traditionally the jury has consisted of 12 people chosen by both sides from a list of voters, and they have determined guilt in criminal cases and liability civil cases by unanimous decision. In recent years, the idea of having juries to supplement the work of judges has come under attack.

It is argued that jury trials consume too much time or that juries lack competence. It is also charged that juries sometimes ignore the legal instructions given them, such as when they are told that plaintiffs in auto accident cases should not collect anything if the plaintiff has been partially negligent regardless of how negligent the defendant may have been. One can counter this criticism by saying that if an old law is unjust, as this rule of contributory negligence may be, the jury system often softens its harsh effects by applying a more contemporary community sense of justice.

The defenders of the jury system point out that a jury trial is more likely to free the innocent than a bench trial because all approximately 12 jury members must agree to convict and because jurors tend to be more like defendants than judges are. Judges and juries agree approximately 83 percent of the time in criminal cases, but when they disagree the jury is nearly always pro-defendant and the judge pro-prosecutor. This and other findings about jury behavior have been developed as part of the research of the University of Chicago Jury Project.

Defenders also argue that the jury system by providing public participation encourages respect for the law. It has, for instance, been found

---

[10]For further detail on judicial election, see R. Watson and R. Downing, *The Politics of the Bench and the Bar: Judicial Selection Under the Missouri Non-partisan Court Plan* (New York, John Wiley, 1969) and E. Haynes, *The Selection and Tenure of Judges* (New York: National Conference of Judicial Councils, 1944).

in before-and-after tests that being a juror does improve one's attitude toward the legal system. This public participation also enables ambiguities in the facts or law to be resolved in the direction of general public opinion.

As a compromise between the attackers and the defenders of the jury system, the trend seems to be in the direction of juries smaller than twelve men deciding by less than unanimous vote. This trend has been especially present in civil cases, and the Supreme Court has recently held it to be constitutional for criminal cases.[11]

JUDICIAL REVIEW

After pretrial release, appointment of counsel, possible delay, newspaper reporting, picking of a judge and the jury's decision, there comes the stage of a possible appeal to a higher court. The most controversial aspect of appellate-court decision-making, although it can also occur at the trial court levels, is the potential nullification by the court of a state or federal statute or administrative regulation. This process of judicial review is peculiar to countries whose constitutions are embodied in a single written document (unlike Great Britain) and is partly attributable to the personality of John Marshall as manifested in his Marbury v. Madison decision.[12]

Many arguments favor giving the courts the power of judicial review rather than leaving it to Congress and the people to determine the constitutionality of legislative acts. It is argued that Congress cannot be trusted to police itself since it has a vested interest in its own legislation. Another strong point is that unpopular minority viewpoints need the courts to protect them. It is also said that constitutional interpretation requires technical legal training which the courts have, and that the courts have less political bias than legislatures do.

Arguments against judicial review emphasize that Congress is more responsive to public opinion, although in the long run the courts are also somewhat responsive, at least via personnel changes. Attacks in the past on judicial review have also stressed the conservatism of the courts, particularly with regard to economic regulation. It is further noted that the lack of

---

[11]Williams v. Florida, 399 U.S. 78 (1970). For further details on the jury system, see H. Kalven and H. Zeisel, *The American Jury* (Boston: Little Brown, 1966); C. Joiner, *Civil Justice and the Jury* (Englewood Cliffs, N.J.: Prentice-Hall, 1962)

[12]Marbury v. Madison, 1 Cranch 137 (1803)

preciseness in the Constitution makes it more a political than a legal document, and that there have often been substantial differences between Democratic and Republican judges in constitutional interpretation.

Between the positions of complete judicial review over all types of statutes and no judicial review at all, there are many intermediate positions. It could be made more difficult for the courts to exercise judicial review by (1) requiring more than a simple majority of judicial votes or (2) allowing for congressional overruling, as with presidential vetoes. Other intermediate positions seek to make the Supreme Court more responsive by having it (1) composed of representatives from all three branches of government as in some West European systems, (2) an elected or shorter-term court, or (3) composed of representatives from all 50 states (a suggestion proposed in a constitutional amendment which many states have passed).

Further intermediate positions involve judicial review only over legislation relating to (1) the judiciary where the court has a special protective interest, (2) state legislation, in order to preserve American federalism, or (3) civil liberties matters where ideological, ethnic, or other minority interests need protection. The trend is decidedly toward the latter position of a civil liberties-oriented judicial review. Big business, which received so many of the benefits of judicial review in the past, can more adequately protect itself in the legislative process.[13]

There are other fields of reform in the American system of justice. For example, prior to the bail stage there is considerable controversy over how to make the police more efficient in apprehending criminals while at the same time complying with constitutional requirements relating to searches and interrogation.[14] Likewise subsequent to the appeal and judicial review stage, there is considerable controversy over how to make prisons more rehabilitative while at the same time providing a negative deterrent to criminality.[15]

---

[13]For further detail on judicial review, see H. Dean, *Judicial Review and Democracy* (New York: Random House, 1966) and R. Carr, *The Supreme Court and Judicial Review* (New York: Rinehart, 1942).

[14]For further detail on police efficiency, see O.W. Wilson, *Police Administration* (New York: McGraw Hill, 1963); J. Skoonick, *Justice Without Trial: Law Enforcement in a Democratic Society* (New York: John Wiley, 1967).

[15]For further detail on prison reform, see D. Glaser, *The Effectiveness of a Prison and Parole System* (Indianapolis: Bobbs-Merrill, 1964); P. Tappan, *Crime, Justice, and Correction* (New York: McGraw-Hill, 1960).

A CHANGING ENVIRONMENT

The fact that reform is needed does not necessarily indicate that the American system of justice has been inefficient or discriminatory as measured by past standards. It does indicate that the American environment is changing with regard to organization which affects efficiency, and that middle class Americans are becoming more sensitive to discriminatory injustices that were formerly tolerated. It is certainly encouraging to note that in recent years the courts and other policy-making bodies have instituted numerous innovations to attempt to resolve the problems raised by pretrial release, legal aid, court delay, pretrial reporting, judicial selection, the jury system, and judicial review, although more still remains to be done.[16]

---

[16]For further detail on judicial or justice reform in general, see H. James, *Crisis in the Courts* (New York:McKay, 1969); A. Vanderbilt, *Minimum Standards of Judicial Administration* (New York: National Conference of Judicial Councils, 1949); American Bar Association, *Minimum Standards for Criminal Justice* (Institute of Judicial Administration, a series of booklets published from 1967 on). More recent books on judicial and legal reform include Jay Sigler and Benjamin Beede, *The Legal Sources of Public Policy* (Lexington-Heath, 1977); Ethan Katsh (ed.), *Taking Sides: Clashing Views on Controversial Legal Issues* (Dushkin, 1991); Fannie Klein (ed.), *The Improvement of the Administration of Justice* (American Bar Association, 1981); Nan Aron, *Liberty and Justice for All: Public Interest Law in the 1980s and Beyond* (Westview, 1989); Philip Dubois (ed.), *The Analysis of Judicial Reform* (Lexington-Heath, 1982); James Q. Wilson (ed.), *Crime and Public Policy* (Transaction, 1983); Herbert Jacob (ed.), *The Potential for Reform of Criminal Justice* (Sage, 1974); and Joel Handler, *Social Movements and the Legal System: A Theory of Law Reform and Social Change* (Academic Press, 1978).

PART TWO:

THE SOCIAL SCIENCE OF OPTIMIZING

SECTION C:

FINDING AN OPTIMUM CHOICE

6

OPTIMUM CHOICE WITHOUT PROBABILITIES

The general purpose of this chapter is to discuss some of the problems involved in making an optimum choice among discrete policy alternatives. By "discrete policy alternatives" we mean a set of political or governmental choices that have no inherent order, such as releasing or not releasing a defendant prior to trial or choosing among 5,000 legally acceptable ways of redistricting a state legislature. Discrete alternatives can be contrasted with continuum alternatives where the choices do have inherent order, such as deciding an optimum jury size between 6 and 12 jurors inclusively, or deciding how to allocate a 5,000 dollar budget among a variety of places or activities. Twelve jurors is inherently larger than six jurors, and 2,000 dollars given to a place is inherently larger than 1,000 dollars. Continuum decisions are often referred to as optimum level and optimum mix decisions, whereas discrete decisions are simply referred to as optimum choice decisions although both continuum and discrete decisions involve optimum choices. Making decisions with discrete alternatives, however, involves a different and generally simpler logic than making decisions with continuum alternatives.

The basic logic for making optimum decisions with discrete alternatives is to determine the benefits minus costs for each alternative, and then pick the alternative that has the best B-C score. Sometimes the benefits and/or the costs are contingent on the occurrence of an event, and they thus need to be discounted by the probability of the event occurring. Under those circumstances, one should determine the discounted benefits minus the discounted costs for each alternative. Discounting benefits or costs may simply mean determining B and C on the assumption that the event will occur, but then multiplying B and C by the probability of the event occurring. One then picks the alternative that has the best PB-PC score, where each P is a different probability or combination of probabilities. There are also more specialized principles, such as those for (1) discounting the time one has to wait to receive benefits or costs, (2) calculating thresholds for P, B, or C above which one of two alternatives is preferred and below which the other is preferred, and for (3) shortcutting the analysis by eliminating some alternatives for which it is not necessary to calculate benefits and costs.[1]

There are a variety of ways of classifying situations involving the making of an optimum choice without probabilities. One can look at (1) whether or not there are decisional constraints with regard to mutual exclusivity or limited budgets, (2) whether the price and quantity components of the benefits and costs involve interval or binary measurement, and (3) whether the alternatives and goals involve multiple or dichotomous categories.

DECISIONAL CONSTRAINTS

MUTUAL EXCLUSIVITY

Table 6-1 provides data for a set of five projects. The object is to allocate scarce resources among one or more projects in order to make the optimum use of those scarce resources. For each project, we indicate the benefits for given costs, the net benefits or profitability, and the benefit/cost ratio or efficiency measure. Each project is a lump-sum project in the sense that one can only buy one unit of the project, not multiple units and not fractions of units. That occurrence is more typical of public sector problems than business problems. For example, a typical set of government projects involving benefit-cost analysis is a set of alternative dams within a river segment. At any given

---

[1]On reaching optimum decisions in general, see Edith Stokey and Richard Zeckhauser, *A Primer for Policy Analysis* (New York: Norton, 1978); Peter Rossi, Howard Freeman, and Sonia Wright, *Evaluation: A Systematic Approach* (Beverly Hills, Ca.: Sage, 1979); Michael White, *et al., Managing Public Systems: Analytic Techniques for Public Administration* (Belmont, Ca.: Duxbury, 1980); and S. Nagel and M. Neef, *Policy Analysis: In Social Science Research* (Beverly Hills, Ca.: Sage, 1979).

TABLE 6-1. MUTUAL EXCLUSIVITY AND LIMITED BUDGETS
AS DECISIONAL CONSTRAINTS IN OPTIMUM CHOICE
WITHOUT PROBABILITIES*

Project	Benefits (in dollars)	Rank	Costs (in dollars)	Rank	B–C (in dollars)	Rank	B/C	Rank
D	4.20	5	3.00	4	1.20	5	1.40	4
E	13.50	1	10.00	1	3.50	1	1.35	5
F	3.50	4	2.00	5	1.50	4	1.75	1
G	9.00	2	6.00	2	3.00	2	1.50	3
H	6.40	3	4.00	3	2.40	3	1.60	2
Totals	36.60		25.00		11.60		7.60	
Averages	7.32		5.00		2.32		1.52	

*Notes to the Figure:

(1)If the projects are mutually exclusive, Project E is the best buy, provided that one can afford the 10 dollar cost.

(2)If the projects are not mutually exclusive, all the projects should be bought provided that one can afford the 25 dollar total cost.

(3)If the projects are not mutually exclusive and one had only 10 dollars available, the best or most profitable combination is G and H, even though they are individually not the most profitable, efficient, effective, or least expensive.

place in the river, it is meaningless to build two duplicative dams, one behind the other or one on top of the other since one dam does all the good that can be done. Similarly, it is meaningless to build half a dam, since the water can flow over half a dam as easily as no dam. Alternative dams are thus not only lump sum projects, but they are also mutually exclusive.

To begin using data from Table 6-1, we can compare Project E or Dam E which has the highest net benefits, with Project F or Dam F, which has the highest efficiency. One basic principle in policy evaluation is to prefer high net benefits over high efficiency. By doing so, we will be better off after that choice is made, assuming other things remain constant. To be more specific, if we invest 10 dollars in Project E, then at the end of the relevant time period we will have the equivalent of 10 dollars in principal and 3.50 dollars in interest, for total assets of 13.50 dollars. If, however, we invest 2 dollars in Project F, then at the end of the time period we will have 2 dollars in principal, 1.50 dollars in interest, and 8 dollars in idle funds, for total assets of only 11.50 dollars. The 8 dollars in idle funds may or may not be able to fund an alternative investment opportunity that pays interest at a rate higher than the .75 of Project F or the .35 of Project E. An alternative perspective is to say, if we buy Project E we will have 13.50 dollars in benefits, whereas if we buy Project F we will have 3.50 dollars in benefits plus 8 dollars in unspent funds, for a total of only 11.50 dollars. In other words, we come out behind by going with the more efficient Project F than by going with the more profitable Project E, regardless of whether we view the situation from the perspective of an investor or a consumer. Thus if the projects were mutually exclusive, Project E would be the best buy, provided that we could afford it.

The situation becomes a bit more complicated, but more interesting, if the projects are not considered mutually exclusive, so that we can buy more than one project. An example of a set of five nonmutually exclusive lump-sum projects might be five different ways of notifying or reminding released defendants to appear in court. The projects could include (1) sending defendants postcards a few days before their trials, (2) phoning them within that time period, (3) going to their homes, (4) having them report to a court officer within that time period, and/or (5) putting a general notice in the newspaper emphasizing that people who fail to appear for their court dates get arrested. It would not be meaningful to go to their homes twice in that time, or only go halfway to their homes. Deliberately notifying only some of the defendants might be unconstitutional treatment. The data in Table 6-1 could be thought of as applying to those five notification projects rather than to five alternative dams. The benefits would be the dollars saved by not having to rearrest no-shows, as contrasted to the flood damage avoided. If we had an unlimited budget (i.e., a budget of 25 dollars or more) that is capable of buying all the projects, then we would buy all of them since they are all profitable.

LIMITED BUDGETS

Suppose we only have 10 dollars available to spend for those five notification projects. Which ones are the best to buy or invest in? One might think we should use the 10 dollars to buy the first most profitable project, then the second, and so on until we exhaust our 10 dollars. That, however, would be fallacious reasoning since we would then spend all our 10 dollars on Project E for a profit of only 3.50 dollars. By distributing our 10 dollars among other less profitable projects, we could make more total profit. For example, we could buy projects F, H, and D. They would collectively cost us only 9 dollars, leaving 1 dollar left over. Buying those three would include the first and second most efficient projects. More important, the sum of the net benefits for those three projects adds to 5.10 dollars, which is substantially more than the 3.50 dollars we would get by spending our 10 dollars on the single most profitable project. In other words, what is most profitable to do with mutually exclusive lump-sum projects may not be most profitable when the projects are not mutually exclusive.

Although buying F, H, and D with our 10 dollars makes more sense than just buying F, it is still not the most profitable way to allocate our 10 dollars, although it may be a highly efficient way, since it yields 5.10 dollars for an investment of only 9 dollars. It has the defect though of allowing 1 dollar to remain idle that otherwise might be profitably spent. We could use our whole 10 dollars to buy projects G and H. At first glance, that looks irrational, because those projects individually do not score best on benefits, costs, net benefits, or efficiency. At second glance, however, one can see that the G and H combination will produce a total profit of 5.40 dollars, which is higher than one can produce by any other combination of 10 dollars worth of projects, including F, H, and D. More specifically, the G and H combination gives us, at the end of the time period, total assets of 15.40 dollars, which consists of 10 dollars in principle and 5.40 dollars in interest. The F, H, and D combination, on the other hand, gives us at the end of the time period, total assets of only 15.10 dollars, which consists of 9 dollars in principle, 5.10 dollars in interest, and 1 dollar in idle funds.

The general rules that one might derive from this analysis are first, if a government agency is interested in maximizing the good that it does, then it should spend its whole budget, or as much as possible. Second, spend the budget for each of the projects in the order of their efficiency. Those two rules together should lead to an optimum allocation of one's scarce resources among the lump-sum projects, which are often present in governmental decision making.

One might object to the difficulty of measuring both benefits and costs in the same units, especially monetary units. With varying degrees of effort, however, one can usually assign a monetary value to controlling floods, getting the average defendant to show up for a trial date, or obtaining other public sector benefits. The human mind implicitly makes such calculations in deciding whether benefits are worth the costs. Thus, quantifying benefits in terms of cost units is only a matter of making that kind of thinking more explicit. A common alternative is to talk in terms of maximizing benefits subject to a maximum cost constraint, or sometimes minimizing costs subject to a minimum benefit constraint, rather than maximizing benefits minus costs. These alternatives may sometimes be satisfactory, but they are not as desirable, as is indicated by their inapplicability in deciding between projects E and F if the benefits for those two projects were not both measured in dollars. In other words, 3.5 F units for 2 dollars could be worth more or less than 13.5 E units for 10 dollars, but 3.50 dollars is clearly worth less for 2 dollars, than 13.50 dollars is for 10 dollars. The desirability of maximizing benefits minus costs applies to both business firms and government agencies, although business firms may generally find it easier to measure benefits and costs in dollars as a common unit.[2]

BENEFITS AND COSTS AS PRICE TIMES QUANTITY

INTERVAL MEASUREMENT ON PRICE AND QUANTITY

Benefits are like total revenue in economics. As such, benefits can be considered as being equal to the value or average price of each unit of

[2]On benefit-cost analysis as applied to discrete projects, see Mark Thompson, *Benefit-Cost Analysis for Program Evaluation* (Beverly Hills, Ca.: Sage, 1980); Guy Black, *The Application of Systems Analysis to Government Operations* (New York: Praeger, 1968); Roland McKean, *Efficiency in Government Through Systems Analysis* (New York: Wiley, 1958), pp. 1-102; Ezra Mishan, *Cost-Benefit Analysis* (New York: Praeger, 1976); and Peter Sassone and William Schaefer, *Cost-Benefit Analysis: A Handbook* (New York: Academic Press, 1978).

benefits, multiplied by the quantity of units. Similarly, costs can be considered equal to the value or average price of each unit of costs, multiplied by the quantity of units. As in economics, price can range over a wide interval, rather than only being a dichotomy of relatively high versus relatively low.

To understand better this type of analysis, it is helpful to have a concrete example. One example is the problem situation of deciding how to decrease the occurrence of illegal searches by the police. One alternative that the courts have adopted is to exclude or throw out illegally obtained evidence from courtroom proceedings in criminal cases, on the theory that doing so will deter the police from using illegal methods to obtain evidence. Prior to 1961, the U.S. Supreme Court allowed the state courts and legislatures to decide themselves whether to adopt this exclusionary rule. In 1961, the Supreme Court in the case of *Mapp v. Ohio* declared that the fourth amendment required that illegally seized evidence by inadmissible in all U.S. criminal cases, at least when objected to by defense counsel.

In 1963, a mailed-questionnaire survey was made of one randomly selected police chief, prosecuting attorney, judge, defense attorney, and ACLU official in each of the 50 states to determine, among other things, their perceptions of changes in police behavior before and after *Mapp v. Ohio*. The experiment was aided by virtue of the fact that 24 of the 50 states had already adopted the exclusionary rule before *Mapp v. Ohio*, and respondents from those states could thus serve as a control group. Three states had partially adopted it, and they were not used in the analysis.

Table 6-2 shows that 57 percent of the respondents from the control group of states reported an increase in police adherence to legality in making searches since 1961, whereas 75 percent of the respondents from the experimental group of newly adopting states reported an increase. This 18 percentage points difference cannot be readily attributed to a chance fluke in the sample of respondents since there is less than a five out of 100 probability that one could distribute 104 respondents over the six cells in Table 6-2 purely by chance and come out with a +.18 relation. This +.18 relation is also not readily attributable to a misperception of reality on the part of the respondents since there was such a high correlation among the different kinds of respondents from the same state or type of states on the empirical question of police adherence to legality, even though there was great disagreement on the normative question of the desirability of the exclusionary rule. The +.18 relation between newly adopting the exclusionary rule and increased police adherence to legality in searches seems to be largely attributable to the fact that the states that newly adopted the exclusionary rule also disproportionately

TABLE 6-2
BENEFITS AND COSTS AS QUANTITY TIME PRICE
(Interval Measurement)

A. The Relation Between Adopting the Exclusionary Rule and Increased Police Adherence to Legality in Making Searches

		Exclusionary Rule		
		Had All Along (Control Group)	Newly Adopted (Experimental Group)	
Police Adherence to Legality	Increase since 1961	57%	75%	+ 18 percentage points difference
	No change	34%	21%	
	Decrease	9%	4%	
	Number of Respondents	48	56	104

B. Alternative Policies and Goals Involved in Increasing Policy Adherence to Legality in Making Searches

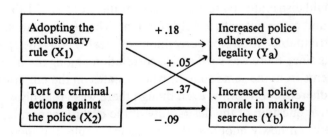

reported an increase in programs designed to educate the police regarding search-and-seizure law, which in turn correlates highly with increased police adherence to legality. States that already had the exclusionary rule also often underwent an increase in police adherence to legality possibly because of the stimulus of the publicity given in *Mapp v. Ohio*, and because of long-term public opinion trends demanding higher standards of police behavior.

Table 6-2 shows the relation between alternative policies and alternative goals involved in the problem of increasing police adherence to legality when making searches. The top part of Table 6-2b shows that the exclusionary rule (X_1) should be adopted if increased police adherence to legality (Y_a) is one's only goal, since there is a positive relation between X_1 and Y_a. Many judges and others (including Felix Frankfurter in his dissenting opinion in *Mapp v. Ohio*) have argued that criminal and damages actions against the police are more effective than adopting the exclusionary rule as a means of increasing police adherence to legality. The questionnaire asked the respondents how often damages or criminal actions had occurred against the police in their communities for making illegal searches. If one divides the respondents into those relatively few who said there had been at least one such action in recent years versus those who said there had been none, then there is only a +.05 relation between the occurrence of such actions and increased police adherence to police legality. The low relation and the low occurrence of such actions may be attributable to the fact that prosecutors are reluctant to prosecute the police who have been aiding them, and searched individuals are reluctant to sue because of the time, cost, embarrassment, unsympathetic juries, police discretion, and difficulty of assessing collectible damages. Thus the exclusionary rule (X_1) should be preferred over damages or criminal actions (X_2) if increased adherence to legality (Y_a) is one's only goal (and the decision-maker cannot adopt both policies), since there is a greater positive relation X_1 and Y_a then there is between X_2 and Y_a.

An additional goal one might have in dealing with the problem of increasing police adherence to legality in making searches is the goal of simultaneously increasing police morale, or at least not decreasing it. The mailed questionnaire asked the respondents about changes in police morale before and after *Mapp v. Ohio*. The relation between being a respondent from a state that had newly adopted the exclusionary rule (X_1) and reporting increased police morale (Y_b) in making searches was a -.37. The negative relation may be attributable to the fact that when evidence is thrown out that the police have worked hard to obtain through what they may have considered a lawful search, this is demoralizing to their enthusiasm for making future searches. If the relation between X_1 and Y_b had been positive, like the relation between X_1 and Y_a, then it would be easy to decide in favor of adopting X_1. However, since the relation between X_1 and Y_b is negative, one must decide whether that negative relation is enough to offset the positive relation between X_1 and Y_a. The matter is not resolved simply by noting that the X_1 and Y_b relation is greater than the X_1 and Y_a relation. This is so because it is unlikely that one would weigh Y_a and Y_b equally. If the Y_a goal has a weight of 3 times or less than the Y_b goal, then the -.37 relation would not be enough to offset the +.18 relation in view of the fact that 3 times .18 is greater than 1 times .37. On the other hand, if the Ya goal has a weight of 2 times or less than the Y_b goal, then the 0.37 relation would be enough to offset the +.18 relation. In other words, if the relation between X_1 and Y_a (times the weight of Y_a) plus the relation between X_1 and Y_b (times the weight of Y_b) is greater than zero, then X_1 should be adopted if Y_a and Y_b are one's only goals.

The most complicated problem situation involves both multiple policies and multiple goals, but even this situation is simple to resolve conceptually after going through the above problem situations. Suppose the weight of Y_a is 3 times greater than the weight of Y_b as determined by a scientific psychological survey of public, legislative, or judicial opinions. Note also that the relation between the occasional occurrence of damages or criminal actions against the police and increased police morale was a -.09. Thus, the exclusionary rule (X_1) should be preferred over damages or criminal actions (X_2) if increased adherence to legality (Y_a) and increased police morale (Y_b) are one's only goals (and the decision-maker cannot adopt both policies), since in Table 6-2; +.18 x 3 plus -.37 x 1 is greater than +.05 x 3 plus -.09 x 1. In other words, .54 + plus -.37 is greater than +.15 plus -.09.

The weight of each goal can be considered a price. The regression coefficients between each policy and each goal can be interpreted like a marginal rate of return (MRR) or a quantity of goal units to be achieved as a result of a one unit increase in the policy. Thus, the total revenue from policy X_1 is equal to P times Q on goal Y_a, and the total cost from policy X_1 is equal to P times Q on goal Y_b. The relation between X_1 and Y_a is a benefit since the MRR or Q is positive, but it is a cost on Y_b since the MRR or Q there is negative. To compare X_1 with X_2, one logically compares the benefits minus costs which each policy produces. Instead of talking in terms of benefits and costs, one could simply talk in terms of effects. Policy X_1 has some positive effects and some negative effects. ONe can determine the algebraic sum of the positive effects (P x Q for Y_a) and the negative effects

(P x Q for Y_b). One can do likewise for X_2, and then compare the net effects of X_1 and X_2 to determine which is better if they are mutually exclusive, or which are profitable if they can both be adopted.

The weight of each goal can be considered a price. The regression coefficients between each policy and each goal can be interpreted like a marginal rate of return (MRR) or a quantity of goal units to be achieved as a result of a one unit increase in the policy. Thus, the total revenue from policy X_1 is equal to P times Q on goal Y_a, and the total cost from policy X_1 is equal to P times Q on goal Y_b. The relation between X_1 and Y_a is a benefit since the MRR or Q is positive, but it is a cost on Y_b since the MRR or Q there is negative. To compare X_1 with X_2, one logically compares the benefits minus costs which each policy produces. Instead of talking in terms of benefits and costs, one could simply talk in terms of effects. Policy X_1 has some positive effects and some negative effects. One can determine the algebraic sum of the positive effects (P x Q for Y_a) and the negative effects (P x Q for Y_b). One can do likewise for X_2, and then compare the net effects of X_1 and X_2 to determine which is better if they are mutually exclusive, or which are profitable if they can both be adopted.

BINARY MEASUREMENT ON PRICE AND QUANTITY

In policy analysis, unlike economics, measurement often tends to be difficult to obtain with more degrees on either quantity or price than simply relatively high versus relatively low. This is the equivalent of binary measurement or of having quantities or values that only fit into two categories. The two categories can be arbitrarily labeled 0 and 1, - and +, or any other pair of labels. Having such measurement is accurate if the relation between X_1 and Y_a is truly greater than the relation between X_2 and Y_b. It does, however, mean losing some information that may or may not be valuable concerning how much greater the first relation is over the second. Similarly, having such measurement is accurate if the value of Y_a is greater than the value of Y_b, although some information is lost concerning how much more valuable Y_a is than Y_b. Fortunately, policy analysis solutions are often insensitive to that unavailable information, since the same solutions would often be reached if the information were available. This is so because policy evaluation solutions typically take the form of X_1 is better than X_2, or X_1 is the best of the policy alternatives. Such statements do not require that we know how much better X_1 is than X_2.

The policy problem of how to provide counsel to the poor in civil cases might be a good example to illustrate how insights can be obtained even when relations are only expressed in terms of direction, rather than magnitude or shape. Three competing alternatives for providing counsel to the poor in civil cases are (1) attorneys who volunteer to be on a list of free attorneys available when poor people have legal problems, (2) attorneys who are salaried by a government agency like the Legal Services Corporation for representing poor people, generally on a full-time basis, and (3) attorneys who represent poor people and are reimbursed for doing so by the government as part of a judicare system analogous to medicare. Four basic goals might be considered in comparing those three policy alternatives, namely being (a) inexpensive, (b) visible and accessible, (c) politically feasible, and providing (d) specialized competence plus reasonably aggressive representation.

For each goal, we can indicate the policy alternative that is relatively more positive, meaning the alternative that most achieves the goal. On being inexpensive, the volunteer system gets a plus, with the salaried attorney and especially the judicare system getting relative minuses. On being visible and accessible, the salaried attorney gets a relative plus, with judicare and especially the volunteer attorney system getting relative minuses. On being politically feasible, both the judicare and especially the volunteer systems create no substantial political problems, and might thus be scored pluses, but the salaried attorney system has had political problems, which gives it a minus. The salaried attorney system, though, tends to result in specialized competence and more aggressive representation which gives it a plus, with minuses to the volunteer and judicare systems on that goal. These relations are summarized in Table 6-3.

With that information, one can say that the volunteer and salaried systems seem to be tied with two pluses apiece. The volunteer system scores well on being inexpensive and politically feasible, whereas the salaried system scores well on being visible/accessible and being specialized/aggressive. To resolve that tie, those goals need relative weights. A conservative evaluator or policy maker would probably place relatively more weight on being inexpensive and politically feasible, and would thus tend to favor the government salaried system. Like most policy analysis, no conclusions can be reached without specifying the relative weights of the goals, even if there is agreement on what the goals are. The policy analyst can, however, clarify what policy is best in light of given goals and value weights. The important thing in this context is that insights can sometimes be obtained concerning what policy is best by working with relations between policies and goals that are only expressed in terms of relative direction without specifying the exact

TABLE 6-3
BENEFITS AND COSTS AS A QUANTITY TIMES PRICE
(Binary Measurement)

PROVIDING LEGAL COUNSEL TO THE POOR IN CIVIL CASES

Goals	Weights	Policies and Relations		
		Volunteer (X_1)	Salaried (X_2)	Judicare (X_3)
Y_a. Inexpensive	less (0)	+	−	−
Y_b. Visible and accessible	more (1)	−	+	−
Y_c. Politically feasible	less (0)	+	−	+
Y_d. Specialized competence and aggressive representation	more (1)	−	+	−
Unweighted sum of pluses		2	2	1
Weighted sum of pluses		2 −	2 +	1 −

+ = Yes, relative to the other alternative policies (or 1)

− = No, relative to the other alternative policies (or 0)

magnitude of the relations.

Like the search and seizure problem, the above right-to-counsel problem can be viewed as a problem of determining which policy has the highest score on benefits minus costs, or the highest score by summing algebraically and the weighted positive or negative effects of each policy. Each effect can be expressed as a quantity times price relative to each goal. In this context, each quantity is either a 1 or a zero. For example, on being inexpensive, the volunteer system gets a 1 and the other two policies get zeros. Also, in this context, each value or price is a 1 or a zero. Thus, the value of being inexpensive gets a relative zero to liberals and a 1 to conservatives. Therefore, each of the three policies $(X_1, X_2,$ and $X_3)$ can be given a total score equal to $(QP)_a + (QP)_b + (QP)_c + (QP)_d$, which shows the benefits or costs which the policy achieves on each of the four goals. The policy which has the highest total score is the best policy, assuming the Q scores are accurate and that one accepts the value of the P scores. One could probably move without difficulty from a binary zero and 1 scoring to a rank-order scoring. The Q scores can then receive ranks of 1, 2, or 3, depending on how well each policy scores relative to the other two policies. The P scores can then receive ranks of 1, 2, 3, or 4, depending on how well each goal scores relative to the other three goals.[3]

DICHOTOMOUS AND MULTIPLE POLICIES AND GOALS

THE MEANINGFULNESS OF DICHOTOMOUS ALTERNATIVES

In making optimum choices, one can talk in terms of the nature of the measurement of the policy-goal relations (Q for quantity or r for relation) and the values of the goals (P for price or w for weight). That measurement can

---

[3]See any elementary economics textbook on the treatment of total revenue as price times quantity, and the treatment of total cost as average cost times quantity, such as in Paul Samuelson, "Equilibrium of the Firm: Cost and Revenue," in *Economics: An Introductory Analysis* (Highstown, N.J.: McGraw-Hill, 1980). For further details on the study of the relations between the exclusionary rule and increasing police adherence to legality in making searches, see S. Nagel, "Effects of Excluding Illegally Seized Evidence," in *The Legal Process from a Behavioral Perspective* (Homewood, Ill.: Dorsey, 1969). For further details on the study of the relations between various goals and alternative ways of providing legal counsel to the poor, see S. Nagel, "How to Provide Legal Counsel for the Poor: Decision Theory," in *Analyzing Poverty Policy*, ed. Dorothy James (Lexington, Mass.: Lexington-Heath, 1975).

include dichotomies, ranks, or interval measurement. One can also talk in terms of the number of alternatives available when discussing the policies (Xs) or the goals (Ys). A good example might be the policy problem of determining how judges should be selected and for what lengths of terms. There are thus two policy dimensions. One is method of selection, which can be meaningfully dichotomized into selection by the electoral process or selection by gubernatorial appointment. The second dimension is length of term before re-election or reappointment, which can be dichotomized into above or below a national average. There are many goals that one might have in this context, but two that may be especially important are the liberalism/conservatism of judicial decisions in economic policy matters and liberalism/conservatism in civil liberties matters.

One can determine how elected judges differ from appointed judges by comparing (1) elected judges with (2) interim appointed judges, serving on the same state supreme courts hearing the same cases. One can also determine how relatively long-term judges differ from relatively short-term judges by finding state supreme courts where both types of judges are serving simultaneously. If more than two categories were used for method of selection or for length of term, then finding appropriate state supreme courts would be difficult on which those multiple categories might be represented. Comparing judges who are not sitting on the same cases would not be so meaningful, since any differences among them might be due to differences in the cases they hear, rather than to differences in method of selection or length of term.

Applying that kind of analysis to state supreme court judges tends to show that elected judges are more liberal on economic matters than appointed judges, but do not differ substantially on civil liberties matters. That finding holds true even when comparing elected and appointed judges from within the same political party. The explanation might be that elected judges are more likely to come from lower income backgrounds and rise through the party ranks, whereas appointed judges may be more likely to be plucked from prominent law firms partly for their monetary contributions. The analysis also tends to show that long-term judges are more liberal on civil liberties matters than short-term judges, but do not differ substantially on economic matters. The explanation might be that long-term judges are less sensitive to majoritarian pressures which may run contrary to freedom of speech, equal treatment for minorities, and criminal procedure safeguards.

With that information, one can conclude that the best method of selection and length of term depends on one's preferences with regard to liberalism and conservatism in economic and civil liberties matters. More specifically, if one prefers liberal results on both dimensions, the best judges would be elected and long-termers. If one prefers conservative results on both dimensions, the best judges would be appointed and short termers. If one prefers judges who are likely to be liberal on economic matters but conservative on civil liberties matters, then the best judges might be those who are elected and short-termers. Similarly, if one prefers conservatives on economic matters but liberals on civil liberties matters, then appointing judges for long terms may be the best solution. The important thing from a policy analysis perspective is that one can say some meaningful things about the important issues of how judges should be selected and for what terms, by using a measurement perspective that is no more complex than a simple dichotomy on each of the policy variables and a simple dichotomy on each of the goal variables.

MULTIPLE ALTERNATIVES AND METHODS FOR HANDLING THEM

Discrete choices are not always few in number. In the problem of legislative redistricting, for example, there may be millions of patterns for combining counties or precincts into the desired number of legislative districts in a state. A wasteful approach to handling that problem would be to try every possible pattern and see how it scores on a total-score measure. The total score might be the average deviation between each district's population and the population of the average district. With perfect equality all districts would have zero deviations, which means they would all have the same population. One could facilitate determining how each pattern scores on that kind of equality measure by arranging for a computer to go through every possible pattern and calculate its equality or inequality score. Even with a computer, the amount of work for a realistic redistricting problem would be prohibitive if all the possible redistricting patterns were checked.

To reduce the number of patterns or alternative policies to be checked on their equality scores, a number of methods can be simultaneously used, such as:

1. Stop the checking when a pattern is found that satisfies a maximum inequality constraint, although doing so will result in a satisfying solution rather than an optimizing one. Such a constraint might be phrased as, no district should have a population that exceeds the average population by more than plus or minus three percent.

2. Do a contiguity check on each pattern before doing the more complicated equality check, and then eliminate any pattern that does not provide for contiguity. By contiguity, we mean that one should be able to go from any place in any district to any other place in the same district without having to leave the district. To check for contiguity requires informing the computer as to which precincts or counties touch each other before any redistricting patterns are tried.
3. Try working with larger geographical units as the building blocks out of which the districts are to be made. The larger the units, the fewer possible patterns there are. Thus, working with counties is better than working with precincts for reducing the policy alternatives, although that might miss some alternative patterns that can provide better equality.
4. Start with the existing pattern as the base from which to create alternative districting patterns, rather than start with some arbitrary random pattern. By starting with the existing pattern, one is likely to be closer to the desired equality than a random pattern would be, and is also more likely to ease the anxieties of incumbent legislators.

The redistricting problem not only involves numerous or even millions of alternative policies, but also numerous conflicting goals. The goals might include:

1. Equality of Population across districts as measured by:
   a. A maximum allowable inequality constraint like the three percent figure mentioned above.
   b. Minimizing an average deviation from equality, which may conflict with the maximum allowable constraint.
2. Compactness of districts as measured by:
   a. Contiguity as mentioned above, which is a constraint that normally must be satisfied allowing no deviation.
   b. Minimizing an average deviation from the perfect compactness of circular districts, or from having everybody living in one place in each district.
3. Political criteria, such as:
   a. Giving each political party a proportion of the total seats equal to the proportion of party members in the state.
   b. Having competitive districts. This conflicts with the proportionality principle above, which requires having safe rather than competitive districts.

c. Minimizing disruption to incumbents. This may conflict with all the other goals, but may be politically important.

There are basically three ways of handling multiple goals like the above, either simultaneously, sequentially, or both. The typical approach is to try first to satisfy both the contiguity constraint and the maximum allowable inequality constraint. After doing that and locking the solution in, one can then seek to satisfy political criteria. Another alternative is to create a composite criterion consisting of the product of (1) the average deviation from equality; and (2) the average deviation from compactness; with (3) the equality measure receiving an exponent weight to indicate how much more important it is than the compactness measure. That alternative may have some mathematical significance in terms of developing an optimum districting pattern, but it may lack both legal and political significance. Legally, no matter how low the average deviation is from equality, if there is at least one district that exceeds the maximum allowable constraint, the whole pattern is likely to be declared unconstitutional. Politically, no matter how equal and compact the districting pattern is, the pattern is not likely to be adopted by a state legislature if there are other patterns that can satisfy contiguity and the maximum allowable inequality constraint, which can also give a better break to incumbents and possibly provide some roughly proportional representation.[4]

---

[4]On dichotomous measurement, see M. Dutta, "Dummy Variables" in *Econometric Methods* (Cincinnati: South-Western, 1975). On reducing number of policy or independent variables, see S. Nagel and M. Neef, "Methods of Reducing the Number of Variables and Making Composite Variables" in *Policy Analysis in Social Science Research* (Beverly Hills, Ca.: Sage, 1979). On combining goals, see Allan Easton, *Complex Managerial Decisions Involving Multiple Objectives* (New York: Wiley, 1973). For further details on the study of alternative methods of selecting judges, see S. Nagel, *Comparing Elected and Appointed Judicial Systems* (Beverly Hills, Ca.: Sage American Politics Series, 1973). For further details on alternative methods of legislative redistricting, see S. Nagel, "Computers and the Law and Politics of Redistricting" in *Improving the Legal Process: Effects of Alternatives* (Lexington, Mass.: Lexington-Heath, 1975).

7

OPTIMUM CHOICE WITH PROBABILITIES

At least four purposes can be meaningfully present in analyzing optimum choices with probabilities, although those same purposes can apply to other kinds of choices. The purposes consist of (1) making decisions, (2) influencing decisions, (3) predicting decisions, and (4) measuring decisional propensities.

MAKING DECISIONS

WITHOUT TIME DISCOUNTING

A good example of where the principles of optimum choice with probabilities are applied is the decision making of personal injury plaintiff lawyers in choosing whether or not to accept a client and whether or not to accept an offer from the other side. The reasoning involved in accepting a client tends to implicitly or explicitly proceed through the following question and answer steps:

1. What damages are likely to be awarded? Suppose that the out-of-pocket medical expenses are 300 dollars for this applicant desiring legal services. By a rough rule of thumb, that means that if the attorney wins the case, about 3,000 dollars in damages will be collected or 10 times the medical expenses. That extra money is awarded by juries to cover lost wages, pain

and suffering, and possibly the attorney's one-third fee. Predicting damages awarded from medical expenses can be done more accurately by consulting the loose-leaf service of the Jury Verdict Research Corporation. That service indicates the predicted damages awarded from medical expenses for various types of injuries. The predictions are based on numerous cases which the JVR researchers gather from around the country. The cases are then processed through a statistical regression analysis to develop regression prediction information, which is communicated in simple language to practicing lawyers through the loose-leaf service.

2. What is the probability of winning this case? By a rough rule of thumb, one can use a .65 figure, since that is about the average victory probability in personal injury cases. Predicting victory probabilities can be done more accurately by also consulting the loose-leaf service of the Jury Verdict Research Corporation. The same case samples are used to indicate victory probabilities for various types of cases. A practicing lawyer can combine those probabilities to obtain conditional or joint probabilities, or can simply use them in their raw form by finding the single case-type that best fits his case.

3. What is the expected value to the attorney of this case? If the predicted damages are 3,000 dollars and the predicted victory probability is .65, then the expected value to the plaintiff is 1,950 dollars. The lawyer, however, only gets one-third of what the plaintiff obtains. Therefore, the expected value of the lawyer's fee would be .33 times 1,950 dollars, or 644 dollars.

4. How much are the lawyer expenses likely to be in this case? This requires evaluating how many hours the case will probably consume. The estimated answer might be 20 hours. Unfortunately, there is no loose-leaf service that is helpful on hours consumed for different types of cases, or on the more important matter of relating hours consumed to damages awarded, like relating medical expenses to damages awarded. If such information were available, it could be useful in enabling lawyers to allocate their time better. Answering the expenses question also requires the lawyer to think in terms of how much an hour of time is worth. The answer might be whatever the market rate is, which might be 30 dollars an hour. The lawyer, however, might be willing to work for less than the market rate, where he is having difficulty filling his time with clients at that rate, or where he is receiving nonmonetary satisfaction. In light of those numbers, the hourly expenses for this case would be about 20 hours times 30 dollars, or 600 dollars in variable expenses, which do not include

overhead or other variable expenses besides the lawyer's time. For simplicity, we can ignore the fact that those costs are contingent on the case going to trial and should be discounted by that probability.

5. Should the attorney take the case? If the expected value or incremental income is 644 dollars, and the expected incremental expense is 600 dollars, then the case seems worth taking. Cases like this will, on the average, cover the value of the attorney's time and provide something for other case-related expenses plus overhead. The case, however, should be rejected if other cases are available that are even better on benefits minus costs, and the attorney does not have the time for all of them. The important thing for our methodological purposes is that this situation does illustrate how the principles of optimum choice with probabilities can be applied in a practical way to both routine and important decisions. The same reasoning could be applied to cases in which a nonmonetary judgment is involved, such as a criminal prosecution or a civil liberties defense, but then one would have to decide whether the nonmonetary benefits are worth the monetary costs.

TIME DISCOUNTING

The above illustration does not take into consideration that the 3,000 dollars in damages may not be awarded for a few years. There may be no need to consider the future element when deciding whether to accept a client, since the main expenses of working on the case may also not occur for a few years until the case comes to trial. There are, however, many situations where a personal injury lawyer should consider the future element. Considering it means making an adjustment to recognize that 3,000 dollars a few years from now may not be worth as much as 2,500 dollars at the present time, since the 2,500 dollars can be invested so that it might earn interest or a profit, making it worth more than 3,000 dollars in a few years.

For example, suppose a personal injury plaintiff could follow the alternative of going to a federal court (on the jurisdictional grounds that the plaintiff and defendant are from different states), or go to the state court in which the defendant can be sued. Suppose further if the plaintiff goes to the federal court, the case will be heard within one year, and if victorious the plaintiff will collect about 15,000 dollars, but with only a 20 percent chance of winning. If, on the other hand, the case goes to the state court, it will be heard within two years, and the plaintiff, if victorious will collect 10,000 dollars, but with a 40 percent chance of winning. Which alternative should be followed?

The expected value of the federal alternative is 3,000 dollars (i.e., 15,000 dollars discounted by the .20 probability of winning it) without considering the time element, and the expected value of the state alternative is 4,000 dollars (i.e., 10,000 dollars discounted by the .40 probability of winning it). If, however, we take into consideration that one has to wait two years for the 10,000 dollars from the state court, its value substantially decreases. More specifically, the present value of a future amount is calculated by the formula $P = A/(1 + r)t$ where r is the interest rate that could be obtained by putting money in a savings account for t years. If we assume the interest rate is 6 percent, then the present value of the state's 10,000 dollars two years from now is 8,900 dollars. If we now discount that present value by the .40 probability of achieving it, the expected value of the state case becomes 3,560 dollars. Applying the same formula to the federal case, the present value of its 15,000 dollar award would be 14,151 dollars since 14,151 dollars $= 15,000/(1 + .06)^1$. If we now discount the present value by the .20 probability of achieving it, the expected value of the federal alternative becomes 2,830 dollars which is still less than the state alternative, but not as much less as the difference with time consumption taken into consideration. We, of course, could have offered a hypothetical example where taking time consumption into consideration reverses the rank order as to which is the better alternative.

Another time-discounting application occurs when, for example, the defendant in a civil case is told by a plaintiff that the plaintiff will withdraw his lawsuit if the defendant will pay 3,000 dollars. The defendant figures if the case goes to trial five years from now and the defendant loses, for which there is a 2/3 chance, the plaintiff will be awarded 6,000 dollars. The defendant thus perceives the case as having an expected value of 4,000 dollars. The question then becomes, is the defendant better off paying the plaintiff 3,000 dollars now or 4,000 dollars five years from now? Answering that

---

[1]On making decisions in light of contingent probabilities, see Ruth Mack, *Planning on Uncertainty: Decision Making in Business and Government Administration* (New York: Wily, 1971); Wayne Lee, *Decision Theory and Human Behavior* (New York: Wiley, 1971); and Bruce Baird, *Introduction to Decision Analysis* (Belmont, Ca.: Duxbury, 1978). On discounting future benefits or costs in light of the passage of time, see Ezra Mishan, Investment Criteria," in *Cost Benefit Analysis* (New York: Prager, 1976). For further details on the analysis of the decisions to accept a legal client or to accept an offer from the other side, see S. Nagel and M. Neef, *Decision Theory in the Legal Process* (Lexington, Mass.: Lexington-Heath, 1979), pp. 141-46. 232-35.

question involves working with the equation, $A = P(1 + r)t$, and the current interest rate which we might assume is .06. The equation thus becomes $A = 3,000(1.06)5$, and A thus equals 4,015 dollars. The defendant would therefore be better off putting his 3,000 dollars into a savings account at 6 percent, waiting 5 years, and then paying 4,000 dollars to the defendant and having 15 dollars left over, than he would be by paying the 3,000 dollars to the plaintiff. For simplicity, we can ignore the fact that the inflation rate may be greater than the interest rate which means the invested money would lose value over time, and that the damages awarded may need to be adjusted upward.

In this illustration, the defendant is comparing a present benefit with a future one, whereas in the other illustration it was a choice for the plaintiff between two future benefits. In this illustration, the defendant (who is paying) is mainly concerned with the future value of a present investment; whereas in the other one, the plaintiff (who is being paid) was mainly concerned with the present value of a future amount. Both are common examples of time-discounting in the legal process. Both have counterparts in numerous public sector situations, where benefits or costs are substantially delayed. The present value of future benefits is often considered by the Army Corps of Engineers in building alternative dams, some of which can be finished sooner than others. The present value of future costs may be a consideration in postponing the burden of supporting a Social Security system, or postponing the suffering from lack of energy conservation. Unfortunately, the present generation may overly discount those future costs.[2]

INFLUENCING DECISIONS

Another purpose for analyzing optimum choices with probabilities is for understanding and influencing decisions rather than making decisions. Two examples include (1) trying to influence judges to release rather than hold

---

[2]On the use of probabilistic decision theory to influence or deter decisions, see Lee McPheters and William Stronge (eds.), *The Economics of Crime and Law Enforcement* (Springfield, Ill.: Thomas, 1976). For further details concerning the use of decision theory to influence judges to do more pretrial releasing, see S. Nagel and M. Neef, "The One-Person Decision Situation: Bond Setting" in *Decision Theory and the Legal Process* (Lexington, Mass.: Lexington-Heath, 1979). For further details on the use of decision theory to influence prosecutors to make more time-saving decisions, see S. Nagel and M. Neef, "Time-Oriented Models and the Legal Process: Reducing Delay and Forecasting the future," 1978 *Washington Law Quarterly* 467-528 (1978).

pretrial defendants, when there is doubt about the probability of the defendant appearing in court; and (2) trying to influence prosecutors to make time-saving rather than time-lengthening decisions, when there is doubt concerning the imposition of the rewards or punishments. Each example involves a somewhat different methodological orientation.

WHERE COSTS ARE MISSED BENEFITS, AND BENEFITS ARE COSTS AVOIDED

The pretrial release problem can be viewed as reaching a decision under conditions of risk, as is shown in Table 7-1. That figures indicates that there are basically two choices available to a judge, namely, to either (1) release the defendant on his own recognizance or low bond; or (2) hold the defendant with no bond or a high bond. Which is the better choice depends on whether the defendant would appear in court if released, or would fail to appear. There are two kinds of errors that could be made. A defendant could be held who would have appeared if he were released (a holding error), or a defendant could be released who fails to appear (a releasing error). The first error is referred to as a type 1 error, because it is the more serious in the eyes of the law. The second error may be less serious legally, but is likely to be considered more costly to judges, since only releasing errors can be detected in individual cases. If the average judge considers a releasing error to be more costly, we can give it a numerical value of -100 in order to have a benchmark for saying something about the relative value of a holding error. Suppose the average judge says he finds a releasing error to be personally twice as upsetting as a holding error. This means a holding error should then have an average numerical value of -50.

If the holding error cost is symbolized as -A, then releasing a defendant who does appear can be symbolized +A, since releasing a defendant who does appear avoids the holding error cost. Similarly, if the releasing error cost is symbolized -B, then holding a defendant who would have failed to appear can be symbolized +B, since it avoids the releasing error cost. The expected value of releasing is equal to (1) the expected benefits of releasing plus (2) the expected negative cost, as is shown at the end of the releasing row in Table 7-1. Similarly, the expected value of holding is equal to (1) the expected benefits of holding plus (2) the expected negative costs, as is shown at the end of the holding row. If the expected value of releasing is set equal to the expected value of holding, then by setting those two algebraic expressions equal to each other, one can solve for P with the solution

TABLE 7-1
OPTIMUM CHOICE ANALYSIS FOR INFLUENCING DECISIONS
(Where Costs are Missed Benefits, and Benefits Are Avoided Costs)

**INFLUENCING JUDGES TO DO MORE
PRETRIAL RELEASING**

Probability of Appearance

		Would Appear (P)	Would Fail to Appear (1-P)	Expected Values
Alternative Decisions Available	Release via ROR or Low Bond	+A	Type 2 Error −B	$EV_R =$ $(+A)(P) +$ $(-B)(1-P)$
	Hold Via No or High Bond	Type 1 Error −A	+B	$EV_H =$ $(-A)(P) +$ $(+B)(1-P)$

There are three general approaches to widening the positive difference between EV_R and EV_H:

I. Raise and clarify the probability of appearance (i.e., increase P).
   A. Raise P through better screening and notification.
   B. Clarify P through statistical studies of what percentage of various types of released defendants appear in court.
   C. More vigorously prosecute those who fail to appear.
II. Make more visible the type 1 errors and costs of holding defendants who would appear (i.e., increase A)
   A. Publicize for each judge the percent of defendants held and the appearance percent attained. (Judges vary widely on percent held, but appearance percentages tend to be about 90 percent.)
   B. Make more visible how much it costs to hold defendants in jail.
      1. Jail maintenance   4. Families on welfare
      2. Lost income   5. Increased conviction probability
      3. Bitterness from case dis- 6. Jail riots from overcrowding
         missed after lengthy wait
III. Decrease the costs of type 2 errors of releasing defendants who fail to appear (i.e., decrease B)
   A. Make rearrest more easy through pretrial supervision.
   B. Decrease the time from arrest to trial.
      1. More personnel, more diversion, and shorter trial stage.
      2. Better sequencing of cases.
      3. Shorter path from arrest to trial.
   C. Decrease pretrial crime committing.
      1. Increase probability of being arrested, convicted, and jailed.
      2. Decrease benefits of successful crime committing.
      3. Increase costs of unsuccessful crime committing.

indicating the judge's threshold probability for releasing or holding. Doing that algebra reveals that the threshold probability is simply $B/(A + B)$. That means the average judge, as mentioned above, has a threshold probability of $100/(50 + 100)$, or .67. In other words, for the average judge, the average defendant needs to be perceived as having better than a .67 probability of appearing in order to be released.

In light of that kind of analysis, we can see that in order to move judges toward doing more releasing when in doubt, there are only three alternatives available. One is to increase the probability that the defendant will appear. The second is to increase the holding error cost, and the third is to decrease the releasing error cost. In the figure, specific proposals are offered to influence each of those three variables, which in turn influences the likelihood of judges to arrive at releasing decisions. A similar type of analysis can be applied to other stages in the legal process where the law says, when in doubt decide in favor of the defendant. The decision maker, however, may be more likely to decide against the defendant, because a pro-defendant error is likely to be viewed as more costly to the decision maker. This is true of judges deciding to imprison rather than grant probation, of parole boards deciding to retain in prison rather than grant parole, and of judges deciding to convict rather than to acquit. The same kind of analysis can also be applied to influence the would-be criminal into deciding against committing a crime rather than in favor of committing one. All those examples involve (1) raising and clarifying the probability of some socially desired outcome; (2) increasing the perceived cost of a type of error that society especially wants avoided; and (3) decreasing the perceived cost of an opposite type of error that society is less sensitive to.

WHERE EACH DECISION HAS ITS OWN BENEFITS AND COSTS

The problem of trying to influence prosecutors to make time-saving rather than time-lengthening decisions can also be viewed as reaching a decision under conditions of risk, as is shown in Table 7-2. That figure indicates there are basically two choices in many of the decisions made by prosecutors with regard to moving ahead on a case or delaying action that will dispose of the case. To influence prosecutors toward the time-saving alternative over the time-lengthening one, requires that they perceive the benefits minus costs derived from making a time-saving decision as greater than the benefits minus costs derived from making a time lengthening decision. Unlike the pretrial release example, the benefits from timesaving are not merely the avoidance

TABLE 7-2

OPTIMUM CHOICE ANALYSIS FOR INFLUENCING DECISIONS
(Where Each Decision Has Its Own Benefits and Costs)

INFLUENCING PROSECUTORS TO MAKE MORE TIME-SAVING DECISIONS

		Alternative Occurrences		Benefits Minus Costs
		Being Penalized for Lengthening Time (P)	Not Being Penalized for Lengthening Time (1-P)	
Alternative Decisions	Time Saving Decision (S)	B_S Benefits from S	C_S Costs from S	$B_S - C_S$
	Time Lengthening Decision (L)	C_L Costs from L	B_L Benefits from L	$(B_L)(1-P) - (C_L)(P)$

Abbreviations: P = probability of being penalized. B = benefits. C = costs. S = time saving decision. L = time lengthening decision.

To Increase the Likelihood That Time Saving Decisions Will Be Chosen:

I. Increase the benefits from making time-saving decisions (i.e., increase B_S).

   For example, reward assistant states attorneys with salary increases and promotions for reducing the average time consumption per case.

II. Decrease the costs of making time saving decisions (i.e., decrease C_S).

   For example, establish a computerized system that informs assistant states attorneys concerning actual and predicted times at various stages for all cases to minimize the trouble involved to the attorney in keeping track of cases. Also, provide more investigative and preparation resources.

III. Increase the costs incurred from making time-lengthening decisions (i.e., increase C_L).

   For example, provide under the speedy trial rules for absolute discharge of the defendant whose case extends beyond the time limit rather than just release on recognizance.

IV. Decrease the benefits from making time-lengthening decisions (i.e., decrease B_L).

   For example, increase release on recognizance so that lengthening the pretrial time will not make the jailed defendant more vulnerable to pleading guilty.

V. Raise the probability of the decision-maker being penalized for lengthening time (i.e. increase P).

   For example, allow fewer exceptions to the speedy trial rules such as suspending their application "for good cause" or "exceptional circumstances."

of the costs of time-lengthening, and similarly the benefits of time-lengthening are not merely the avoidance of the costs from time-saving. Each of the two decisions has its own benefits and costs independent of the other alternative decision. The key contingent probability in this context is the probability of being penalized for making a time-lengthening decision. The main penalty under the new Speedy Trials Acts is the discharge of the defendant from jail or from prosecution if the time-lengthening exceeds a certain maximum constraint. This penalty, however, is only imposed if the defendant raises the issue and a judge finds the time-lengthening was not justified.

The formula is different here for determining the threshold probability above which the prosecutor would be better off reaching a time-saving decision than a time-lengthening one. However, it can be calculated the same way. It is only a matter of solving for P when the expression for the benefits minus costs of a time-saving decisions are set equal to the expression for the benefits minus costs of the alternative time-lengthening decision. Similarly, one can calculate a threshold value for any of the benefits or costs when they are expressed in terms of all the other variables after setting those two expressions equal to each other. The importance of this example, though, is not to aid a prosecutor in calculating a threshold probability or threshold values. Instead, the example is designed to illustrate how thinking in terms of making optimum choices with probabilities can generate ideas for influencing decisions. In other words, the five sets of ideas shown in table 7-2 might not all have been generated if ways of encouraging timesaving decisions were merely listed without the organized framework which optimum choice analysis provides.

This framework emphasizes a five-part check list that includes: (1) increasing the benefits of rightdoing; (2) decreasing the costs of rightdoing; (3) increasing the cost of wrongdoing; (4) decreasing the benefits from wrongdoing; and (5) increasing the probability of wrongdoers being penalized. The same kind of analysis can apply where there are three or more alternative decisions, with one especially favored that we want to influence, although we then have more benefits and costs that need to be increased or decreased. Similarly, we can have two or more contingent probabilities that need to be increased or decreased to stimulate favorable decisions.[3]

---

[3]On using decision theory for predictive purposes, see Robert McIver, "Cause as Incentive" in *Social Causation* (New York: Harper, 1964). For further details on the use of decision theory for predicting the effects of judicial process changes on plea bargaining settlements, see S. Nagel and M. Neef, "The Two-Person Bargaining Situation: Plea Bargaining" in *Decision*

PREDICTING DECISIONS

ESTABLISHING THE DECISIONAL MODEL

A third purpose that can be served from analyzing optimum choice with probabilities is to predict better what decisions are likely to be made given certain likely or contemplated system changes. A good example involves the modeling of the plea bargaining between prosecutors and defense counsel. By plea bargaining we mean an out-of-court settlement whereby the defendant agrees to plead guilty to the original charge or a lesser charge in return for the prosecutor agreeing to reduce the charges or to recommend a sentence perceived as lighter than what the defendant would have received after a trial. A high percentage of all criminal cases are settled through explicit plea bargaining. Explicit plea bargaining involves actual negotiations between the prosecutor and either defense council or the defendant. Implicit plea bargaining involves no negotiations but rather an implicit understanding that if he pleads guilty, the prosecutor will recommend a less severe sentence than if the defendant goes to trial and is found guilty. Because of the importance of plea bargaining in the criminal justice system, it needs to be taken into consideration in order to predict the effects of almost any judicial reform.

A simple but meaningful way of modeling the decision-making in plea bargaining is that shown in the top of Table 7-3. The defendant's best interests will be maximized by accepting the prosecutor's offer of a given sentence if the sentence is less than that which the defendant perceives would be received if convicted by a trial (symbolized S_d), discounted by the probability of being convicted (symbolized P_d), with a bonus added to reflect a settlement that avoids the defendant's costs of going to trial (symbolized C_d). Similarly, the prosecutor's best interests will be maximized by accepting the defendant's offer of a given sentence if the sentence is more than the sentence that the prosecutor perceives the defendant would get if convicted by a trial (S_p), discounted by the probability of being convicted (P_p), with a discount deducted to reflect that defendant's upper limit equals $(SP - C)_d$, and the prosecutor's lower limit equals $(SP - C)_p$. They will reach a settlement if, and only if, the defendant's upper limit exceeds the prosecutor's lower limit. The sentencing level of the settlement (or how high or low the agreed sentence will be) depends on how high or low the numerical values of S, P, and C are.

Theory and the Legal Process (Lexington, Mass.: Lexington-Heath, 1979).

TABLE 7-3
OPTIMUM CHOICE ANALYSIS FOR PREDICTING DECISIONS

Defense Counsel Strategy:	**Prosecutor's Strategy:**
1. Accept offer if less than: (perceived probability of conviction)	1. Accept offer if greater than: (perceived probability of conviction)
times (sentence if convicted)	times (sentence if convicted)
plus (% bonus to avoid litigation)	minus (% discount to avoid litigation)
2. Otherwise go to trial	2. Otherwise go to trial

Judicial Process Changes that Affect:

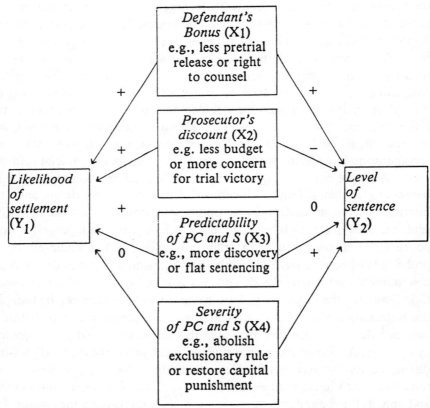

Meaning of symbols

" + " means an increase in X causes an increase in Y, or a decrease in X causes a decrease in Y.

"-" means an increase in X causes a decrease in Y, or a decrease in X causes an increase in Y.

"0" means X is not related to Y. All three types of relations assume other variables are held constant.

DETERMINING THE EFFECTS OF SYSTEM CHANGES ON THE DECISIONS

With that decisional model, we can now predict the effects of a variety of judicial process changes on the likelihood of a settlement being reached and the sentencing level of the settlements that are reached. In order to make those predictions, we need to know how the judicial process changes affect C, P, and S for both the defendant and the prosecutor. Table 7-3 summarizes the various possible relations. They are:

1. Anything that increases the defendant's costs of going to trial, such as less pretrial release or more expensive counsel, will increase the likelihood of a settlement and the level or length of the sentence. Similarly, anything that decreases the defendant's costs of going to trial will decrease the likelihood of a settlement and the level of the sentence.
2. Anything that increases (or decreases) the prosecutor's costs of going to trial, such as changes in the budget or the chances of winning, will increase (or decrease) the likelihood of a settlement. However, if costs go up the prosecutor will then be willing to give a bigger discount that will lower the level of the sentence. Thus, the prosecutor's costs vary directly with the likelihood of a settlement, but inversely with the level.
3. Anything that improves predicting the probability of conviction and the sentence upon conviction should increase the likelihood of a settlement. This is so because if both sides have the same P and the same S, then they are likely to reach a settlement since the defendant's costs move the defendant's upper limit up, and the prosecutor's costs move the prosecutor's lower limit down. Conviction probabilities can be made more predictable if both sides have access to each other's evidence. Sentences can be made more predictable if statutes require judges to give a non-discretionary sentence upon conviction for a given crime. The level of the sentence, however, should not be influenced by improved predictability so long as the improved predictability has not increased or decreased the conviction probability or the likely sentence.
4. Anything that increases the severity of the likely sentence or increases the conviction probability is likely to increase the level of sentence, such as restoring capital punishment or allowing defendants to be convicted with illegally seized evidence. Increasing the severity of S and P, however, should not affect the likelihood of a settlement if both sides are equally perceptive as to how much S and P have increased, since that means the

defendant's limit and the prosecutor's limit will equally rise and thereby still allow the same amount of room for a settlement to be reached.

One could expand the model to include any kind of judicial process change, not just the examples given, as long as one can say something meaningful about the effect of the change on C, P, and S of the defendant and prosecutor. The same model could also be used to aid prosecutors and defense counsel in making plea bargaining decisions and to influence them toward accepting each other's offers. The model, however, seems most useful as a predictive model for judicial planning. The previous models that relate to personal injury lawyers, pretrial release, and timesaving can also serve multiple purposes, but they seem especially useful in the context of aiding or influencing decision-making.[4]

MEASURING DECISIONAL PROPENSITIES

DEVELOPING THE MEASUREMENT SYSTEM

A fourth purpose that can be served by analyzing optimum choice with probabilities is the purpose of measuring decisional propensities. A decision-theory model serves that purpose by asking decision makers questions about how they value various outcomes in order to predict how they would be likely to decide, rather than asking them directly how they would be likely to decide. For example, it would not be so meaningful to ask judges, lawyers, or even lay people how high the probability of guilt has to be before they would vote to convict a defendant. It would not be very meaningful because too many people might answer about .90 since they might know that .90 probability roughly corresponds to the conviction standard of "beyond a reasonable doubt." In other words, they might respond by giving what they consider to be the answer that society or the legal system considers the right answer, rather than indicating how they would actually vote, which they may not even be adequately aware of.

---

[4]On measuring attitudes in policy-analysis research, see Marlene Henerson, Lynn Morris, and Carol Fitz-Gibbon, *How to Measure Attitudes* (Beverly Hills, Ca.: Sage, 1978). For further details on measuring decisional propensities among would-be jurors, see S. Nagel, D. Lamm, and M. Neef, "Decision Theory and Juror Decision Making" in *The Trial Process*, ed. Bruce Sales (New York: Plenum, 1981).

An appropriate system of questioning might involve informing respondents that if they were jurors they could vote either to convict or acquit and the defendant could be either innocent or guilty. Thus there are four possible occurrences: (a) voting to convict a defendant who is truly guilty; (b) voting to convict a defendant who is actually innocent; (c) voting to acquit a defendant who is actually guilty; or (d) voting to acquit a defendant who is truly innocent.

The respondents are then asked which of those four possible occurrences they consider undesirable and which they consider desirable. Most respondents say that (b) and (c) are undesirable, and (a) and (d) are desirable. We then ask, "Of the undesirable occurrences, which is the most undesirable?" Most respondents indicate occurrence (b), which is convicting an innocent defendant. Then we ask, "If we position the most undesirable occurrence at -100 on a scale from 0 to -100, then where would you position the other undesirable occurrence?" (voting to acquit a guilty defendant). Respondents are likely to say anything from about -5 to -95.

With that information, we can easily calculate the would-be juror's threshold probability for convicting. The formula with the above set of questions is simply $100/(100+X)$, where the X represents the value the respondent places on the less desirable of the two undesirable occurrences.

William Blackstone, for example, once said that it is 10 times as bad to convict an innocent defendant as it is to acquit a guilty one. If he were answering these questions consistently with that statement, he would give acquitting a guilty defendant a score of -10 on a 0 to -100 scale, where convicting an innocent defendant has a score of -100. Thus, his threshold probability would be $100/(100+10)$ or $100/110$, which equals .91. For William Blackstone, the defendant's probability of guilt would have to be greater than .91 before Blackstone would be willing to convict.

APPLYING THE MEASUREMENT SYSTEM

Perhaps the most interesting kind of application of the above measurement system involves applying it to a sample of people, some of whom have been given one set of judicial instructions, and some of whom have been given another set. This can aid in obtaining insights into how different judicial instructions might influence the propensity to convict. Perhaps the most interesting instructions might be those designed to increase the sensitivity of would-be jurors to avoiding errors of convicting innocent defendants and designed to decrease differences among different types of jurors.

There does seem to be a need for developing such instructions because when the measurement system is applied to a sample of fairly knowledgeable and liberal college students, their threshold probabilities for voting to convict tend to be close to about 51 percent, rather than close to about 90 percent which judges tend to associate with the meaning of the legal requirement of only voting to convict when the defendant appears to be guilty beyond a reasonable doubt. If knowledgeable and liberal college students have values that are relatively insensitive to avoiding conviction errors, then the general public may be even less sensitive to such errors, as contrasted to acquittal errors. Similarly, instructions that would decrease differences among types of jurors also seem to be needed because when the measurement system is applied to certain types of people responding to certain types of cases, substantial differences are sometimes revealed. For example, the threshold probabilities of males differ substantially from females in rape cases in the direction that males require a much higher probability of guilt before they will vote to convict, although males and females do not necessarily differ in other cases.

One type of instruction that increases sensitivity to conviction errors is informing the would-be jurors that the legal system expects them to vote for a conviction only when the defendant appears to be guilty beyond a reasonable doubt. That instruction, however, does not substantially decrease the difference between males and females in rape cases, although it does raise both their threshold probabilities. One type of instruction that decreases differences is informing the would-be jurors that decisional studies have shown that (1) male jurors are less likely to convict a rape defendant, (2) female jurors are more likely to convict a rape defendant, and (3) both males and females should be sensitive to whether they are voting in accordance with the facts or in accordance with whether they identify with the male defendant or the female victim. That instruction, however, does not substantially raise the overall threshold probability, although it may raise the female threshold probability with an offsetting reduction of the male threshold probability. The type of instruction that seems to be capable of both raising low thresholds and equalizing differences across types of jurors is an instruction that informs the would-be jurors that society considers convicting an innocent defendant to be ten times as undesirable as acquitting a guilty defendant, and that jurors should feel about ten times as confident of their accuracy if they vote to convict as they would if they vote to acquit.

The important point for our methodological purposes is not the substance of these findings in terms of low thresholds, differing thresholds, and how lowness and differences can be reduced. Rather, the point is that a measurement system based on making optimum choices under conditions of risk can reveal underlying values that might otherwise not be as accurately expressed, and that such measurement can then be used to obtain insights concerning would-be jurors in general, different types of would-be jurors, and different types of instructions to would-be jurors. The same kind of subtle, but meaningful, measurement system might also be applied to other kinds of decision making, where individuals vote or decide among discrete alternatives under conditions of risk, and where there is a policy controversy over whether they are applying legal or proper standards in reaching decisions.

SOME CONCLUSIONS

The simple logic which this chapter proposes for solving optimum choice problems involving discrete policy alternatives can be summarized in nine basic rules as follows:

1. Determine the benefits minus costs for each policy alternative, and then pick the alternative that has the best B-C score (relevant to the section on "Mutual Exclusivity" in Chapter 6).
2. In calculating the benefits or costs for each policy alternative, bear in mind that the benefits or costs can often be more meaningfully understood by considering them as representing price times quantity, or a relative value-weight times a marginal rate of return (relevant to the section on "Benefits and Costs as Price Times Quantity" in Chapter 6).
3. In working with alternative policies, it is often meaningful to think in terms of only two alternative choices, although some problems may involve so many policies that special reduction methods need to be adopted to make the choices more manageable (relevant to the section on "Dichotomous and Multiple Policies and Goals" in Chapter 6).
4. In working with goals or effects to maximize (i.e., benefits) or goals to minimize (i.e., costs), it is often meaningful to think in terms of only two positions on a goal (e.g., relatively high versus relatively low), although some problems may involve numerous conflicting goals requiring special methods for handling them simultaneously and/or sequentially (relevant to that same section).
5. Where the benefits or costs are contingent on the occurrence of an event, then the benefits or costs need to be discounted or multiplied by the

probability of that event occurring (relevant to the section on "Making Decisions" in the present chapter).

6. Where the benefits or costs are not received or incurred for some time, they may need to be discounted for the fact that a given benefit or cost later is generally not as beneficial or as costly as the same benefit or cost now (relevant to that same section).

7. Where individuals reach decisions in light of expected benefits minus expected costs, one can encourage the individuals to reach more favorable decisions by seeking to manipulate those benefits, costs, and probabilities (relevant to the section on "Influencing Decisions" in the present chapter).

8. Where individuals reach decisions in light of expected benefits minus expected costs, one can predict what decisions will be reached by knowing how changes affect those benefits, costs, and probabilities (relevant to the section on "Predicting Decisions" in the present chapter).

9. Where individuals reach decisions in light of expected benefits minus expected costs, one can measure their propensity to reach certain decisions by inquiring how they value certain beneficial or costly outcomes (relevant to the section on "Measuring Decisional Propensities" in the present chapter).

Many examples can be given for each of those nine rules such as deciding among alternatives relevant to (1) building dams or notifying released defendants to appear in court; (2) increasing police adherence to legality in making searches or providing legal counsel to the poor in civil cases; (3 and 4) selecting judges or redistricting legislatures; (5 and 6) accepting a personal injury client or an offer from the other side; (7) encouraging more pretrial release by judges or more time-saving decisions by prosecutors; (8) predicting the effects of judicial process changes on plea bargaining; and (9) measuring the propensity of would-be jurors to convict. Those examples have emphasized legal policy problems, but examples could be given from a variety of other subject matter areas. Indeed, what may be especially needed in this context is for more political and social scientists to apply these general principles to a variety of subjects. The collective experience of doing so is likely to provide increased benefits and decreased costs for optimum choices among discrete policy alternatives.

SECTION D:

FINDING AN OPTIMUM LEVEL OR MIX

8

OPTIMUM LEVEL LOGIC

The purpose of this chapter is to show how virtually any public policy problem can be solved through simple logic and algebra once the relation has been established between the goal to be achieved and various policy levels. By an "optimum policy level problem" is generally meant a problem in which doing either too much or too little on a policy is undesirable in the sense of producing unduly decreased benefits and/or increased costs.[1]

---

[1] On the general methodology of optimum level analysis, see Michael Brennan, *Preface to Econometrics* (Cincinnati: South-Western, 1973), pp. 111-82; Samuel Richmond, *Operations Research for Management Decisions* (New York: Ronald, 1968), pp. 40-124; and William Baumol, *Economic Theory and Operations Analysis* (Englewood Cliffs, N.J.: Prentice-Hall, 1978), pp. 1-71. The examples in these three books are, however, all from business situations rather than governmental policy situations.

The governmental policy analysis literature tends to slight optimum level analysis. For example, the popular book, Edith Stokey and Richard Zeckhauser, *A Primer for Policy Analysis* (New York: Norton, 1978) only mentions the important problem of arriving at an optimum policy level (where doing too much or too little is undesirable) on pp. 140-1 out of its 356 pages. There is no mention at all in such books as John Gohagan, *Quantitative Analysis for Public Policy* (Hightstown, N.J.: McGraw-Hill, 1980); and Edward Quade, *Analysis for Public Decisions* (New York: Elsevier, 1975). Of the many policy analysis books published from 1975

A typical optimum level problem might be one in which a government agency is concerned with how strongly to enforce a set of regulations relating to pollution, crime, delay, consumer protection, or other matters. If enforcement is pushed too far, there may be heavy enforcement costs of both a monetary and nonmonetary nature. On the other hand, if enforcement is allowed to be too lenient, there may be considerable damage costs in terms of the kind of damage that can be done by pollution, crime, or other negative social indicators. The object is generally to arrive at a policy level where the sum of the enforcement costs plus the damage costs is minimized. At this point, benefits minus costs are maximized in terms of enforcement benefits (i.e., damage costs avoided) minus enforcement costs, or damage benefits (i.e., enforcement costs avoided) minus damage costs. Although a typical policy level problem may involve a valley-shaped total cost curve or a hill-shaped total benefit curve, such problems also can involve one-directional relations between policies and goals. Here the object is to obtain as much of the policy as possible within economic and other constraints, assuming the policy relates positively to a desirable goal.

To simplify the discussion, the set of symbols that we will frequently use is defined as follows:

Y = the degree of overall goal achievement. It may represent a composite of subgoal achievements. It may represent total benefits, total costs, or benefits minus costs.

Y_1 = the degree of goal achievement on one of the subgoals of the overall goal. It too may represent a composite, and it can also be a benefit or a cost. The Y_1 curve also means the curve that is positively slowing between Y and X.

Y_2 = the degree of goal achievement on a second subgoal of the overall goal. It is generally an opposite type of benefit or cost in the sense

through 1980, the one with the most material on the subject, although the treatment is still quite shallow, is Michael White, *et. al.*, *Managing Public Systems: Analytic Techniques for Public Administration* (Duxbury, 1980), pp. 178-90. But also see the excellent case study of "The Optimum Speed Limit" in Duncan MacRae and James Wilde, *Policy Analysis for Policy Decisions* (Belmont, Ca.: Duxbury, 1979), pp. 133-56.

Earlier, more abbreviated attempts than this present chapter to develop a logic and algebra for optimum policy-level analysis include S. Nagel, "Finding an Optimum Mix or Optimum Level for Public Policies," in Frank Scioli and Thomas Cook (eds.), *Methodologies for Analyzing Public Policies* (Lexington, Mass.: Lexington-Heath, 1975), pp. 79-87; and S. Nagel and M. Neef, "A Simplified Approach to Solving Optimum Level Problems," in *Policy Analysis: In Social Science Research* (Beverly Hills, Ca.: Sage, 1979), pp. 157-59.

that if Y_1 increases when X increases, then Y_2 generally decreases, and vice versa. It can also be opposite in the sense that Y_1 is a benefit from increases in X, and Y_2 is a cost; or Y_1 is a cost, and Y_2 is a benefit. The Y_2 curve also means the curve that is negatively sloping between Y and X.

X = the degree of policy input for achieving the overall goal.

X* = the optimum degree of policy input for maximizing the overall goal where Y is a benefit, or for minimizing the overall goal where Y is a cost.

Y* = the overall goal achievement when the degree of policy input is at an optimum land likewise with $Y*_1$ and $Y*_2$).

a or A = the Y-intercept of the scale coefficient in a linear or nonlinear equation relating Y to Z. Lower case letters refer to one kind of cost or benefit (Y_2).

b or B = the slope or other regression coefficient in a linear or nonlinear equation relating Y to X. In this context, subscripts 1, 2, and 3 refer to other such coefficients in the same Y to X equation, rather than to other sub-goals.

W = the relative value-weight of Y_1 versus Y_2 where they are not both measured in the same units.

The discussion begins with the simplest situations which may be almost too simple. They are presented, however, because they are used to build more complex situations that one normally would think could not be solved by simple logic and algebra, but only by a more sophisticated knowledge of calculus or nonlinear programming routines. This chapter does not explicitly use calculus reasoning or symbols, although the proofs of some statements do require calculus. One, however can use those statements without a previous background in calculus or any awareness of what the calculus proofs might involve. There might be some optimum level situations that this chapter has not included, but they are probably too uncommon to be worth including. The author, however, welcomes learning of such situations so as to be able to further extend this logical approach to the analysis of optimum policy levels.

ONE-DIRECTIONAL RELATIONS BETWEEN A POLICY AND A GOAL

The simplest optimum level situation is one in which adopting more of a given policy consistently produces more of a given goal, or consistently produces less of a given goal, although not necessarily at a constant rate. If that type of relation were graphed with Y on the vertical axis and X on the horizontal axis, the graph might show a positively sloping diagonal line, or a negatively sloping diagonal line. Each of these lines not only moves in one direction but each also moves at a constant rate. They, however, do slope as contrasted to a perfectly horizontal or perfectly vertical line, neither of which has a definable slope.

An example of a one-directional linear relation between a policy and a goal might be the relation between the policy of restricting newspaper reporting concerning pending criminal trials (X) and the goal of assuring defendants a fair trial in being free of prejudicial newspaper reporting (Y). In that example, as X increases, Y increases although not necessarily at a constant rate.[2]

Graphing the relation between Y and X could also show various types of smooth curves that move in one direction, but at a decreasing or increasing rate. Such curves can take four shapes, namely: (1) a positive-concave curve that is steep up and then flattens out, like the left side of a hill; (2) a positive-convex curve that is flat at first and then steep up, like the right side of a valley; (3) a negative-convex curve that is steep down and then flattens out, like the left side of a valley; and (4) a negative-concave curve that is flat at first and then steep down, like the right side of a hill. All these curves are steep at one end and plateau out at a diminishing rate at the other end.

The S-shaped curve is the third type of one-directional relation that often occurs in relating goals to policies. Variations on S-shaped curves all are steep at the beginning and the end, but plateau in the middle, or they plateau at the beginning and end, but are steep in the middle. Such curves can also take four shapes, namely: (1) a positive S-curve that is steep up, flattens out, and then steep up again; (2) a positive S-curve that is flat at first, the steep up, and then flattens again; (3) a negative S-curve that is flat, steep down, and then flattens again; and (4) a negative S-curve that is steep down, flattens, and then steep down again.

Regardless whether straight lines, diminishing-returns curves, or S-shaped curves best show the relation between goal achievement and adopting more of a given policy, the decision rules are fairly simple for determining the optimum policy level. They are as follows:

---

[2]On the free press, fair trial example, see S. Nagel and M. Neef, *Legal Policy Analysis: Finding an Optimum Level or Mix* (Lexington, Mass.: Lexington-Heath, 1977), pp. 281-316.

1. If Y is a benefit (and there is a positive relation), or if Y is a cost (and there is a negative relation), then adopt as much of X as is possible within the economic, legal, political, or other constraints under which one is operating.
2. If Y is a benefit (and there is a negative relation), or if Y is a cost (and there is a positive relation), then adopt as little of X as is possible within the constraints under which one is operating.

TWO-DIRECTIONAL RELATIONS BETWEEN A POLICY AND A GOAL

A two-directional relation between a goal and a policy when graphed produces a hill-shaped curve or a valley-shaped curve. Such curves are generally obtained by combining two one-directional relations such as a positive-convex cost curve (Y_1) and a negative-convex cost curve (Y_2) which produce a valley-shaped total cost curve (Y). Sometimes, however, it is meaningful to relate a goal to a policy using a type of relation which is inherently hill-shaped or valley-shaped without involving a combination of one-directional curves. The most common type of curve like that is a quadratic curve which algebraically is of the form:

$$Y = a + b_1X + b_2X^2 \tag{1}$$

An example of a two-directional relation between a policy and a goal might be the relation between school integration (Y) and busing levels (X). School integration can be measured by determining the extent to which the black student percentage in each school deviates from the overall black student percentage in the district. Busing levels can be measured by determining how much money is spent per student for busing, or how many miles the average student is bused with an adjustment to take into consideration the total size of the district if comparisons are going to be made across districts. The relation between busing level and integration may be a hill-shaped relation. When busing is relatively unused, there may be relatively little integration. As the busing level increases, school integration may also increase up to a point. Beyond that point enough "white flight" may occur so that the increased busing has fewer whites to integrate, with a resulting decrease in integration. The policy problem can thus be viewed as finding the peak or tipping point on that hill-shaped curve.[3]

The numerical values for a, b_1, and b_2 in Equation 1 can be determined through a statistical analysis in which data is obtained on Y and X for many places at one-point-in-time, for many time-points in a single place, or by a combination of both approaches. The numerical values for the parameters of this equation and for other equations relating Y to X can also sometimes be determined by carefully asking knowledgeable people what they perceive the parameters to be and then averaging their responses. By knowing the numerical parameters for other related equations, one can also sometimes deduce what the parameters should be for the equation in which one is interested. Under certain circumstances, it might also be reasonable to assume certain values for the parameters, as where one assumes that when \$X is zero, Y is also zero.[4]

If we have a meaningful relation like that shown in Equation 1, then

---

[3]On the school busing example, see Gary Orfield, *Must We Bus?* (Washington, D.C.: Brookings, 1978).

[4]On determining the numerical parameters (for the equations giving in this chapter) through the use of statistical regression analysis, see Jacob Cohen and Patricia Cohen, *Applied Multiple Regression/Correlation Analysis for the Behavioral Sciences* (Hillsdale, N.J.: Erlbaum, 1975), especially pp. 212-64; Don Lewis, *Quantitative Methods in Psychology* (Iowa City: U. of Iowa Press, 1966), especially pp. 51-136; and Edward Tufte, *Data Analysis for Politics and Policy* (Englewood Cliffs, N.J.: Prentice-Hall, 1974), especially pp. 65-134.

In seeking the perceptions of knowledgeable people, one would ask such questions as, "If X is zero, what do you think the value of Y would tend to be?" for determining "a" in Y = a + bX; or "If X increases by one unit, then by how many units do you think Y would tend to increase or decrease?" for determining "b". One could also ask such questions as, "If X is one unit, what do you think the value of Y would tend to be?" for determining "a" in $Y = aX^b$; or "If X increases by one percent, then by how much of a percent do you think Y would tend to increase or decrease?" for determining "b".

A deductive approach to determining the numerical parameters might involve knowing the relation between X and Z and the relation between Z and Y, and then deducing the relation between X and Y, or deducing the parameters from a purely mathematical model as in the jury size example discussed later under exponential relations. See S. Nagel, "Deductive Modeling in Policy Analysis," in *Policy Analysis: In Social Research* (Beverly Hills, Ca.: Sage, 1979), pp. 177-96. On the making of assumptions to arrive at the numerical parameters, see S. Nagel and M. Neef, *Legal Policy Analysis: Finding an Optimum Level or Mix* (Lexington, Mass.: Lexington-Heath, 1977), pp. 232-34 and pp. 242-43.

The numerical parameters should reflect causal relations between the goals and the alternative allocations, not just spurious correlations. On causal analysis, see Hans Zeisel, *Say It With Figures* (New York: Harper and Row, 1968); Hubert Blalock, *Causal Influences in Non-Experimental Research* (Chapel Hill: U. of North Carolina Press, 1964); and S. Nagel and M. Neef, "Determining and Rejecting Causation," in *Policy Analysis: In Social Science Research* (Beverly Hills, Ca.: Sage, 1979), pp. 69-102.

we can easily arrive at an optimum level of X which will maximize Y (if it is a benefit), or minimize Y (if it is a cost). Doing so first requires determining the slope of the relation between Y and X. Since Equation 1 generates a hill-shaped or valley-shaped curve, the slope is not constant. If a hill is involved, the slope is positive at first, then zero where the hill reaches a peak, and then negative where the hill is going down. Similarly, if a valley is involved, the slope is negative at first, then zero where the valley reaches bottom, and then positive where the valley is going up. Thus the slope of Y relative to X depends partly on X.

To find the slope of Y relative to X requires applying two rules governing slopes. Rule 1 says, if the relation between Y and X is of the form, $Y = a + bX$, then the slope is b. Rule 2 says, if the relation between Y and X is of the form $Y = aX^b$, then the slope is baX^{b-1}. This baX^{b-1} is the slope of any of the straight lines that could be drawn tangent to the curve which would be produced by plotting $Y = aX^b$. Applying those two rules to Equation 1 involves recognizing that the equation is like a combination of three equations, namely: (1) $Y = a$; (2) $Y = b_1X$; and (3) $Y = b_2X^2$. The slope for the first equation is zero following Rule 1, since the slope of a constant is horizontal and thus has no slope. The slope for the second equation is b_1, also following Rule 1. The slope for the third equation is $2b_bX^{2-1}$, following Rule 2. That slope simplifies to $2b_2X$. Putting those three slopes together gives us $b_1 + 2b_2X$ which is the slope of Y relative to X for all of Equation 1.

What now do we do with that information? The logical thing to do is to set that slope equal to zero, and then solve for X. By doing that, we are recognizing that we want to know the value of X when Y hits a peak on a hill-shaped curve or hits bottom on a valley-shaped curve. At either of those two points, the slope of Y relative to X is zero. Setting that slope equal to zero, and solving for X, involves the following steps:

1. $b_1 + 2b_2X = 0$
2. $2b_2X = -b_1$ (Subtracting b_1 from both sides)
3. $X^* = -b_1/2b_2$ (Dividing both sides by $2b_2$)

The third step tells us that the optimum value of X is $-b_1/2b_2$. That means that if we can determine the numerical values for b_1 and b_2, then we will be able to maximize benefit Y or minimize cost Y by adopting X at the $-b_1/2b_2$ level.

COMBINING ONE-DIRECTIONAL RELATIONS
TO MAKE A TWO-DIRECTIONAL RELATION

IN GENERAL

As mentioned in the beginning of this chapter, the most common optimum level problem is one in which a total cost or total benefit curve is determined by combining two subgoal curves. Each subgoal curve is likely to involve a one-directional relation, and the combination is likely to involve a two-directional relation like a hill-shaped curve or a valley-shaped curve. There are various ways of classifying such relations. One dimension relates to whether we are (1) adding opposing costs; (2) adding opposing benefits; or (3) subtracting costs from benefits. Another dimension relates to whether we are combining (1) linear relations; (2) nonlinear relations that proceed at an increasing or decreasing rate, but not both; or (3) nonlinear relations that are S-shaped. A third dimension relates to whether the optimum level on the overall goal can be found (1) through a decision rule without solving an equation; (2) through an equation where X can be made to stand by itself on the left side of the equals sign; or (3) through an equation that requires reiterative guessing of values for X until the optimum level is found.

As for the first method of classification, the combination of two one-directional relations may involve adding two opposing costs as, for example, where one sums (1) a holding cost curve, showing the relation between (a) the percentage of defendants held in jail prior to trial and (b) holding costs, including the cost of incarceration, lost gross national product, and some amount to consider the bitterness generated by being held in jail without being found guilty; plus (2) a releasing cost curve, showing the relation between (a) the percentage of defendants held in jail and (b) the releasing costs, including the cost of crimes committed by released defendants and the cost to rearrest no-shows. The combination may also involve adding two opposing benefits as for example, where one sums (1) an acquittal accuracy curve showing the number of innocent defendants acquitted (Y_1) as jury sizes (X) increase since larger juries are less likely to convict under a unanimity rule; plus (2) a conviction accuracy curve showing the relation between the number of guilty defendants convicted (Y_2) as jury sizes (X) decrease since smaller juries are more likely to convict under a unanimity rule. The combination may also involve subtracting cost relation from a benefit relation as, for example, where one subtracts (1) an S-curve showing the relation between the probability of being held in jail (Y_1) and various dollar bond levels (X), from (2) an S-curve showing the relation between the probability of appearing in court (Y_2) and various dollar bond levels (X).[5]

Which of these three types of combinations to use is largely a matter of semantics, since they are all interchangeable depending on whether one talks about (1) achieving benefits; (2) missing benefits that could have been achieved; (3) incurring costs; or (4) avoiding costs. In the analysis which follows, the examples will emphasize combinations that involve adding what might be called type 1 costs to type 2 costs in order to obtain a total cost curve. It is easier to work with addition than with subtraction, and policy problems generally or often involve trying to decrease negative social indicators like crime, pollution, disease, and jury errors. One, however, can reword the rules which follow to cover examples in which the combinations involve summing benefits or subtracting costs from benefits.

Another meaningful way of classifying combinations is not in terms of whether they involve adding costs, adding benefits, or subtracting costs from benefits, but rather in terms of whether the one-directional relations are linear or nonlinear. Within the nonlinear relations, it is helpful to know whether the one-directional relations involve curves that move at an increasing or decreasing rate (like diminishing-return curves), but not partly at a decreasing rate and partly at an increasing rate (like S-shaped curves). Curves that move at a decreasing or increasing rate, but not both, can be classified in terms of the form of their equations as being semi-log functions, power functions, or exponential functions, each of which will be defined shortly. That kind of classification is useful for informing one how to express the slope of the relation between Y and X in a combination curve regardless whether it is a total-cost, total-benefit, or benefit-minus-cost curve.

Table 8-1 uses an equation form to show 15 common optimum level situations where one-directional relations are combined. There are five types of one-directional relations that one may be likely to encounter in public policy analysis. One is linear and four are nonlinear. Of the nonlinear, three involve decreasing or increasing returns but not both, and one involves both. Going from the northwest corner of the table toward the southeast, the combinations move from the easier to the more difficult along the main

---

[5]On the example of determining an optimum percentage of defendants to hold in jail prior to trial, see S. Nagel and M. Neef, *Legal Policy Analysis* (Lexington, Mass.: Lexington-Heath, 1977) at pp. 1-74. On the example of determining an optimum jury size, see the same book at pp. 75-158. On the example of determining an optimum dollar-bond level in pre-trial release, see S. Nagel and M. Neef, *Decision Theory and the Legal Process* (Lexington, Mass.: Lexington-Heath, 1979), pp. 1-70.

TABLE 8-1
COMMON OPTIMUM LEVEL SITUATIONS WHERE
ONE-DIRECTION RELATIONS ARE COMBINED

	Linear	Semi-Log	Power	S-Shape	Exponential
Linear	1 D	2 A	4 A	7 A	11 A
Semi-Log	2 A	3 D	5 A	8 G	12 G
Power	4 A	5 A	6 A	9 G	13 G
S-Shape	7 A	8 G	9 G	10 A	14 G
Exponential	11 A	12 G	13 G	14 G	15 G

diagonal, which consists of situations 1, 3, 6, 10, and 15. The numbering of the combinations or situations is also roughly from the simpler to the more difficult, but trying to keep together those relations that involve similar equations. Each situation above the main diagonal is duplicated below it. Each situation involves a combination of two relations or equations. We sometimes use the word function or curve, instead of equation or relation. In that context, a function is the right side of an equation with Y on the left side. A curve is the equation plotted.

The easiest combinations are those in which an optimum policy level can be determined by a decision rule like the two rules mentioned above in discussing a one-directional relation between a policy and a goal. Of the 15 situations, there are only two such situations, and they are designated by a D in the lower right-hand corner of their cells. Easy solutions, but not quite as easy, are those in which X can be made to stand by itself on the left side of an equation with numerical parameters on the right side, like the situation described above in discussing a two-directional relation between a policy and a goal. There are seven such situations. They are designated in a table by an A for analytic solution. The relatively more difficult situations require reiterative guessing to determine an optimum value of X, although those guesses can be quickly checked with a programmable calculator against fairly simple criteria so that even those solutions are not difficult. There are six such situations designated by a G in the table. Even they can be avoided by expressing relations between policies and goals through the use of simpler relations where they are applicable.

LINEAR RELATIONS

The first situation in Table 8-1 involves combining two linear relations. One relation might show how holding costs go up when the percentage of defendants held in jail prior to trial goes up. The other relation might show how releasing costs go up when the percentage of defendants held in jail goes down. The first relation might be graphed as a positively sloped diagonal line (Y_1) and the second relation might be graphed as a negatively sloped diagonal line (Y_2). If one then sums these two lines, one obtains a total cost curve that is also a diagonally sloped straight line. It is positively sloped if the first relation has a steeper slope than the second relation, and it is negatively sloped if the opposite is true. In other words, if the first linear relation is expressed as:

$$Y_1 = a + bX, \tag{2a}$$

and the second relation is expressed as:

$$Y_2 = A + BX, \tag{2b}$$

then the sum of those two relations will be positively sloped if b is greater than B, and negatively sloped if the opposite is true.

In view of the fact that combining two linear relations results in a linear total cost curve, the decision rules that apply to one-directional relations between a policy and a goal also apply here. This means that:

1. If b is greater than B, this tells us that Y_1 cost curve is steeper than the Y_2 cost curve, and that total cost will be a positively-sloped line. More important, it tells us to adopt X to as small a degree as possible since the more X we adopt, the more the total cost increases.
2. If B is greater than b, this tells us that the Y_2 cost curve is steeper than the Y_1 cost curve, and that the total cost will be a negatively sloped line. More important, it tells us to adopt X to as large a degree as possible, since the more X we adopt, the more the total cost decreases.

Such a combination of straight lines may fit some policy situations. It, however, may be a generally unrealistic situation for two reasons. First, it ignores diminishing returns in the sense that if an increase in X causes an increase in Y_1 costs, then as X goes down Y_1 should also go down, but at a diminishing rate. Similarly, if a decrease in X causes an increase in Y_2 costs, then as X goes up, Y_2 should go down, but at a diminishing rate. One, however, may find linear relations to be present over short intervals on an X policy variable. Second, working with a combination of straight lines may be politically unrealistic, as well as lacking empirical reality. These combinations tend to result in solutions that say X should be zero present or 100 percent where X is a percent, or that X should be negative or positive infinity where X has a complete range of numbers. Solutions like that may be too extreme to be meaningful. For example, where we are talking about the optimum percentage of defendants to hold in jail prior to trial, we can predict in advance that an all-linear approach will result in an optimum point (where total costs are minimized) of zero percent or 100 percent, which means unrealistically recommending that no one be held or that everyone be held.

SEMI-LOGARITHMIC RELATIONS

To improve the realism of the way we relate costs (or benefits) to policy levels, we can work with semi-logarithmic equations of the form:

$$Y = a + bLogX \qquad (3)$$

The numerical values for a and b can be determined for that equation (or any of the other equations in this chapter) by using statistical regression analysis, questioning of knowledgeable people, deductive reasoning, or reasonable assumptions, as was mentioned in discussing two-directional quadratic relations. If b is a positive number, then when Equation 3 is plotted, it will generate a positively-sloped diminishing returns curve that is steep up at first and then flattens out. If b is a negative number, then when Equation 3 is plotted, it will generate a negatively-sloped diminishing returns curve that is steep down at first and then flattens out. Semi-log curves are useful for relating costs or benefits to policies where one wants a curve rather than a straight line, but an especially simple curve in terms of the easy slope rule that is associated with a semi-log curve.

If we combine a semi-log relation and a linear relation, we get an equation of the form, $Y = a + bX + A + BX$. Given that equation, the slope of Y relative to X is (b) + (B/X). The first part follows from Rule 1, which says, if $Y = a + bX$, then the slope is b. The second part follows from Rule 3, which says, if $Y = a + bLogX$, then the slope of Y to X is b/X. Therefore, if we set that slope equal to zero in order to find where the combination total-cost curve bottoms out, we would go through the following steps:

1. (b) + (B/X) = 0
2. B/X = -b (Subtracting b from both sides)
3. X/B = 1/-b (Inverting both sides)
4. X* = B/-b (Multiplying both sides by B)

This tells us that in Situation 2, the optimum value for X is B/-b, since that value will minimize total costs. If the goals were worded differently, B/-b would maximize total benefits, or maximize benefits minus costs.

Saying X* = B/-b actually means that if we sum a linear curve and a semi-log curve, we will obtain either a hill-shaped or a valley-shaped summation curve, and the peak or bottom of that curve will occur where X equals B/-b. A hill-shaped summation curve results from a positively-sloped semi-log curve and a negatively-sloped line where the hill shows total benefits. A valley-shaped summation curve results from combining a negatively sloped semi-log curve and a positively sloped line. It is that kind of combination relation which we want to emphasize in analyzing the combination relations, namely those that result in valley-shaped summation curves.

The next situation in Table 8-1 is Situation 3 which involves combining a positively-sloped semi-log curve and a negatively-sloped one. Doing so produces an equation of the form $Y = a + b \text{ Log } X + A + B \text{ Log } X$. One can, however, show such a combination of two semi-log curves like the combination of two straight lines produces a one-directional total costs curve or total benefits curve. The easiest way to show that is by substituting any values for a, b, A and B, and then allowing X to move up from .001 to 1,000. Doing so reveals that Y is constantly increasing or decreasing, although at a decreasing rate, but never changing direction. Thus, Y never reaches a peak or a bottom. It is therefore meaningless to determine the slope of the above equation, set that slope equal to zero, and then solve for X, since there is no point where the slope of Y relative to X is zero. The optimum value of X under these circumstances must be determined by a decision rule analogous to the decision rule for determining the optimum X value when combining two straight lines. The appropriate decision rule is:

1. If b (the positive coefficient) is greater in magnitude than B (the negative coefficient), then as X increases, Y will also increase. Therefore, adopt as little X as possible, assuming Y is a cost rather than a benefit.
2. If B is greater in magnitude than b, then as X increases, Y will decrease. Therefore, adopt as much X as possible, assuming Y is a cost.
3. If b and B are both positive, then as X increases, Y will increase; and if b and B are both negative, then as X increases, Y will decrease. We should then act accordingly with regard to the degree of X to adopt.

POWER FUNCTION RELATIONS

Many relations between costs (or benefits) and policies are shown by equations of the form:

$$Y = aX^b \qquad (4)$$

The "a" or scale coefficient represents the value of Y when X is 1. The "b" or elasticity coefficient represents the percent that Y changes when X changes 1 percent. Unlike semi-log curves which can only be positive concave or negative convex, power functions can be positive concave (if b is greater than zero, but less than 1), linear (if b is 1), positive convex (if b is greater than 1), or negative convex (if b is less than 0). Power function curves are useful for relating costs or benefits to policies where one wants to allow for all those possibilities, and when one wants the easy interpretation of the b or elasticity coefficients.

In Situation 4, we combine a linear relation with a power function relation. The straight line can be a positively sloping cost, and the power function can be a negative convex cost. Another alternative that will yield a valley-shaped total cost curve is for the straight line to be negatively sloping, and for the power function to be positive convex. Under either situation, the combination yields an equation of the form $Y = a + bX + AX^B$. Given that equation, the slope of Y relative to X is $b + BA(X)^{B-1}$. Setting that slope equal to zero and solving for X involves the following steps:

1. $b + BA(X)^{b-1} = 0$
2. $BA(X)^{B-1} = -b$
3. $(X)^{B-1} = -b/BA$
4. $X^* = -b/BA$ raised to the power $1/(B-1)$

Thus, if we have an optimum policy level problem involving a combination of a linear cost and a power-function cost and we can determine the numerical values of b, B, and A, then all we have to do to find the optimum X level is insert those values in the above formula in step 4.

In Situation 5, we combine a semi-log cost curve with a power function cost curve. That means a negative convex semi-log curve with a positive convex power curve. Such a combination has the form, $Y = a + bLog X + AX^B$. Its slope is $(b/X) + (BAX^{B-1})$. Setting that slope equal to zero to find the value of X when Y bottoms out involves:

1. $(b/X) + (BAX^{B-1}) = 0$
2. $BAX^{B-1} = -b/X$
3. $(X)(X)^{B-1} = -b/BA$
4. $X^{1+(B-1)} = -b/BA$
5. $X^B = -b/BA$
6. $X^* = -b/BA$ raised to the power $1/B$

That formula can be used to find a peak or a bottom for any combination of a semilog curve and a power curve, although the only combination that will yield a valleyshaped curve is a negative-convex semi-log curve and a positive-convex power function.

In Situation 6, we combine a positively sloping power function and a negatively sloping one in order to obtain a valley-shaped total cost curve. The combination curve is thus an equation of the form, $Y = aX^b + AX^B$. Such an equation has a slope of the form, $baX^{b-1} + BAX^{B-1}$. Setting that expression equal to 0 and solving for X yields:

1. $baX^{b-1} + BAX^{B-1} = 0$
2. $baX^{b-1} = -BAX^{B-1}$
3. $(X)^{b-1}/(X)^{B-1} = (-BA)/(ba)$
4. $(X)^{(b-1)-(B-1)} = (-BA)/(ba)$
5. $(X)^{b-B} = (-BA)/(ba)$
6. $X^* = (-BA)/(ba)$ raised to the power $1/(b- B)$

Summing two power functions to obtain a total cost curve or a total benefits curve is especially common in policy analysis. It is also common to subtract a cost curve from a benefits curve, where both are power functions. The formula in step 6 applies to either kind of addition. If the combination involves subtraction, then the combination equation is simply $Y = aX^b - AX^B$. The two slopes then have a minus sign between them instead of a plus sign, and in the sixth step showing X^*, there is no minus sign to the right of the equals sign.

A common variation on the power function is to work with an equation of the form $Y = c + aX^b$. The advantage of that variation is that it enables one to show that when nothing is spent on X (or X is operating at the zero level), then there are still fixed benefits or costs obtained. Determining the value of c may involve inspecting the dots of a scattergram to determine "c," and then using $Y - c$ as the dependent variable in a statistical regression analysis to determine "a" and "b." Doing that, however, has no effect on the optimizing procedure since c is a constant, and thus the slope of $Y = c + aX^b$ is baX^{b-1}, just as much as it is when $Y = aX^b$. The same is true if a constant "c" is added to an exponential relation of the form $Y = ab^x$. There is already a constant "a" in a linear, semi-log, quadratic, and S-shaped relation.

S-SHAPED RELATIONS

In policy analysis, many relations between policies and either benefits or costs can be best shown by equations of the form:

$$Y = a + b_1X + b_2X^2 + b_3X^3 \tag{5}$$

Equations like that are especially useful for policies that have little effect at first, then a substantial effect, and then plateau out. An example might be the level at which bail bonds are set (as the policy variable, X) and the probability of defendants being held in jail (as a cost variable that we would like to hold down, Y_1). As the bond level goes up, the probability or percentage of defendants held in jail stays low, at least while the bond level is going up at a low level. At some point, however, increases in the bond level do result in substantial increases in defendants being held in jail. At another point, the bond level becomes so high that virtually everyone gets held in jail, as being unable to meet the bond level. At that point, increases in the bond level have little effect on increases in the percentage of defendants held in jail.

If we combine a positively sloped S-shaped curve with a negatively sloped straight line, we get an equation of the form, $Y = a + bX + A + B_1X + B_2X^2 + B_3X^3$. One can think of the negatively-sloped straight line as representing the probability of nonappearance in court for trial, which is a kind of cost curve that goes down when the bond level goes up. The slope of that combination valley-shaped curve is an expression of the form, $b + B_1 + 2B_2X + 3B_3X^2$. That expression simplifies to $c + dX + eX^2$, where $c = b + B_1$, $d = 2B_2$, and $e = 3B_3$. To solve for the value of X, when that valley-shaped curve hits bottom, we set that expression equal to zero. Doing so, however, yields a quadratic equation that is more easily solved by a formula than by trying to get X to stand by itself, on the left side of the equation. The formula for solving a quadratic equation in the above form is:

$$X^* = [-d \pm (d^2 - 4ce)^5]/2e \tag{6}$$

To use this formula, we insert the numerical values of the parameters for the simply two curves, namely a, b, B_1, B_2, and B_3, after they have been translated into the symbols c, d, and e. After making those insertions, we will obtain two solutions for X^*. One will indicate where the combination curve reaches a peak of maximum costs, and the other will indicate where a combination curve reaches a bottom of minimum costs. It is, of course, the value of X

where the curve reaches bottom that interests us. If, however, we were summing two benefit curves, or dealing with the difference between a benefits and a cost curve, then we would be interested in knowing the value of X where the combination curve reaches a peak.

In Situation 8, we combine an S-shaped curve with a semi-log curve. As in Situation 7, the S-shaped curve could relate the probability of being held in jail to alternative bond levels, and the semi-log curve could relate the probability of nonappearance to the bond levels. The equation representing that combination is $Y = a + b \log X + A + B_1X + B_2X^2 + B_3X^3$. The slope for that equation is $b/X + B_1 + 2B_2X + 3B_3X^2$. If, however, we set that expression equal to zero and try to solve for X, we will find that it is algebraically impossible to get X to stand by itself, on the left side of the equals sign. The quadratic equation formula is also no help, since it requires that all the exponents be either zero, 1, or 2, with no decimal or negative exponents. The first addend in that slope is the algebraic equivalent of bX^{-1}, which involves a negative exponent. To solve for X when the above slope is set equal to zero might best be done on a programmable calculator. We would insert into the calculator the numerical values for b, B_1, B_2, and B_3, and show how they are related to each other in the above slope expression. In place of X in that expression, we would use whatever we insert as a guess into calculator storage register No. 1. We then insert a guessed value into that storage register, push the start button, and observe the display to see what value the expression has with that guess. If the value of the expression is above zero, we try a lower guess. If the value of the expression is below zero, we try a higher guess. Only a few seconds of calculation are required between guesses until our guessing is able to make the expression equal to zero. The guess at that point is the optimum value of X because it is X when the slope of Y is zero, indicating in this context that Y has reached the bottom of a valley-shaped total cost curve.

In Situation 9, we combine an S-shaped curve with a power function. That combination yields an equation like $Y = aX^b + A + B_1X + B_2X^2 + B_3X^3$. The slope for that equation is $baX^{b-1} + B_1 + 2B_2X + 3B_3X^2$. Setting that slope equal to zero and solving for X requires the same kind of reiterative guessing approach as in Situation 8. The subsequent tenth situation, however, can be solved through the analytic solution method. It involves summing two S-shaped curves, one that might represent the probability of being held, with the second representing the probability of nonappearance. Nonappearance may be graphed as a negatively sloping S-shaped curve, in the sense that at low bond levels there is a *high* probability of nonappearance, until some point is reached when it becomes worthwhile to show up in order to get one's bond money back, rather than treat the small bond forfeiture as a substitute for a fine. At extremely high bond levels, there may be a continuously *low* probability of nonappearance, at least in misdemeanors or traffic violations, since the average defendant is probably as likely to appear to collect a 20,000 dollar bond as a 25,000 dollar bond. The equation which represents the sum of two such S-shaped functions has a form like Equation 5, with lower-case letters for its parameters added to a similar equation with upper case letters. The slope of such an equation looks like the slope of the quadratic equation for Situation 7, except $c = b_1 + B_1$, $d = 2b_2 + 2B_2$, and $e = 3b_3 + 3B_3$. Also like Situation 7, the solution for X when that slope is set equal to zero requires the use of the quadratic formula given in Equation 6.

EXPONENTIAL RELATIONS

In policy analysis, some relations between policies and costs or benefits are best expressed by an exponential curve. Such curves have the form:

$$Y = ab^X \tag{7}$$

The numerical parameters can be arrived at through a statistical analysis by obtaining scores for persons, places, or things on the Y variable and the X variable, and then inputting that data into a regression analysis with just the dependent variable logged. For a power function, one logs both Y and X; whereas for a semi-log function, one just logs the X variable. The numerical parameters may also be obtained by deductive mathematical reasoning, as in the policy analysis problem of finding an optimum jury size. In that problem, X is the number of jurors to be solved, b is the probability that an average juror will vote to convict, and the "a" coefficient is relative normative weight that one places on obtaining accurate convictions versus accurate acquittals. In an exponential function, the unknown or the policy level to be found is an exponent, whereas in a power function the unknown policy level is the base which is raised to a power.

Situation 11 combines a linear function with an exponential function. The positive exponential function might show that as the number of jurors increases, the errors of guilty defendants who are not convicted increases at an exponential rate, since it is much more difficult to obtain a unanimous conviction with more jurors. The straight line would be negatively sloped in the opposite direction and show that the number of errors of innocent persons being convicted goes down as the number of jurors increases, since the number of defendants convicted in general goes down as the number of jurors increases. Such a pair of relations when combined generates an equation of the form $Y = a + bX + AB^X$. To find the slope for that equation requires Rule 4. The previous three rules dealt with a linear relation, a power function, and a log function. The S-shaped curve required no new rule, since it is a combination of linear and power-function terms. Rule 4 says that if $Y = ab^X$, then the slope of Y relative to X is $(LNb)(ab^X)$. The expression LN b means find the natural logarithm of b, which can easily be done on an inexpensive calculator. The common logarithm of 100 is 2, since 100 is 10 squared. The natural logarithm of 100 is 4.61 since 100 is e (or 2.72) raised to the power 4.61. Knowing Rule 4 enables us to determine that the slope of the combination equation is $b + (LN\ B)(AB^X)$. Setting that slope equal to zero and solving for X involves the following steps:

1. $b + (LN\ B)(AB^X) = 0$
2. $(LN\ B)(AB^X) = -b$
3. $(AB^X) = -b/(LN\ B)$
4. $B^X = -b/[(LN\ B)(A)]$
5. $Log(B^X) = Log\ -b[(LN\ B)(A)]$
6. $X(Log\ B) = (Log\ -b) - Log[(LN\ B)(A)]$
7. $X(Log\ B) = (Log\ -b) - [Log(LN\ B) + Log\ A]$
8. $X(Log\ B) = (Log\ -b) - Log\ (LN\ B) - Log\ A$
9. $X^* = [(Log\ -b) - Log(LN\ B) - Log\ A]/Log\ B$

Optimum policy-level formulas similar to that one were actually used to arrive at a tentative optimum jury size between 6 and 12. That analysis was favorably referred to by the U.S. Supreme Court in the case of Ballew v. Georgia, 435 U.S. 233 (1978).

The rest of the situations number 12 through 15 can easily be developed by combining the separate equations for an exponential function and a semi-log function (Situation 12), a power function (Situation 13), an S-Shaped function (Situation 14), and another exponential function (Situation 15). All four of those situations generate slopes that require the reiterative guessing approach in order to solve for X when the slopes are set equal to zero. That reiterative guessing will indicate the numerical value X should have in order to minimize the sum of Y_1 plus Y_2. By slightly varying the analysis, one can also determine the numerical value of X in order to maximize the sum of Y_1 and Y_2 (where they are benefits rather than costs), or maximize $Y_1 - Y_2$ or $Y_2 - Y_1$ (where one is a benefit and the other is a cost).

OTHER COMBINATIONS

The other main combination that has a reasonable likelihood of occurring in policy analysis involves a combination of a one-directional relation (like any of the five just discussed) and a two-directional relation (like a quadratic relation in the subsequent section). An example of this type of combination might be finding an optimum school busing level where we are concerned with two goals. One goal is that of integration (Y_1), as measured by the average deviation between the black student percentage of each school and the black student percentage in the district. A second goal (although a negative one) might be the dollar costs (Y_2) at various busing levels for fuel, drivers and equipment. The first goal might be related to busing levels by way of a hill-shaped quadratic relation of the form, $Y = a + b_1X + b_2X^2$, as previously discussed.

The second goal might be related to busing levels as a positively sloped linear, semi-log, power, S-shaped, or exponential function. The object of the analysis is to find the busing level that maximizes the Y_1 benefit minus the Y_2 cost.

One problem in this analysis, which often occurs in any kind of optimum level analysis, is how to measure Y_1 and Y_2 in the same units so that Y_2 can be meaningfully subtracted from Y_1, or how to develop a coefficient to indicate the relative importance of a one-unit increase in integration versus a one-unit increase in busing costs. Although the problem is frequent, it seems more obvious here because we are combining two substantially different kinds of curves and because it seems almost unethical, inequitable, or unconstitutional to assign a dollar value to increases in integration. The problem arises whenever two goals are combined which may be measured in different units, or even when the same units have different meanings. An example of the latter situation is where we combine conviction errors (Y_1) and acquittal errors (Y_2) in arriving at an optimum jury size. They are both measured in "errors," but a conviction error clearly does not have the same meaning as an acquittal error. Even in the simple one-directional linear relation of the form, $Y = a + b^X$, there may be a problem of combining goals since Y may be a composite of various subgoals.

This measurement problem may not be as difficult as it at first seems for at least three reasons. First, people deal with this kind of problem almost every day in satisfactory ways as when, for example, a shopper decides to buy a can of beans for 1 dollar, rather than two cans of asparagus for 1 dollar. In doing so, the shopper is in effect saying that one can of beans has more value than two cans of asparagus. That implicitly involves some kind of value scale on which beans and asparagus can be compared. Shoppers are also capable of deciding between one can of beans at 1 dollar and two cans of asparagus at more or less than 1 dollar. Putting integration units (measured in percentage points) and busing costs (measured in 1,000s of dollars) on roughly the same scale should not be so much more difficult. Second, psychologists and economists have been studying the problems of combining goals, and they have developed simple and not-so-simple methods for doing so. Third, to do the combining does not necessitate that integration percentage points be converted into dollars, that busing dollars be converted into percentage points, or that both units be converted into something else like utility or satisfaction units. All one needs to make the combination meaningful is to get agreement or an average opinion of relevant people on how many times more or less is the relative value of a one-unit increase in integration versus a one-unit increase in busing costs.[6]

A more concrete example can help clarify the problem, especially how it might be resolved through the relative-value approach. Suppose we have three schools in a district, and one is 10 percent black, the second is 20 percent, and the third is 30 percent black. The average black percentage is thus 20 percent, which is the same as the percentage of black students in the district if each school has the same population. The first school deviates from the average by 10 percentage points, the second school by zero, and the third school also by 10, for an average deviation of 20/3 or 7 percentage points. If we subtract those 7 percentage points from 100, we can meaningfully say that this district is 93 percent integrated, although we would have to explain how the 93 percent was calculated. If busing costs are measured in 1,000 dollar units, then the measurement question becomes how many times more than 1,000 dollars in government expenditure is it worth to the community or district to move from 93 percent integrated to 94 percent integrated.

---

[6]On the methodology of combining goals, see J. P. Guilford, *Psychometric Methods* (New York: McGraw-Hill, 1954); Allan Easton, *Complex Managerial Decisions Involving Multiple Objectives* (New York: Wiley, 1973); and Peter Gardiner and Ward Edwards, "Public Values: Multi-attribute Utility Measurement for Social Decision Making," in Martin Kaplan and Steven Schwartz (eds.) *Human Judgement and Decision Process* (New York: Academic Press, 1975).

Perhaps a survey of relevant people to that question might produce an average response of 10. If so, then when it comes time to subtract predicted Y_2 from predicted Y_1 in order to calculate Y, we would use an equation like $Y = 10Y_1 - Y_2$. If Y_1 is a quadratic function and Y_2 is a linear function, the equation can also be expressed as $Y = 10(a + b_1X + b_2X^2) - (A + BX)$. Inserting 10 for W (or weight) does not complicate the analysis. It simply means that the a, b_1, and b_2 get multiplied by 10. We can also ignore the 10 and consider that $a = 10a$, $b_1 = 10b_1$, and $b_2 = 10b_2$. To be more sophisticated, we can also recognize that the weight of 10 may not be a constant. In other words, W may be 10 when we move from 93 percent and 94 percent, but less than 10 when we move 97 percent to 98 percent. If W moves down as the integration percentage (P) moves up, the relation might have the form, $W = aP^b$, with b being a negative number. If so, then we would substitute a(P)b for the W of 10 in the above equation.

To combine such a weighted quadratic relation with a linear relation is no problem in light of the previously described procedures. We simply note that given those two relations, the slope of Y relative to X is $b_1 + 2b_xX - B$. If we set that slope equal to zero, we get:

1. $b_1 + 2b_2X - B = 0$
2. $2b_2X = B - b_1$
3. $X^* = (B - b_1)/2b_2$

That third step indicates that if one can determine those numerical parameters for B, b_1, and b_2, then by inserting them into that equation, one can determine an optimum busing level that will maximize the integration benefits minus the busing costs. If, however, that analysis shows X^* will yield an integration score of only about 40 percent, then that X value might be outside the feasible region in the sense that the Supreme Court may not tolerate an integration percentage that low. The Supreme Court has specified maximum deviations in legislative redistricting cases, but it has not yet indicated precise constraints or outer limits in school integration cases.

To combine a weighted quadratic-relation with a semi-log, power, S-shaped, or exponential busing cost-relation involves basically the same kind of reasoning. The combination with a semi-log cost-curve, however, leads to a slope equation of the form, $b_1X + 2b_2X^2 - B = 0$, which is best solved by the quadratic formula. Similarly, when one combines a quadratic and an S-shaped relation, and then sets the slope of the combination equal to zero, one also obtains an equation that is best solved by the quadratic formula. When one combines either a power function or an exponential function (to represent the relation between busing levels and busing costs) with a quadratic function (to represent the relation between busing levels and integration), one gets the kind of equation which can only be solved by reiterative guessing after setting the slope of the combination equal to zero.

One might ask how it is possible to have so many different relations between busing costs (Y_2) and busing levels (X). If busing levels are measured in terms of dollars spent per student, then the relation between Y_2 and X would have to be linear, since Y_2 would equal the number of students times X. If, however, busing levels are measured in terms of miles per student, we could have a positively sloped diminishing-returns curve between Y_2 and X. In other words, busing costs could keep going up as the number of miles increases, but at a diminishing rate since many of the costs are fixed costs for equipment, rather than variable costs like fuel. With this subject matter, however, an S-shaped curve does not seem meaningful since it requires costs to move up at a decreasing rate and then at an increasing rate, or to move up at an increasing rate and then a decreasing rate. Neither of those occurrences seems to fit the realities here, although these occurrences may apply to other policy analysis problems.

In discussing optimum policy-level problems, one might also ask about curves that are more than two-directional, including curves that have more than one bend as in a business cycle curve. Those curves may be quite meaningful when relating time (on the horizontal axis or as the independent variable) to changes in either a social indicator goal (Y) or to changes in a policy (X) (on the vertical axis or as the dependent variable). These curves, however, do not seem to fit any relations between a social indicator goal (as a dependent variable) and a policy (as an independent variable). One partial exception might be that when two of the curves previously discussed are combined together, the result may be an S-shaped curve on its side. Such a curve goes down to a bottom, up to a peak, and then down again, or else up to a peak, down to a bottom, and then up again. That type of combination curve can, for example, occur when a positively sloped S-shaped curve is combined with a negatively sloped straight line. The result may be a combination curve that has both a bottom indicating minimum costs and a peak indicating maximum benefits. Both points, as previously mentioned, can be found through the use of the quadratic formula. One simplifying reality about policy analysis, as compared to natural science or pure mathematics, is that there are so few curves that do realistically fit policy analysis data. It also helps that those curves can be expressed as variations on linear regression analysis and as curves for which slopes can easily be determined.

With regard to other combinations, it may be quite reasonable to have an optimum level problem in which the valley-shaped total cost curve or hill-shaped total benefit curve is generated by combining more than two curves. For example, in the optimum speed limit problem of Duncan MacRae (mentioned in note 1 above), three curves are combined to generate a valley-shaped total cost curve. They are (1) time saved as a benefit which is a negative convex power function; (2) operating costs including fuel which is a positive-linear function; and (3) accidents cost which is also shown as a positive-linear function. All three subgoal variables are measured in dollars which eases the goal-combining problem. Other optimum level problems could conceivably involve any number of benefit curves and cost curves that are algebraically and geometrically summed to get a total curve with a bottom or a peak. One, however, might sum the cost curves to get a total cost curve, sum the benefit curves to get a total benefit curve, and then get a net benefits curve by subtracting the total costs curve from the total benefits curve. One might also sum the positively sloping cost curves, sum the negatively sloping cost curves, and then sum these two opposite cost curves to get a total cost curve, or do similarly where all the effects are expressed in terms of benefits like the time saved rather than time lost. Once one obtains the total curve that has a bottom or a peak, the slope of its equation can be set equal to zero, and a solution found for X which will indicate the optimum policy level.

SOME CONCLUSIONS

The simple logic and algebra which this chapter proposes for solving optimum policy-level problems can be summarized in three sets of rules, dealing with equations, slopes and optimization. With regard to curve-fitting equations, the rules indicate the type of equation one should or could use for showing certain types of relations between goals and policies. The rules are as follows:

1. If the relation increases or decreases at a constant rate, the equation should read, $Y = a + bX$, or variations on that relation with control variables.
2. If the relation increases or decreases at an increasing or decreasing rate, but not both, the equation should read:
   a. $Y = a + b \text{ Log } X$, when we want simplicity in expressing a diminishing returns slope.

b. $Y = aX^b$, when we want a coefficient that will relate a percentage change in Y to a one percent change in X.

c. $Y = ab^X$, when the subject matter is such that it makes sense for the policy variable to be an exponent.

3. If the relation produces a valley-shaped or hill-shaped curve without combining relations, the equations should read, $Y = a + b_1X + b_2X^2$.

4. If the relation increases or decreases at both an increasing and a decreasing rate roughly in the shape of an S, the equation should read $Y = a + b_1X + b_2X^2 + b_3X^3$.

There are other comparative reasons for using these various equations in policy analysis, but these are probably the most frequent ones.

With regard to slopes, the rules are:

1. If $Y = a + bX$, then the slope of Y relative to X is b.
2. If $Y = a + b \text{ Log } X$, then the slope is b/X.
3. If $Y = aX^b$, then the slope is baX^{b-1}.
4. If $Y = ab^X$, then the slope is $(LN\ b)(ab^X)$.
5. If $Y = a + b_1X + b_2X^2$, then the slope is $b_1 + 2b_2X$.
6. If $Y = a + b_1X + b_2X^2 + b_3X^3$, then the slope is $b_1 + 2b_2X + 3B_3X^2$.

Rules 5 and 6 are combinations of rules 1 and 3.

With regard to optimization, the rules are:

1. If a curve showing the relation between degrees of policy adoption (X) and either total benefits, total costs, or benefits minus costs (Y) is a straight diagonal line or a one-directional curve, then adopt as much or as little as possible of the policy within the constraints depending on whether moving up or down on the policy is desirable.

2. If the curve showing the relation between degrees of policy adoption (X) and either total benefits, total costs or benefits minus costs (Y) is a valley-shaped or hill shaped curve, then adopt the policy up to the point where one reaches the minimum on the valley shaped curve or the maximum on the hill-shaped curve. Doing so involves:

   a. Expressing the relation between X and Y as a quadratic equation of Type 3 above, or a combination of any two of the above equations.

   b. Determining the slope of that equation or combination of equations.

   c. Setting that slope equal to zero, and

(1)   solving for X by getting X to stand by itself on the left side of the equation, or

(2)   solving for X by using reiterative guessing with a programmable calculator.

With that set of six equations, four slope rules, and three optimization rules (linear, analytic solution, and reiterative guessing), plus the numerical parameters from a statistical, deductive or other analysis, one should be able to arrive at an optimum policy level through simple logic and algebra. Obtaining those numerical parameters, including relative value weights, is not easy. The work involved in obtaining them, however, should be more meaningful if one knows better what is going to be done with that kind of numerical information after it has been obtained. Too often in policy analysis, data is gathered for what is intuitively viewed as an optimum policy-level problem, where doing too much or too little would be undesirable, but the data gatherers may only have in mind showing the extent to which a given policy has achieved its intended goals. Such data gathering and analysis may miss the opportunity to go further and say something about what might be the optimum policy level under various normative constraints and empirical coefficients. It is hoped that this chapter will help clarify what is involved in optimum policy-level analysis so that more policy-relevant data gatherers will apply their data to developing optimum policy level models.

9

ALLOCATION LOGIC

The purpose of this chapter is to show how virtually any public policy problem that involves allocating scarce resources to activities or places can be solved through simple logic if two prerequisites are met. First, one should be able to express quantitatively (1) the goal to be maximized, and (2) the constraints to be complied with. Second, the goal and the constraints should be expressed as statistical, mathematical, or other functions (i.e., equations or inequalities) of (1) the potential allocations to the alternative activities, or (2) the potential allocations to the alternative places. Solving such problems normally does not require the use of complicated and sometimes unreliable linear or nonlinear programming routines. By using a logical approach, one can also obtain better insights into what is happening which in turn can improve the policy recommendations.[1]

---

[1]On the general methodology of allocating scarce resources, see David Himmelblau, *Applied Nonlinear Programming* (Hightstown, N.J.: McGraw-Hill, 1972); Philip Kotler, *Marketing Decision Making: A Model Building Approach* (New York: Holt, 1971); Sang Lee, *Linear Optimizing for Management* (Princeton, N.J.: Petrocelli/Charter, 1976); Robert Llwellyn, *Linear Programming* (New York: Holt, 1963); and Claude McMillan, Jr., *Mathematical Programming: An Introduction to the Design and Application of Optimal Decision Machines*

SITUATIONS, SYMBOLS, AND SOLUTIONS

To better understand the allocation methodology being presented, it is helpful to classify our government allocation problems. Table 9-1 provides us with a 6 by 4 classification scheme that yields 24 common allocation situations. The main dimension (on the top) is whether the relation between the goals and the allocations are linear or nonlinear. Within each of those two categories, we can talk in terms of whether we are seeking to maximize benefits subject to a maximum cost constraint, or seeking to minimize costs subject to one or more minimum benefit constraints. A third dimension (shown on the side) is whether we are allocating to interacting activities, or allocating to non-interacting places. Within each of those two categories, we can talk in terms of whether or not there are minimum (and possibly maximum) constraints on what can be given to the activities and places. Each of the 24 situations involves a somewhat different reasoning process. There are also variations on these basic 24 situations which will be discussed.

To simplify the discussion, it would be helpful to define a set of symbols that we will frequently use. They are as follows:

Y = the overall goal to be achieved.

Y_1 = the first subgoal, or the amount of Y achieved by Place 1.

Y_2 = the second subgoal, or the amount of Y achieved by Place 2.

X_1 = the dollars allocated to Activity 1 or Place 1.

X_2 = the dollars allocated to Activity 2 or Place 2.

G = the grand total of dollars-available to be allocated to the activities or places after the minimums have been allocated or considered. G can be a given or an amount to be calculated.

M_1 = the minimum amount to be allocated to Activity 1 or Place 1.

M_2 = the minimum amount to be allocated to Activity 2 or Place 2.

$M\%_1$ = the minimum percent of G to be allocated to Activity 1 or Place 1.

$M\%_2$ = the minimum percent of G to be allocated to Activity 2 or Place 2.

X^*_1 = the optimum amount to allocate to Activity 1 or Place 1.

X^*_2 = the optimum amount to allocate to Activity 2 or Place 2.

Y^* = the overall goal achievement when optimum amounts are allocated

―――――――――――――――

(New York: Wiley, 1970). In addition to the authors of the above books, I would like to thank such people as Judith Liebman and Wayne Davis of the University of Illinois, Rob Dembo of Yale, Paul Zipkin of Columbia, and Leon Lazdon of the University of Texas for their helpful suggestions concerning linear and nonlinear programming.

TABLE 9-1. COMMON ALLOCATION SITUATIONS

ACTIVITIES	LINEAR RELATIONS Maximize Y Minimize TC			NONLINEAR RELATIONS Maximize Y Minimize TC		
	(One Y)	(2Y's)		(One Y)	(2Y's)	
Unconstrained	1	5	9	13	17	21
Constrained	2	6	10	14	18	22
PLACES						
Unconstrained	3	7	11	15	19	23
Constrained	4	8	12	16	20	24

Y_2 = the second subgoal, or the amount of Y achieved by Place 2.

X_1 = the dollars allocated to Activity 1 or Place 1.

X_2 = the dollars allocated to Activity 2 or Place 2.

G = the grand total of dollars-available to be allocated to the activities or places after the minimums have been allocated or considered. G can be a given or an amount to be calculated.

M_1 = the minimum amount to be allocated to Activity 1 or Place 1.

M_2 = the minimum amount to be allocated to Activity 2 or Place 2.

$M\%_1$ = the minimum percent of G to be allocated to Activity 1 or Place 1.

$M\%_2$ = the minimum percent of G to be allocated to Activity 2 or Place 2.

X_1^* = the optimum amount to allocate to Activity 1 or Place 1.

X_2^* = the optimum amount to allocate to Activity 2 or Place 2.

Y^* = the overall goal achievement when optimum amounts are allocated to activities when optimum amounts are allocated to activities or places (and likewise with Y_1^*, Y_2^*, and G^*).

a or A = the Y-intercept in a linear function, or the scale coefficient in a nonlinear function. Lower case letters refer to Place 1 or Goal 1, and upper case to Place 2 or Goal 2.

b or B = the slope in a linear function, or the elasticity coefficient in a nonlinear function. Subscript 1 refers to Activity 1, Place 1, or Goal 1 depending on the context.

to activities or places (and likewise with $Y*_1$, $Y*_2$, and $G*$).

a or A =   the Y-intercept in a linear function, or the scale coefficient in a non-linear function. Lower case letters refer to Place 1 or Goal 1, and upper case to Place 2 or Goal 2.

b or B =   the slope in a linear function, or the elasticity coefficient in a non-linear function. Subscript 1 refers to Activity 1, Place 1, or Goal 1 depending on the context.

The discussion begins with the simplest situations which may be almost too simple. They are presented, however, because they are useful on which to build more complex situations that one normally would think could not be solved by simple logic, and instead would require a computerized optimizing routine. Even nonlinear relations with many activities and/or places to be allocated to and many constraints can usually be solved through simple logic and algebra. The solutions recommended below at least provide good starting points in the allocation reasoning process. One possibly may be able to devise unusual hypothetical situations where the decision rules may not apply. The author welcomes learning of such situations so as to be able to further extend this logical allocation approach.

LINEAR RELATIONS BETWEEN GOALS AND ALLOCATIONS

By linear relations between goals and allocations, we mean that it is meaningful to express the relation between the Y's and the X's by an equation of the following form for two interacting activities:

$$Y = a + b_1X_1 + b_2X_2 \tag{1}$$

The analogous form for two noninteracting places is:

$$Y_1 = a + bX_1 \tag{2a}$$
$$Y_2 = A + BX_2 \tag{2b}$$

The numerical values for a, b_1, and b_2 in Equation 1 and for a, b, A, and B in equations 2a and 2b can be induced from statistical analysis or deduced from accepted premises. The numerical parameters for an activities equation often come from an analysis across agencies or places. The numerical parameters for the places equations often come from an analysis over time for each place. One can also carefully ask knowledgeable people what they perceive the parameters to be and average their responses. The Y-intercept generally should be fixed at zero since spending nothing should generally produce no benefits. That would be an example of arriving at one of the numerical parameters by way of an assumption rather than through induction or deduction.[2]

MAXIMIZING TOTAL GOAL ACHIEVEMENT

The simplest set of situations is probably the set that involves maximizing Y subject to a maximum cost constraint. If we are allocating to the activities in the context of Equation 1, we should give all of G or the grand total of dollars available, to the activity with the highest positive slope and nothing to any of the other activities, unless there are some minimum or maximum constraints. If there are two activities tied for best in terms of their slopes, then they should divide G equally. If there are minimum constraints, we should give each activity the minimum to which it is entitled, and then allocate all of the

---

[2]For examples of allocation problems that emphasize linear relations, see Edward Beltrami, *Models for Public Systems Analysis* (New York: Academic Press, 1977); C. Laidlaw, *Linear Programming for Urban Development Plan Evaluation* (New York: Praeger, 1972); S. Nagel and M. Neef, *The Application of Mixed Strategies: Civil Rights and Other Multiple-Activity Policies* (Beverly Hills, Ca.: Sage, 1976); and S. Nagel, *Minimizing Costs and Maximizing Benefits in Providing Legal Services to the Poor* (Beverly Hills, Ca.: Sage, 1973).

On linear regression analysis, see Allen Edwards, *An Introduction to Linear Regression and Correlation* (San Francisco: Freeman, 1976); and Jacob Cohen and Patricia Cohen, *Applied Multiple Regression/Correlation Analysis for the Behavioral Sciences* (Hillsdale, N.J.: Erlbaum, 1975). On asking questions designed to elicit perceptions of slopes or marginal rates of return, see Kotler, op. cit., and George Huber "Methods for Quantifying Subjective Probabilities and Multi-Attribute Utilites," in 5 *Decision Sciences* 430-58 (1974). Meaningful questions might include, "If X is zero, what do you think the value of Y would tend to be?" or "If X increases by one unit, then by how many units do you think Y would tend to increase or decrease?" A deductive approach to determining the numerical parameters might involve knowing the relation between X and Z and the relation between Z and Y, and then deducing the relation between X and Y. See S. Nagel and M. Neef, "Deductive Modeling in Policy Analysis," in *Policy Analysis: In Social Science Research* (Beverly Hills, Ca.: Sage, 1979), pp. 177-96. On the making of assumptions to arrive at the numerical parameters, see S. Nagel and M. Neef, *Legal Policy Analysis: Finding and Optimum Level or Mix* (Lexington, Mass.: Lexington-Heath, 1977) pp. 232-34, 242-43. The numerical parameters should reflect causal relations between the goals and the alternative allocations, not just spurious correlations. On causal analysis, see Hans Zeisel *Say It With Figures* (New York: Harper & Row, 1968); Hubert Blalock, *Causal Inferences in Non-Experimental Research* (Chapter Hill: U. of North Carolina Press, 1964); and S. Nagel and M. Neef, "Determining and Rejecting Causation," in *Policy Analysis: In Social Science Research* (Beverly Hills, Ca.: Sage, 1979).

remainder to the activity with the highest positive slope. If there is a maximum constraint, then we can only allocate up to that maximum and then switch to the activity with the next to highest positive slope, and so on. The same rules apply if we are allocating to places where linear relations are involved and the goal is to maximize benefits subject to a budget constraint.

This applies to situations 1 through 4. One variation on the basic idea that cuts across all 24 situations is dealing with an objective that is to be minimized, like crime, rather than an objective that is to be maximized, like cases resolved. When the goal is a bad rather than a good, one simply reverses the rules and concentrates on the activities or the places that have the highest negative slope with Y rather than the highest positive slope. Another variation involves more than two activities or two places, but the same rules often apply, as they do here. One could also talk in terms of allocating to both activities and places. This might simply involve allocating first to activities and then suballocating those allocations among the places, or allocating first to places and then suballocating within those places to their activities. Another variation involves expressing the minimum constraints in terms of percentages rather than dollar amounts. In this first set of situations, that would merely involve calculating the minimums for each activity or place by applying their minimum percentages to the grand total to be allocated and then allocating the remainder to the activities or places with the best slopes.

In all 24 situations, it is assumed that X_1, X_2, and other activities or places must have values of zero or more, meaning there are implicit non-negativity constraints. If we are allocating a budget or effort to activities or places, there is no meaningful way we can give an activity or place less than nothing. We could take away something previously given, but allocation problems by definition only refer to giving, not taking. If an activity or place could be allocated a negative amount, rather than a zero amount, then one could develop nonsense solutions analogous to being able to divide zero by zero. For example, with Equation 1, if b_1 is greater than b_2, the logical solution would be to give a large negative amount to X_2 and the same large positive amount to X_1. By doing so, we would achieve a large amount of Y while spending nothing, since the sum of the expenditures on X_1 plus X_2 would be zero.

MINIMIZING TOTAL EXPENDITURES

Satisfying One Goal Constraint

In Situation 5, we are still working with Equation 1. Now, however, we do not want to give all of G to the X that has the best slope, but just enough to achieve whatever the minimum Y level is. In other words, if b_1 is greater than b_2, then give nothing to X_2, and solve for X_1 in the equation Minimum Y = $a + b_1X_1$. It is possible that there is no value of X_1 that will achieve the minimum Y level. In any of these allocation problems, there may be no solution given the realities of the actual situations. The solution under those circumstances may be:

1. Obtain more G to allocate.
2. Set a lower minimum Y level.
3. Set lower minimum allocations to the activities or places.
4. Improve the efficiency of the activities or places, which means increasing their slopes so they produce more Y with less money.

Situation 6 involves minimum constraints on the activities. Thus with Equation 1, one would give the required minimum X_2 and then solve for X_1 in the equation, Minimum Y = $a + b_1X_1 + b_2(M_2)$. If the minimums to be given to X_1 and X_2 are expressed as percentages (like .20 per X) rather than dollar amounts, one would solve for G in an equation, for example, Minimum Y = $a + b_1(.80G) + b_2(.20G)$. A more general statement would be, Minimum Y = $a + b_1[(1 - M\%_2)(G)] + b_2[(M\%_2)(G)]$. After solving for G in this equation, X^*_1 is the numerical value of what is in the first set of brackets, and X^*_2 is in the second set.

Situations 7 and 8 involve the same kind of reasoning as situations 5 and 6 except the total goal achievement equals Y_1 plus Y_2. Thus in Situation 7, one would give nothing to X_2 if b_1 is greater than b_2. One would determine X^*_1 by solving for X_1 in the equation, Minimum $(Y_1 + Y_2) = a + bX_1$. In Situation 8, one would determine the optimum allocation to X_1 by solving for X_1 in the equation Minimum $(Y_1 + Y_2) = a + bX_1 + A + B(M_2)$.

Satisfying Two or More Goal Constraints

Allocating to Activities. The problem becomes slightly more complicated if we have two goals or two kinds of benefits on which we want minimum achievement levels. In Situation 9, for instance, the problem might be to minimize total costs while providing a minimum Y_1 level and minimum Y_2 level. Suppose, for example, the problem is one of reaching a minimum client satisfaction level (Y_1) and a minimum lawyer satisfaction level (Y_2) in the allocation of dollars to law reform work (X_1) and routine case handling (X_2) in the Office of Economic Opportunity Legal Services Agencies. That might mean a pair of constraints like the following:

$$a + b_1X_1 + b_2X_2 \geq \text{Minimum } Y_1 \tag{3a}$$
$$A + B_1X_1 + B_2X_2 \geq \text{Minimum } Y_2 \tag{3b}$$

The easiest way to determine at least an initial set of optimum values for X_1 and X_2 is to reason that if we are trying to minimize total costs, then we should not seek more than the minimum Y_1 and Y_2 levels. Doing so means converting the "greater than or equal to" signs in inequalities 3a and 3b into equals signs. If X_1 is better than X_2 in both equations (meaning it has a larger slope), then set X_2 equal to zero and solve for X_1 in both equations. The larger value for X_1 is X^*_1, since that amount is needed to achieve both minimum Y_1 and minimum Y_2 at the lowest total cost. One would do the opposite if X_2 were better than X_1. If, however, X_1 is better in one equation, but worse in the second equation, then something should be given to both X_1 and X_2. To determine what those amounts are, solve both equations simultaneously. The resulting solutions for X_1 and X_2 should be optimum values in the sense of achieving minimum Y_1 and minimum Y_2 while spending a minimum total costs.

If there are minimum constraints on X_1 and X_2 as in Situation 10, then follow the same procedures as in Situation 9, except give the worse X its minimum value rather than nothing. If one X is worse on only one of the two equations, and the equations are solved simultaneously, one may find that one or both of the solutions fall below the minimum level. If, for example, X^*_1 is below M_1, then consider M_1 to be X^*_1, and solve for X_2 in both equations. The higher value for X_2 under those circumstances is X^*_2. That way one satisfies minimum Y_1, minimum Y_2, minimum X_2, and minimum X_2, while minimizing the total expenditures.

If there were three subgoals and thus three inequality constraints instead of two, an appropriate approach would be to simultaneously solve (1) equations 1 and 2, (2) equations 1 and 3, and (3) equations 2 and 3. That would give three pairs of possible optimum values. One should then sum the X_1 and X_2 for each of those three pairs to see which sum is the smallest since we are seeking to minimize total costs. The pair that yields the smallest sum is the optimum pair assuming that pair can also satisfy the third constraint. If not, then one should turn to the pair that yields the next to the smallest sum, and so on. No matter how many such constraints there are, by solving them in pairs one should be able to arrive at the optimum allocation, since that is the equivalent to finding the key corner points in a linear programming graph. By key corner points we mean solutions that involve giving something to each of the activities rather than everything to only one activity. If after giving something to each activity with three subgoals, one finds that an activity like X_1 is not getting its minimum, then substitute M_1 for X_1 and solve for X_2 in the three equations. $X*_2$ then equals the largest of those three solutions, and $X*_1$ equals M_1.

If there are three activities and only two constraints, as in 3a and 3b, we cannot solve a pair of equations simultaneously that has three unknowns. The simple thing to do under those circumstances is to think in terms of allocating only to the X that has the best slope on the second constraint. All the other Xs can be dropped out. We are then left with two equations and two unknowns which should then be capable of being solved if a solution exists. If the same X is best on both equations, then we simply give that activity all the G rather than divide it between two activities.

Allocating to Places. Situations 11 and 12 involve allocating to places rather than to activities. Under those circumstances, the constraints would be like the following, relating each goal to the place allocations:

$$(a_1 + b_1X_1) + (A_1 + B_1X_1) <= \text{Minimum } Y_1 \qquad (4a)$$
$$(a_2 + b_2X_1) + (A_2 + B_2X_2) <= \text{Minimum } Y_2 \qquad (4b)$$

They differ from constraints 3a and 3b in that each place has its own Y-intercept, whereas the activities share a common Y-intercept. The minimum Y_1 is arrived at by summing the Y_1 from Place 1 and the Y_1 from Place 2, and likewise with the minimum Y_2. Therefore, if we want to minimize the total costs and meet these minimum goal constraints, it makes sense to solve both equations simultaneously unless one of the two places is better on both of the subgoals. If so, we would simply give that better place enough of the G so as to achieve at least the minimum desired level on both Y_1 and Y_2. Whatever that optimum allocation might be, it might produce more than the minimum Y_1 in order to get the minimum Y_2 or vice versa.

In Situation 12 where there are minimum amounts that have to be allocated to each place, solve the equations for 4a and 4b simultaneously provided that X_1 is better on one goal and X_2 is better on the other goal. If the solution to X_1 is below M_1, then substitute M_1 for X_1, and solve for X_2. Do the same if the solution for X_2 is below M_2. If X_1 is better on both goals, then give X_2 its minimum (M_2) and determine what is the smallest allocation needed to X_1 in order to achieve at least the minimum on Y_1 and the minimum on Y_2, taking into consideration what has been allocated to X_2 and the slope of X_2. In other words, if Xl has the better slope on both Y_1 and Y_2, then (1) substitute M_2 for X_2 in equations 4a and 4b, and (2) solve for X_1 in each of those two equations. X^*_2 thus equals M_1, and X^*_1 equals the larger of the two solutions for X_1.

Whatever has been said about minimum values on X_1 and X_2 should apply equally to maximum values on X_1 and X_2, although government allocation problems are more likely to specify minimums to activities or places, rather than maximums. For example, in Situation 12, if the solution to X^*_1 exceeds a maximum value, then substitute that maximum value for X^*_1 and solve for X_2, just as one would substitute the minimum value for X^*_1 and solve for X_2 if the original X^*_1 fell below M_1. Similarly, in these various situations, if the minimums are expressed as percentages of G rather than as absolute amounts, then substitute $(M\%_2)(G)$ for X_2 and $(1 - M\%_2)(G)$ for X_1 when X_1 has the better slope in both equations. If X_1 has the better slope in only one of the two equations, then solve the equations simultaneously, and make adjustments to consider $M\%_1$ and $M\%_2$ analogous to the adjustments to consider M_1 and M_2 in Situation 12.

As an additional type of constraint, a problem could conceivably provide for a maximum goal achievement or maximum Y level. Normally, goal achievement has a ceiling placed on it indirectly by a budget constraint. There may, however, be situations where the policy makers are willing to allow goal achievement to rise to a point, regardless of cost or in anticipation that the specified point can be afforded. Such a situation is like 1, 2, 3, or 4, except in those situations G is determined by the budget constraint, rather than by calculating the amount needed to achieve the maximum Y. The maximum Y situation would be resolved by giving nothing to the X or Xs with less than the best slope. One would then solve for the value of the best X in an equation of the form, Maximum Y = a + bX, since the other Xs would be set to zero or set to their minimum values. That is the same approach one would use if the policy problem specified a desired or fixed Y level, rather than a maximum Y level. It is also the same approach when the problem specifies a minimum Y level with one goal as in situations 5, 6, 7, and 8. In other words, the same optimizing analysis can often be applied to substantially different situations by seeing the underlying logical similarities.

NONLINEAR RELATIONS BETWEEN GOALS AND ALLOCATIONS

By nonlinear relations between goals and allocations, we mainly mean relations that involve diminishing returns between inputs and outputs. Such a relation may mean that increasing the inputs will cause increased beneficial outputs, but with a plateau effect like the left side of a hill. A nonallocation example might be dollars spent to provide legal services for the poor with the goal being client satisfaction (Y). An allocation example might involve allocating the budgets of legal services agencies between law reform activities (X_1) and routine case handling (X_2). A diminishing returns relation may also look like the left side of a valley if the output is a detriment like crime (Y), and the inputs are anticrime expenditures to Place 1 (X_1) and Place 2 (X_2).[3]

MAXIMIZING TOTAL GOAL ACHIEVEMENT

Allocating to Interacting Activities

There are a variety of ways of expressing nonlinear relations. The simplest way to show diminishing positive or negative returns where two or more activities are involved is through an equation of the form:

---

[3]For examples of allocation propblems that emphasize nonlinear relations, see Donald Shoup and Stephen Mehay, *Program Budgeting for Urban Policy Services* (New York: Praeger, 1971); Walter Helly, "Allocation of Public Resources, " in *Urban Systems Models* (New York: Academic Press, 1975); S. Nagel and M. Neef, "Finding an Optimum Geographical Allocation for Anticrime Dollars and Other Governmental Expenditures," in *Legal Policy Analysis: Finding an Optimum Level or Mix* (Lexington, Mass.: Lexington-Heath, 1977), pp. 225-74; and S. Nagel, "Optimally Allocating Campaign Expenditures," *Public Choice* (Winter, 1980).

On nonlinear regression analysis, see Don Lewis, *Quantitative Methods in Pyschology* (Iowa City: U. of Iowa Press, 1966); and Edward Tufte, *Data Analysis for Politics and Policy* (Englewoods Cliffs, N.J.: Prentice-Hall, 1974). The use of subjectively perceived parameters or assumed paramters applies to nonlinera relations as well as linear ones. For example, knowledgeable people can sometimes handle questions of the form, "If X is one unit, what do you think the value of Y would tend to be?" where we are trying to ascertain "a" in the nonlinear equation, $Y = aX_b$. Similarly, one can ask, "If X increases by one percent, then by how much of a percent do you think Y would tend to increase or decrease?" Under some circumstances, it might also be reasonable to assume a square-root relation where b = .5, a rectangular hyperbola where b = -1, or a quadratic equation where b = 2.

$$Y = a(X_1)^{b1}(X_2)^{b2} \tag{5}$$

One can obtain the numerical values for the three parameters from the same data used in determining the numerical values for those parameters back in linear Equation 1. The only difference is that when inputting the data into a computer as part of a regression analysis, one instructs the computer to work with the logarithms of Y, X_1, and X_2, rather than their raw scores. Numerical values can also sometimes be deduced from accepted premises.

What makes that type of relationship between goals and activities so easy to work is not only the simplicity of how those values can be used to determine an optimum allocation, as can be illustrated with Situation 13. If b_1 is greater than b_2, one would probably not want to allocate all of one's 100 dollar budget to X_1 because as the relation between Y and X_1 plateaus out, an incremental dollar given to X_1 is likely to produce a smaller return than using that same dollar as the first dollar given to X_2. The object is to allocate the 100 dollars in such a way as to spend all of the 100 dollars, but with a given amount allocated to each activity so that they are in a state of equilibrium, whereby they both have the same incremental rate of return.

To be more specific, we want to solve for X_1 and X_2 simultaneously in the following pair of equations:

$$X_1 + X_2 = G \tag{6a}$$
$$b_1 a X_2^{b2}(X_1)^{b1-1} = b_2 a X_1^{b1}(X_2)^{b2-1} \tag{6b}$$

The first equation says spend all of the grand total on X_1 and X_2. The second equation follows from the fact that if $Y = aX^b$, then the marginal rate of return of Y to X is baX^{b-1}. Thus the second equation is setting the MRR of X_1 equal to the MRR of X_2. If we simultaneously solve both those equations, we will find that $X^*_1 = [b_1/(b_1 + b_2)](G)$, and that $X^*_2 = [b_2/(b_2 + b_2)](G)$. Those solutions tell us we should allocate G to the activities in proportion to their exponents or elasticity coefficients, provided that each activity has a positive exponent and Y is desired. That rule of proportionality also follows from the fact that in Equation 5, the relations between each activity and Y depend solely on their respective exponents since they share a common scale coefficient of "a" value.[4]

If any activity has a negative exponent, then it gets allocated nothing (or whatever minimums are provided in Situation 14), and the remaining G is allocated among the activities with positive exponents in proportion to those exponents. Under Situation 14, (1) the minimums are allocated to all the activities; (2) the sum of the minimums is subtracted from G; and (3) the remainder of G is then allocated to the activities with positive exponents in proportion to their exponents. Activities with positive exponents would normally have exponents with values between zero and 1, which indicates diminishing returns between X and Y. If an exponent in this context equals 1 (showing a linear relation between X and Y) or a number greater than 1 (showing an increasing returns relation), then one still allocates in proportion to those exponents in order to obtain a maximum Y (or goal achievement) for a given G (or amount to be allocated).

In order to keep the allocation system simple, the X_1 and X_2 units should be kept dollars, hours, or other effort units rather than physical units. For example, the system becomes substantially more complicated if we are

---

[4]The simultaneous solution to equations 6a and 6b is as follows:

1. $(X_1)^{b1-1}/(X_1)^{b1} = [b_2 a(X_2)^{b2-1}]/[b_1 a(X_2)^{b2}]$ (X_1 expressed in terms of X_2 using equation 6b)

2. $(X_1)^{b1-1-b1} = [(b_2)(X_2)^{b2-1-b2}]/b_1$ (Cancelling the "a" values and showing division with exponential expressions)

3. $(X_1)^{-1} = [(b_2)(X_2)^{-1}]/b_1$ (Doing the subtraction within the exponents)

4. $1/X_1 = b_2/(b_1 X_2)$ (A -1 exponent is the same as a reciprocal)

5. $X_1 = (X_2 b_1)/b_2$ (Inverting both sides)

6. $[(X_2 b_1)/b_2] + X_2 = G$ (Substituting the right side of step 5 for X_1 in Equation 6a)

7. $X_2[(b_1/b_2) + 1] = G$ (Factoring out X_2)

8. $X_2 = G/[(b_1/b_2) + 1]$ (Dividing both sides by what is in brackets)

9. $X_2 = G/[(b_1/b_2) + (b_2/b_2)]$ (Anything divided by itself equals 1)

10. $X_2 = G/[(b_1 + b_2)/b_2]$ (Addition of fractions)

11. $X_2^* = G[b_2/(b_1 + b_2)]$ (To divide by a fraction, invert and multiply)

12. $X_1 + G[b_2/(b_1 + b_2)] = G$ (Substituting the right side of step 11 for X_2 in Equation 6a)

13. $X_1 G - G[b_2/(b_1 + b_2)]$ (Subtracting from both sides)

talking about allocating a budget of 100 monetary units or 100 dollars between equipment versus labor when equipment is measured in tons and labor in quantity of people. Suppose one ton of equipment costs 5 dollars and one person's labor costs 2 dollars. One could therefore express the budget constraint as $5X_1 + 2X_2 = 100$. We could then be solving for tons of equipment (X_1) and number of employees (X_2), rather than dollars to spend on X_1 and X_2. This would also change the coefficients or parameters in all the equations in this chapter. The change would be contrary to our concern for being able to solve governmental allocation problems through simple logic, algebra, and calculator-aided arithmetic. Once we solve for X_1 and X_2 in dollars, we can always translate those dollars into tons of equipment and numbers of people since we know that one ton costs 5 dollars and one person costs 2 dollars.

If the minimums for X_1 and X_2 are expressed as percentages of G, the logical allocation system has to be modified slightly. Suppose, for example, b_1 in Equation 5 is .2, and b_2 is .4. That tells us the optimum allocation to X_1 is 2/6 of G, and the optimum to X_2 is 4/6 of G. If, however, the minimum constraints specify X_1 must receive .40 G, then we would give .40 G to X_1, rather than .33 G, and X_2 should receive the remainder, or .70 G. If there were an X_3 with a b_3 of .6, then X_1 should receive 2/12 of G, X_2 should receive 4/12, and X_3 should receive 6/12. If, however, the constraints require that X_1 get at least 40 percent, then we have to give .40 to X_1, rather than .17, and allocate the remaining 60 percent between X_2 and X_3. The logical way to do this allocating is in proportion to their elasticity coefficients. Thus, X_2 would get 4/10 of the remaining .60, and X_3 would get 6/10 of the remaining .60. Through a similar reasoning process, one could solve any allocation problem involving (1) the allocation of scarce resources among interacting activities; (2) the objective of maximizing goal achievement; (3) a relation between goal achievement and the activity allocations which is expressed as a nonlinear multivariate power function like Equation 5, and (4) minimum constraints on one or more activities expressed as percentages of the grand total to be allocated. The same reasoning can apply to Situation 16 discussed later.

Allocating to Noninteracting Places

The simplest way to show diminishing positive or negative returns where two or more places are involved (as in Situation 15) is through a set of equations of the form:

$$Y_1 = a + bLogX_1 \qquad\qquad (7a)$$
$$Y_2 = A + BLogX_2 \qquad\qquad (7b)$$

These two equations are analogous to equations 2a and 2b, except they are nonlinear because X_1 and X_2 are logged in determining the numerical values for the parameters through statistical regression or other analysis.

This type of relation between goals and places is also easy to work with in arriving at optimum allocations. If b is greater than B, one would still want to allocate something to X_2 since it might be wasteful to allocate all of G to X_1 when the plateau effect becomes too great. More specifically in this context, we want to solve for X_1 and X_2 simultaneously in the following pair of equations:

$$X_1 + X_2 = G \qquad\qquad (8a)$$
$$b/X_1 = B/X_2 \qquad\qquad (8b)$$

The first equation says spend the grand total on X_1 and X_2. The second equation follows from the fact that if $Y = a + bLogX$, then the marginal rate of return of Y to X is b/X. Thus the second equation is setting the MRR of X_1 equal to the MRR of X_2. If we simultaneously solve both these equations, we will find that X^*_1 equals G multiplied by the ratio between b and the sum of b and B. Similarly, X^*_2 equals G multiplied by the ration between B and the sum of b and B. In other words, we can optimally allocate to noninteracting places by allocating in proportion to their semi-log regression coefficients. This rule also follows from the fact that the marginal rates of return for equation 7a and 7b depend only on the values of b and B. The values of a and A have no bearing on the MRR's, because they are constants, rather than multipliers or exponents of the allocations.[5]

---

[5]The simultaneous solution to equations 8a and 8b is as follows:

1. $X_1/b = X_2/B$ (Inverting both sides of Equation 8b)
2. $X_1 = X_2b/B$ (Multiplying both sides by b)
3. $(X_2b/B) + X_2 = G$ (Substituting the right side of step 2 for X_1 in Equation 8a)
4. $X_2[(b/B) + 1] = G$ (Factoring out X_2)
5. $X_2 = G/[(b/B) + 1]$ (Dividing both sides by what is in brackets)
6. $X_2 = G/[(b/B) + (B/B)]$ (Anything divided by itself is 1)
7. $X_2 = G/[(b + B)/B]$ (Addition of fractions)
8. $X_2^* = G[B/(b + B)]$ (When dividing by a fraction, invert and multiply)

One might ask, why not express the relation between goal achievement and inputs for each place using power functions of the form, $Y_1 = a(X_1)b$ and $Y_2 = A(X_2)B$? The answer is that doing so would greatly complicate the optimum allocations, since it would mean solving a pair of simultaneous equations in which the first equation is of the form $X_1 + X_2 = G$, and the second equation is of the form $ba(X_1)^{b-1} = BA(X_2)^{B-1}$. That pair of equations cannot be solved by simply (1) expressing X_1 in the terms of X_2 using the second equation; (2) substituting that expression for X_1 in the first equation; (3) solving the first equation, which is now one equation, in one unknown (X_2); and then (4) using the first equation to solve for X_1. Doing steps 1 and 2 yields an equation of the form, $c(X^d_2) + X_2 = G$. If d is not an integer, one has to use a reiterative guessing approach until a solution for X_2 is found. That is not too difficult with two places or two unknowns, but becomes virtually impossible to handle with 50 states, 100 cities, or any substantial number of places, where each place or X is an unknown allocation to be solved. The semi-log equations 7a and 7b enable one to allocate easily to any number of places by simply allocating in proportion to their semi-log regression coefficients (i.e., b_i/sigma b], provided that each place has a positive coefficient and Y is desired.

If any place has a negative coefficient, then it gets allocated nothing (or whatever minimums are provided in Situation 16), and the remaining G is allocated among the places with positive coefficients in proportion to those coefficients. Under Situation 16, (1) the minimums are allocated to all the places; (2) the sum of the minimums is subtracted from G; and (3) the remainder of G is then allocated to the places with positive coefficients in proportion to their coefficients. If we are spending to fight crime or a negative goal, then we allocate proportionally to the activities or places with negative exponents or coefficients.

---

9. $X_1 + G[B/(b + B)] = G$ (Substituting the right side of step 8 for X_2 in Equation 8a)

10. $X_1 = G - G[B/(b + B)]$ (Subtracting from both sides)

11. $X_1 = G[1 - (B/b + B)]$ (Factoring out G)

12. $X_1 = G[(b + B)/(b + B) - (B)/(b + B)]$ (Anything divided by itself is 1)

13. $X_1^* = G[b/(b + B)]$ (Subtraction of fractions)

MINIMIZING TOTAL EXPENDITURES

Satisfying One Goal Constraint

Allocating to Activities. Situation 17 involves allocating to two or more activities in such a way as to minimize total expenditures while satisfying a minimum level of Y. This simply involves solving for G in the following equation:

$$\text{Minimum } Y = a[(b_1/\Sigma b)(G)]^{b1} [(b_2/\Sigma b)(G)]^{b2} \tag{9}$$

This equation tells us that what needs solving is the grand total to allocate to the activities. The grand total should be less than the maximum budget available if we are trying to minimize expenditures, rather than maximize goal achievement. This equation also tells us that the percentage of G to be allocated to Activity 1 should be proportionate to the elasticity coefficient of Activity 1, and similarly with Activity 2. We know what minimum Y is supposed to be. We also know values for a, b_1, and b_2 probably from a regression analysis in which all the variables have been logged. Once we solve for G as the one unknown in the above equation, we can easily solve for X^*_1 and X^*_2, since they are the amounts in the first and second set of brackets, respectively. In other words, X^*_1 and X^*_2 are the minimum amounts possible for achieving the desired minimum Y, given the known relations between Y and both X_1 and X_2, as shown in Equation 5. Solving for G can be done by getting G to stand by itself on the left side of the equation by applying the rules of high school algebra, including the rules for simplifying expressions that contain exponents.[6]

---

[6]For example, if a = .5, b_1 = 2, b_2 = 3, and Minimum Y = 10, then

1. $10 = .5[(2/5)(G)]^2[(3/5)(G)]^3$ (Inserting numerical values)
2. $10 = .5(.40G)^2(.60G)^3$ (Doing the division)
3. $10 = .5(.16G^2)(.22G^3)$ (Raising each factor in the parenthesis to the power outside the brackets)
4. $10 = .02G^5$ (Doing the multiplication)
5. $G^5 = 500$ (Dividing both sides by .02)
6. $G^* = 3.47$ (Finding the one-fifth root)
7. $X^*_1 = (.40)(3.47) = 1.39$ (Substituting G^* in the first brackets)
8. $X^*_2 = (.60)(3.47) = 2.08$ (Substituting G^* in the second brackets)

In Situation 18, each activity is entitled to a certain minimum allocation as a matter of equity, politics, law, or other considerations while the remaining funds are allocated in accordance with the relative productivity of each activity. The best way to handle this kind of allocation problem is to solve for G in Equation 9 (as in Situation 17), and then to follow these rules:

1. If X^*_1 is above M_1, and X^*_2 is above M_2, then the solution of Equation 9 for Situation 17 is also the solution to Situation 18.
2. If X^*_1 is below M_1, and X^*_2 is below M_2, then insert M_1 into the first set of brackets as X^*_1, and insert M_2 into the second set of brackets as X^*_2.
3. If X^*_1 is below M_1, and X^*_2 is above M_2, then insert M_1 into the first set of brackets, insert X_2 into the second set of brackets, and solve for X_2.
4. If X^*_1 is above M_1 and X^*_2 is below M_2, then insert M_2 into the second set of brackets, insert X_1 into the first set of brackets, and solve for X_1.

These rules will provide the lowest possible allocations to X_1 and X_2 in order to satisfy both the minimum Y level and the minimum X_1 and X_2 levels.

If the minimums for X_1 and X_2 are expressed as percentages of G, the solutions are even easier than when they are expressed in absolute amounts. Suppose, for example, b_1 is 3 and b_2 is 5, then when we insert those amounts into Equation 9 the first set of brackets will show $(3/8)(G)$, and the second set will show $(5/8)(G)$. That will yield an acceptable solution if $M\%_1$ is equal to or less than .375 and if $M\%_2$ is equal to or less than .625. Suppose, however, $M\%_1$ is .40 and $M\%_2$ is zero, meaning no minimum for X_2. We would then insert into the first set of brackets $(.40)(G)$, insert into the second set of brackets $(.60)(G)$, and then solve for G, assuming we also have a numerical value for the "a" and minimum Y. In other words, $b_i/\Sigma b$ has to be replaced by $M\%_i$ if $M\%_i$ is greater than $b_i/\Sigma b$. By applying that kind of reasoning, we can also handle minimum X_1 and X_2 percentage constraints for places in Situation 20.

Allocating to Places. Situation 19 is like 17 in that it involves allocating to minimize expenditures while satisfying a minimum goal achievement with no minimum constraints on how much can be allocated to each place or activity. Situation 19 is also like 15 in that it involves allocating to places rather than activities, which means working with semi-log functions like 7a and 7b, rather than a power function like that of Equation 5. Thus what is basically involved is solving for G in the following equation:

Minimum $Y = a + bLog\{[b/(b+B)]G\} + A + BLog\{[B/(b+B)]G$ (10)

This equation tells us that all we need to do is solve for G, as in Equation 9. The expression in the first pair of braces is equal to X^*_1 or the optimum amount to allocate to Place 1 in order to achieve the minimum Y level. Similarly, the expression in the second pair of braces is equal to X^*_2. Each place receives an allocation in proportion to its semi-log regression coefficient. Minimum Y is the minimum goal achievement that we want the total allocation to have across both places. If there were more than two places we would simply add a third expression like the two which are now in Equation 10, although we would have to switch using subscripts to distinguish between the places, rather than using lower and upper case letters. Equation 10 can be solved by getting G to stand by itself on the left side of the equation by using the rules of high school algebra dealing with logarithms, especially the rule that says the logarithm of a product is equal to the sum of the log of the first factor plus the log of the second factor.[7]

Situation 20 is like 19, except each place is entitled to a minimum allocation, before allocating additional resources to satisfy the minimum Y level. That means following the same four rules described in connection with situation 18, but substitute "braces" for "brackets" in those rules. Braces are needed in Equation 10 because the sum of the place-coefficients is symbolized (b + B), rather than Σb which is used to show the sum of the activity

---

[7]For example, if $1 = .50$, $b = 2$. $A = .25$, $B = 3$, and Minimum $Y = 10$, then:

1. $10 = .50 + 2Log[(2/5)G] + .25 = 3Log[(3/5)G]$ (Inserting numerical values)
2. $10 = .75 + 2Log(.40G) + 3Log(.60G)$ (Doing the division and some addition)
3. $10 = .75 + 2(-.40+Log(G)) + 3(-.22+Log(G))$ (Taking the log of each factor in the parentheses)
4. $10 = .75 - .80 + 2Log(G) - .66 + 3Log(G)$ (Doing the multiplication)
5. $10 = .71 + 5 Log(G)$ (Doing the rest of the addition and subtraction)

6. $5 Log(G) = 10 + .71$ (Adding +.71 to both sides)
7. $Log(G) = 10.71/5 = 2.14$ (Dividing both sides by 5)
8. $G^* = 138.68$ (Finding 10 raised to the 2.14 power)
9. $X^*_1 = (.40)(138.68) = 55.47$ (Substituting G^* in the first brackets)
10. $X^*_2 = (.60)(138.68) = 83.21$ (Substituting G^* in the second brackets)

coefficients in Equation 9. If the minimum Y level can be satisfied by going below the minimum place or activity allocations, then we have a conflict between the objective that says minimize expenditures, and the constraint that says provide each place with certain minimum allocations. Under those circumstances, it might be appropriate to lower the minimums, since lower allocations will still achieve a minimum Y level. Exactly what the new minimums should be is an equity matter that cannot be deductively determined the way we can logically deduce optimum allocations with various situations (like those specified in Table 1) and various empirical relations (like those specified in equations 1, 2, 5, and 7).

SATISFYING TWO OR MORE GOAL CONSTRAINTS

Allocating to Activities. In nonlinear situations 21 through 24, two or more goal constraints are involved which generally means solving pairs of equations simultaneously, as with linear situations 9 through 12. Allocating to activities under such circumstances means solving simultaneously a pair of equations like the following:

$$\text{Minimum } Y_1 = a(X_1)^{b1}(X_2)b^2 \tag{11a}$$
$$\text{Minimum } Y_2 = A(X_1)^{B1}(X_2)^B2 \tag{11b}$$

This means going through steps like:

1. Use Equation 11b to express X_1 in terms of X_2.
2. Substitute that expression for X_1 in Equation 11a.
3. Solve Equation 11a, which is now one equation in one unknown. This gives X^*_2.
4. After solving for X_2 in Equation 11a, then solve for X_1 in the same equation. This gives X^*_1.

The results represent the lowest possible allocations to X_1 and X_2 that can satisfy Y_1 at its minimum and simultaneously satisfy Y_2 at its minimum. If there is a minimum Y_3 equation, then solve the Y_1 and Y_2 equations, the Y_1 and Y_3 equations, and the Y_2 and Y_3 equations. The best pair of solutions is the pair in which (1) the sum of X_1 and X_2 is the lowest, and (2) all three equations are satisfied.

In situation 22, we not only have minimums on Y_1 and Y_2 to satisfy, but also on X_1 and X_2. The logical approach involves solving equations 11a and 11b simultaneously. In doing so, if X^*_1 and X^*_2 equal or exceed M_1 and M_2 respectively, then situation 22 has been resolved. If X_1 is below M_1, then substitute M_1 for X^*_1, and solve for X_2 in each of the two equations. The larger solution for X_2 is X^*_2. Do the opposite if X_2 is below M_2. If both Xs are below both Ms, then $X^*_1 = M_1$ and $X^*_2 = M_2$.

As an alternative, suppose the minimums are expressed as percentages of G and the solutions to X_1 and X_2 do not satisfy those minimums because, for example, X^*_1 is less than $(M\%_1)(G)$. Under those circumstances, substitute $(M\%_1)(G)$ for X_1 in Equations 11a and 11b, substitute $(1 - M\%_1)(G)$ for X_2, and then solve for G in each equation. G^* is the larger of the two Gs in order to be able to achieve both minimum Y_1 and minimum Y_2. X^*_2 is $(M\%_1)(G^*)$ and X^*_2 is $G^* - X^*_1$. The same reasoning can be applied to other variations on the idea of percentage minimums in situations 22 and 24.

Allocating to Places. In situation 23 where noninteracting places are being allocated to, the pair of equations that needs to be solved separately or simultaneously might be like the following:

$$\text{Minimum } Y_1 = a + bLogX_1 \tag{12a}$$
$$\text{Minimum } Y_2 = A + BLogX_2 \tag{12b}$$

As a concrete example, one can consider the two places to be Chicago and New York. The problem is how to allocate an anticrime budget in such a way as to minimize expenditures while seeing to it that Chicago does not have more than 10 crime units and New York does not have more than 15 crime units. We would thus be talking about a maximum Y_1 and a maximum Y_2, rather than minimums on those two goals, but the logical analysis is still the same. The coefficients would also be negative rather than positive, but that also does not affect the logical analysis. The solution under these circumstances is simply to solve for X_1 in Equation 12a and solve for X_2 in Equation 12b.

To make the problem more challenging, we can move to Situation 24 where Chicago has a minimum allocation of M_1, and New York has a minimum allocation of M_2. If the X^*_1 solution to Equation 12a is below M_1, then $X^*_1 = M_1$, and similarly if the X^*_2 is below M_2. That will mean X^*_1 will produce a higher Y_1 level than if X^*_1 had been above M_1. Doing better than the minimum Y_1 level, however, is consistent with the constraint which says we should do at least as well as minimum Y_1.

As an even more challenging alternative, we can change the problem to say we want certain Y_1 and Y_2 levels across both cities. That might mean solving simultaneously a pair of equations like:

$$\text{Maximum } Y_1 = b_1 LogX_1 + b_2 LogX_2 \tag{13a}$$
$$\text{Maximum } Y_2 = B_1 LogX_1 + B_2 LogX_2$$

The Y_1 in this context might be crimes against property (lower-case slopes) and Y_2 crimes against persons (upper-case slopes). For the sake of simplicity, the "a" and A coefficients here are considered to be zero. Equation 13b can be used to express X_1 in terms of X_2, with this expression substituted in Equation 13a for solving Equation 13a. If there are minimums for X_1 and X_2, they can be handled as previously described in situations 18, 20, and 22.

For a grand finale challenge, we could pose a problem of minimizing expenditures when allocating across places subject to constraints like 13a, 13b, 12a, 12b, and 10. The logical thing to do under those circumstances is solve for X^*_1 and X^*_2 under 10, 12, and 13. This will give three pairs of possible solutions. The best pair is the one in which X_1 plus X_2 is lowest and which is also capable of satisfying the constraints on total crime (Equation 10), crime in Chicago and New York (Equations 12a and 12b), and property-person crimes (Equation 13a and 13b). If we had lots of places to allocate to (not just two), then there would be more calculations and more solutions to check against those criteria. The amount of places or activities, however, should not deter one from using a logical algebraic approach like that advocated here, although a computer or good calculator would be helpful for doing the calculating and checking.

To tie the linear part of this chapter with the nonlinear part, we could pose an allocation problem involving two activities or places, in which the first activity has a linear relation with goal achievement and the second relation, like that shown below:

$$Y = a + bX_1 + A(X_2)^B \tag{14}$$

At first glance, one might think combining both kinds of relations might complicate things. It actually simplifies them. For example, suppose the problem is how to allocate a given budget (G) between X_1 and X_2 in light of Equation 14. The solution simply involves setting the marginal rates of return for X_1 and X_2 equal to each other which means $b = BA(X_2)^{B-1}$. This, however, is just one equation in one unknown, where we can easily solve for

$X*_2$. After doing so, we substitute that value in the budget constraint equation, $X_1 + X_2 = G$, and solve for $X*_1$. For another example, suppose the problem is how to allocate an undetermined budget (G) between X_1 and X_2 so as to minimize expenditures while achieving at least a minimum Y level. Like the previous example, we set the MRRs equal to each other, since we want to be operating efficiently, regardless of whether we are maximizing goal achievement or minimizing expenditures. This enables us to solve for $X*_2$. We can then substitute that value for X_2 in Equation 14, set the left side of the equation at minimum Y, and then solve for $X*_1$.

The other 22 situations are about as easy to figure out by manipulating variations on the three basic equations of: (1) $Y = a + bX_1 + A(X_2)^B$ which shows the relations between goal achievement and the allocations to the activities or places, (2) $b = BA(X_2)^{B-1}$, which equalizes the marginal rates of return or slopes, and (3) $X_1 + X_2 = G$, which shows the relation between total costs and the allocations to the activities or places. The situations can be similarly handled if we combine a linear relation and a semi-log function in Equation 14 (rather than a linear relation and a power function), or a power function and a semi-log function.[8]

SOME CONCLUSIONS

The simple logic which this chapter proposes as a substitute or supplement for more complex linear programming and nonlinear programming methods can be reduced to five general rules as follows:

1. When allocating resources to activities or places with linear relations, allocate to the activity or place that has the best slope with goal achievement and nothing to the other activities or places, unless there are minimum or maximum constraints on the activities or places.
2. When allocating to interacting activities with nonlinear relations, allocate

---

[8]Other combinations could be developed using exponential relations of the form $Y = ab^X$, S-shaped relations of the form, $Y = a + b_1X_1 + b_2X^2_1 + b_3X^3_1$, and quadratic relations of the form $Y = a + b_1X^2_1$. The same basic principles apply for dealing with the 24 types of situations when they consist of or include those relations. Some of these situations, however, cannot be solved through the kind of proportional allocation that this chapter emphasizes, or even through equation-solving where one solves for an unknown by getting it to stand by itself on the left side of an equation. Such situations may require reiterative guessing of values until an optimum is arrived at. This may necessitate or benefit from the use of nonlinear programming routines like those discussed in the books cited in note 1. For further discussion of the applicability of the logic-algebra approach of this chapter to those more complicated relations, see Chapter 8 of the present book.

in proportion to the elasticity coefficients which each activity has in a power function relation between goal achievement and the activity allocations.

3. When allocating to noninteracting places with nonlinear relations, allocate in proportion to the regression coefficients which each place has in a semilog relation between goal achievement and each place allocation.

4. When allocating to either activities or places with either linear or nonlinear relations, allocate all the resources available if one is seeking to maximize goal achievement, but allocate just enough to satisfy a minimum goal level or levels if one is seeking to minimize expenditures.

5. The above rules should be applied after minimum amounts have been allocated to the activities or places, or else the minimums or maximums should be inserted in place of the optimum allocations when the optimums are below the minimums or above the maximums, regardless whether those constraints are expressed as absolute amounts or percentages.

There are a number of benefits or advantages that come from using this type of simple logic approach as contrasted to using linear and nonlinear programming routines for allocation problems. These include:

1. By reasoning out the answer, one obtains insights into the relationships that may enable a revision of the objective function or the constraints.

2. By reasoning out the answer, one can better communicate its meaning to policy makers and policy appliers.

3. By reasoning out the answer, one is more likely to catch nonsense results.

4. Linear and nonlinear programming routines often requires stating the objective and the constraints in an awkward way that increases the likelihood that they will be misstated.

5. Linear programming routines will not work for nonlinear situations.

6. Nonlinear programming routines often get stuck in intermediate solutions especially where there are many activities or places to be allocated to.

7. A logical algebraic approach with a hand calculator saves time by avoiding the punching of cards or the processing of a computer program.

8. A logical algebraic approach is also faster and easier to apply than a graphing approach. Graphing also tends to be confined to two activities or two places, and it is quite inaccurate where nonlinear relations are involved.

In light of these advantages, it is hoped that this chapter will stimulate more analysis and use of a logical algebraic approach to allocation and other optimizing problems. The essence of the approach is to express relations between goals and alternative decisions in terms of simple regression equations that are linear (with none of the variables logged), log-linear (with all of the variables logged), or semilog (with the independent variables logged). Doing so enables one to capture the reality of the relations between goals and alternative decisions, and it enables one to easily manipulate the results to arrive at optimum decisions. More complicated rules may be needed in natural science, engineering, and business problems, but this approach seems well suited to solving government allocation problems through simple logic after the appropriate statistical analysis has been done. What may be needed now is more analysis of the implications of that kind of approach to optimization, and more applications of the relatively simple logical rules which develop from that kind of analysis.

PART THREE:

THE SOCIAL SCIENCE OF
DECISION-AIDING SOFTWARE

SECTION E:

PUBLIC POLICY ANALYSIS

10

CONCEPTUALIZING POLICY ANALYSIS

CONCEPTUALIZING THE FIELD OF POLICY ANALYSIS

DEFINING POLICY ANALYSIS

Public policy analysis can be defined as determining which of various alternative public or governmental policies will most achieve a given set of goals in light of the relations between the policies and the goals.

That definition brings out the four key elements of policy evaluation which are:

1. Goals, including normative constraints and relative weights for the goals.
2. Policies, programs, projects, decisions, options, means, or other alternatives that are available for achieving the goals.
3. Relations between the policies and the goals, including relations that are established by intuition, authority, statistics, observation, deduction, guesses, or other means.
4. Drawing a conclusion as to which policy or combination of policies is best to adopt in light of the goals, policies, and relations.

Other concepts that are often used to mean the same thing as public policy analysis include policy evaluation, policy studies, program evaluation, public management-science, and policy science. One could make distinctions between those concepts as follows:

1. Policy evaluation emphasizes evaluating alternative public policies, as contrasted to describing them or explaining why they exist.
2. Policy studies includes describing policies, explaining their existence, and evaluating them.
3. Program evaluation emphasizes evaluating a specific program like a halfway house in Chicago in 1984, as contrasted to developing general principles of how to evaluate.
4. Public management science emphasizes decision-making that is involved in implementing broader decisions, generally made by legislatures and agencies that have quasi-legislative authority.
5. Policy analysis emphasizes systematic analytic methods which can be quantitative or qualitative.
6. Policy science emphasizes quantitative methods.

Methods of public policy analysis refer to:

1. How to draw a conclusion as to which policy to adopt from information on goals, policies, and relations.
2. How to establish the relations between policies and goals.
3. How to determine what policies are available for adoption and what goals are appropriate to consider.[1]

SOURCES OF ELEMENTS

A frequently asked question in public policy analysis is where do the goals, policies, and relations come from. The main sources are authority, statistics, observation, deduction, and sensitivity analysis.

Authority involves consulting one or more persons, books, articles, or other entities that are considered knowledgeable as to what the relevant goals,

---

[1] For further details on defining policy analysis, see Garry Brewer and Peter deLeon, *The Foundations of Policy Analysis* (Homewood, IL: Dorsey. 1983); Yehezkel Dror, *Public Policy-Making Reexamined* (New Brunswick, NJ : Transaction Books, 1983); Phillip Gregg (ed.), *Problems of Theory in Policy Analysis* (Lexington, MA: Lexington-Heath, 1976); Harold Lasswell, *A Pre-View of Policy Sciences* (New York: Elsevier, 1971); and S. Nagel (ed.), *Encyclopedia of Policy Studies* (New York: Marcel Dekker, 1983), iii-xxii and 3-10.

policies, or relations might be.

Statistical or observational analysis involves analyzing specific instances in order to generalize as to what the goals, policies, or relations might be.

Deduction involves drawing a conclusion from premises that have been established from authority, observation, and/or intuition.

Sensitivity analysis involves guessing the goals, policies, or relations, and then determining what effect, if any, the guessed values have on the bottom line of which policy is best.[2]

TYPES OF RATIONALITY

There are three types of rationality in public policy analysis. They consist of rationality of intentions, consequences, and procedures.

Rationality of intentions refers to people trying to maximize benefits minus costs in whatever they do. That is a tautology or an occurrence that is true by definition. Benefits minus costs is a synonym for net satisfaction, and net satisfaction refers in a circular way to what people are trying to maximize. Although that kind of rationality is present by definition, it is still a useful concept in providing an initial premise at a high level of generality for many examples of policy analysis.

Rationality of consequences refers to being successful in maximizing benefits minus costs in reaching decisions. That is impossible to always do for two reasons. One is that although very little information is often needed to make optimizing decisions, sometimes even the minimum of accurate information is lacking with regard to goals, policies, and/or relations. Second, many policy decisions are based on averages or probabilities of success that may not be so present in a given situation. For example, a decision-maker may choose to go ahead with a project because it truly has a .90 probability of success. The decision-maker, however, may be unlucky enough to hit that one-in-ten chance in which the project fails, and the decision-maker may not get ten chances or even one more chance to come out even.

---

[2]For further details on sources of the elements in policy analysis. see Dickinson McGaw and George Satson, *Political Social Inquiry* (New York: Wiley, 1976) (general); E. E. Schattschneider, et al., *A Guide to the Study of Public Affairs* (New York: Dryden, 1952) (authority); David Hoaglin, et al., *Data for Decisions: Information Strategies for Policymakers* (Cambridge. MA: Abt, 1982) (statistical analysis): Martin Greenberger, et al., *Models in the Policy Process* (New York: Russell Sage, 19761) (deduction); and Carl Moore, *Profitable Applications of the Break-Even System* (Englewood Cliffs, NJ: Prentice-Hall, 1971) (sensitivity analysis).

Rationality of procedures refers to developing a set of procedures that will maximize benefits minus costs if one does have adequate information and average luck. Those procedures in turn refer to such methods as benefit-cost analysis decision theory, optimum level analysis, and allocation theory, as defined below in Section 11-A. Those are the kinds of procedures with which systematic or rational policy analysis is concerned.[3]

OBJECTIONS TO FEASIBILITY

There are three major objections to the feasibility of procedural rationality in public policy analysis. They refer to subjective goals, missing information, and multiple goals/ alternatives.

The goals in public policy analysis are generally highly subjective, difficult to measure, and on different dimensions as compared to the goal of maximizing income minus expenses in business analysis. This objection can be dealt with by a variety of methods for handling nonmonetary benefits and costs such as norming the raw scores of each alternative on each goal by calculating part/whole percentages. The raw scores are thus put on a 0 to 100% scale, and the raw scores on each goal sum to 100%.

Information is more often missing or unreliable in public policy analysis than it is in business analysis. The probabilities of risky events are often especially unknown or unreliable. This objection can often be handled by determining the probability or other score above which one alternative wins and below which another alternative wins. One can then decide whether the true score is above or below that threshold score.

There frequently are many goals and policies to consider in public policy analysis. A typical optimum level or mix problem may involve an infinite number of alternatives, such as ways in which a budget could be allocated among various activities or places. Goals, however, can be composited or aggregated even if they are non-monetary. Likewise multiple policies can be reduced through processes of elimination and by treating allocation problems in terms of the finite number of objects to which resources are being allocated rather than in terms of the infinite number of alternative allocations.

Another objection is that the mathematics of systematic policy analysis

---

[3]On rationality. see Edward Friedland, *Introduction to Concepts of Rationality in Political Science* (Morristown, NJ: General Learning Press, 1974) and Herbert Simon, *Reason in Human Affairs* (Palo Alto, CA: Stanford, 1983).

may be too complicated for the average person to deal with, as contrasted to elementary business calculations. One is not likely, however, to need anything more complicated than an inexpensive hand calculator, a knowledge of the substance being dealt with, and the codified common-sense which the policy analysis field is developing.[4]

TRENDS

Systematic decision-analysis in the public sector began in the 1970s. Trends which have already emerged include the following which relate to goals, means, methods, and the public policy-evaluation orientation or profession.

As for goals, there is a trend toward more taking of goals as givens and then attempting to determine what policies will maximize or optimize them, rather than taking policies as givens and then attempting to determine their effects. Policy analysts are also becoming more sensitive to social values, with more questioning of goals in evaluating alternative policies.

As for means, there is a trend toward showing increased sophistication with regard to the political feasibility of policies being adopted and the feasibility of alternative delivery systems or implementation systems after they are adopted. Policy evaluation is also becoming increasingly interdisciplinary in drawing upon a variety of disciplinary sources as to means or policies for achieving goals. This includes economics, political science, sociology, and psychology among basic disciplines, and includes business administration, planning, public administration, law, social work, and education among applied disciplines.

As for methods, policy evaluation research has been building on business analysis especially with regard to maximizing benefits minus costs. It has, however, been developing its own methodology especially in matters of a measurement, equity, negative social indicators, and administrative psychology. Policy evaluation is also developing increased precision with its methods, but at the same time it is increasingly recognizing that simple

---

[4]On objections to the feasibility of systematic policy analysis see "The Pros and Cons of Systems Analysis in Policy Studies," in S. Nagel (ed.), *Basic Literature in Policy Studies: A Comprehensive Bibliography* (Greenwich, CT: JAI Press, 1984), 33-36. A leading work on the pro side is Daniel Lerner and Harold Lasswell (eds.), *Policy Sciences* (Palo Alto, CA: Stanford, 1951). A leading work on the con side is Ida Hoos, *Systems Analysis in Public Policy: A Critique* (Berkeley, CA: University of California Press, 1972). On possible ways of overcoming each of the four separate objections, see chapters 13 through 16 of S. Nagel, *Public Policy: Goals, Means, and Methods* (New York: St. Martin's, 1984).

methods may be enough for many policy problems. Policy evaluation is also becoming increasingly pro-active or pre-adoption rather than reactive or post-adoption. That distinction partly corresponds to deductive modeling as contrasted to empirical before-and-after analysis.

As for the policy-evaluation orientation, it has undergone substantial growth in training programs, research centers, funding sources, publishing outlets, and scholarly associations. It is also becoming increasingly used by government at the federal, state, and local levels, and in the executive, judicial, and legislative branches. This is indeed an exciting time to be in the field of public policy analysis in view of its growth and vitality.[5]

CONCEPTUALIZING A POLICY ANALYSIS PROJECT

METHODOLOGICAL FORM

There are various ways of classifying the forms of policy analysis. An especially useful classification is in terms of the methods for drawing prescriptive conclusions. There are five main categories consisting of optimum choice, risk, level, mix, and timing analysis.

Optimum choice analysis or basic benefit-cost analysis involves lump-sum alternatives that do not allow for adopting a fraction of an alternative or more than one of the same alternative. The object is to pick the alternative that maximizes benefits minus costs.

Optimum risk analysis or decision theory also involves lump-sum alternatives, but the extent to which they produce benefits or costs is contingent on the occurrence of one or more probabilistic or risky events. The benefits and the costs thus have to be discounted or multiplied by the probability of their occurring.

Optimum level analysis involves a policy which can take many positions along a continuum, but doing too much or too little is considered undesirable. The optimum position is the one that (1) maximizes benefits if all the effects have been stated positively, (2) minimizes costs if all the effects have been stated negatively, or (3) maximizes benefits minus costs if some effects are positive and some negative.

---

[5]For further details on trends in policy analysis see Giandomenico Majone, "Applied Systems Analysis: A Genetic Approach," in Edward Quade and Hugh Miser (eds.), *Handbook of Systems Analysis* (New York: Elsevier, 1984), 12-37.

Optimum mix analysis or allocation theory involves multiple policies, places, activities, persons, or other entities to which a budget, time, or other scarce resources are to be allocated. Part/whole percentaging (as mentioned for norming nonmonetary goals) can be helpful here for calculating allocation percentages with different weights for different goals.

Optimum timing analysis is sometimes referred to as a fifth methodology, although it frequently uses optimum choice, level, or mix analysis. It can be defined as the development of principles for deciding how to minimize time consumption by efficiently controlling the ordering of events, arrival rates, processing rates, critical paths, and other time-relevant items.[6]

POTENTIAL USEFULNESS

There are three major uses to which policy evaluation models can be put. Those uses relate to making, influencing, and predicting decisions. Other important but less frequent uses of policy evaluation models include measuring decisional propensities and deducing motives.

For making decisions, the basic approach involves determining the goals to be achieved, the policies available for achieving them, and the relations between the goals and the policies. In benefit-cost terms, this means determining the benefits and the costs for each policy. The benefits and costs are goals to be increased and decreased, respectively. The quantity of benefits or costs which a policy is predicted as achieving is a measure of the relations between the policies and their goals. From that input data, one should be able to draw conclusions as to the policy or combination of policies that should be adopted or decided upon for maximizing the goals, or for maximizing benefits minus costs.

For influencing decisions, the basic approach involves starting out with a decision that is considered socially desirable, or desirable from the perspective of whoever is seeking to influence decisions. That decision can be considered as the rightdoing decision, and its opposite as the wrongdoing decision. One should then seek to change the reality and the perceptions of the benefits and the costs so as to encourage more rightdoing. This means

---

[6]For further details on the five basic methodologies, see Edith Stokey and Richard Zeckhauser, *A Primer for Policy Analysis* (New York: Norton, 1978); Michael White, et al., *Managing Public Systems: Analytic Techniques for Public Administration* (N. Scituate, MA: Duxbury, 1980); and S. Nagel, *Policy Evaluation: Making Optimum Decisions* (New York: Praeger, 1982).

drawing conclusions as to how to (1) increase the benefits of rightdoing, (2) decrease the costs of rightdoing, (3) increase the costs of wrongdoing, (4) decrease the benefits of wrongdoing, and/or (5) increase the probability that the benefits and costs will be received.

For predicting decisions, the basic approach involves determining what the benefits and costs are considered to be by the relevant decision-makers, as contrasted to what they might actually be. One also needs to determine how those benefits and costs are likely to change or might change. One then draws conclusions as to how the decisions are likely to change in light of various changes in the benefits and costs of the alternative policies, programs, or decisions.

For measuring decisional propensities, the basic approach here is to determine a model that relates decisional outcomes to the perceptions of the benefits and costs of alternative courses of action. Ask people whose decisional propensities one is seeking to measure how they assess the various benefits and costs, instead of asking them directly about their decisional propensities. From data provided by their answers and from the model that relates decisions to benefits and costs, draw a conclusion as to their decisional propensities. The conclusion might be expressed in the form of a threshold probability above which they are likely to decide in one direction and below which they are likely to decide in the opposite direction. The conclusion might also be expressed in the form of a threshold benefit/cost ratio where the questions have mainly dealt with perceptions as to certain facts occurring, rather than questions asking about their values.

For deducing motives, the basic approach is to try to be able to determine what a decision-maker's goals are from knowing what decision he or she reached plus other information. If the information is in the form (1) X decision was reached and (2) the decision-maker perceives that the only effect of X is Y, then we can conclude that if the decision-maker (DM) adopts X, the DM must want to achieve Y. If, however, the DM perceives that X causes Y, but also perceives that X causes Z, then the DM's motivation might be to achieve Z. One can develop a similar pair of rules for deducing the DM's causal perceptions (rather than motivations) if the information is in the form (1) X decision was reached and (2) the DM favorably values Y and only Y. Other rules can be developed which involve combinations of decisions, perceptions, and motivations whereby one can or cannot deduce one of the three elements by knowing something about the other two.[7]

ACTUAL UTILIZATION

Table 10-1 helps to see the concept of research utilization as being a continuum concept, rather than a yes/no concept. Utilization as its lowest level involves doing a policy research project that is not in any way referred to by the people who make policy in the subject matter area. Nor is there any evidence that the policy makers were aware of the project, even though they did not explicitly cite it. That is clearly nonutilization. At the other extreme or the highest level of utilization, the research project converts the decision-makers from being negative to being positive or vice versa on an issue. That is an extremely rare occurrence and may never even occur for controversial issues.

At the next to highest level is research that reinforces preconceived decisions. This is reasonably common. Some skeptics of the value of systematic policy analysis consider that occurrence not to be utilization. Policy researchers should, however, be quite pleased if their research accelerates a worthwhile decision which otherwise might not be made for a while. An example might be the research that showed more defendants could be released prior to trial without increasing the no-show rate, provided there is some systematic screening to determine who is to be released. Liberals found support in such studies since they wanted to see more defendants released in view of the presumption of innocence. Likewise, conservatives also found support in such studies since they wanted to see a reduction in the expensive jail burden on the taxpayers. That kind of reinforcement did accelerate the presumably desirable occurrence of increased pretrial release with a constant or lower no-show rate.

At the next to the lowest level is research that is referred to by the policy-makers orally or by being officially cited. The citing could be by either the majority group among the decision-makers or the minority/dissenters. Either kind of citing is an example of low level utilization, even if the

---

[7]For further discussion and examples of the usefulness of policy evaluation models, see Sheen Kassouf, *Normative Decision Making* (Englewood Cliffs, NJ: Prentice-Hall, 1970) (making decisions); Gary Becker and William Landes (eds.). *Essays in the Economics of Crime and Punishment* (New York: Columbia University Press, 1974) (influencing decisions); Martin Greenberger, et al., *Models in the Policy Process* (New York: Russell Sage, 1976) (predicting decisions); and S. Nagel and M. Neef, *Decision Theory and the Legal Process* (Lexington, MA: Lexington-Heath, 1979) (general).

TABLE 10-1
DEGREES OF UTILIZATION OF A POLICY RESEARCH STUDY

Not Even Referred to	Referred to	Reinforces Values or Decisions	Converts Values or Decisions
(1)	(2)	(3)	(4)

0   100

research cited was not on the winning side, and was not influential enough to convert decisions or even reinforce preconceived decisions. This is also a common occurrence. People who are skeptical of the value of policy research tend to emphasize how common the first two categories are of no citing or citing but no influence. One should, however, recognize that progress in dealing with policy problems may require many unutilized research projects before a research project is developed that does get well used. The policy research system is still a success if only one in ten projects gets used, but that one tends to produce benefits which outweigh the costs of the other nine.[8]

ADOPTION

Table 10-2 shows the relation between the concepts of policy research utilization and policy research adoption. Utilization here is divided into a yes category and a no category. The yes category includes categories 2, 3, and 4 in Table 10-1. That means a research project is considered utilized if it has been cited. One could, however, define the yes category in Table 10-2 as only including categories 3 and 4 from Table 10-1 or even as only including category 4. Common usage, though, would consider a policy research project as having been utilized by the Supreme Court if the Supreme Court cites it, especially since it is relatively easy to determine whether a project has been cited, but relatively difficult to determine whether the project has been influential.

Policy adoption refers to whether the recommendations of the research project have been adopted by the policy-makers, regardless whether the project was referred to. Like utilization, adoption can be thought of as occurring in degrees, and not just as being present or absent. There is more adoption if the federal government or all 50 states adopt a policy than if only one state does. There is more adoption if a policy becomes part of the Constitution, rather than just part of a statute, an administrative regulation, or a judicial opinion, in that order. One can also talk about degrees of adoption in terms of the size of the favorable vote which the policy received in a legislature or other decision-making body without being vetoed or

---

[8]On utilization of policy analysis research, see Albert Cherns, *Using the Social Science and Social Problem Solving* (London: Routledge and Kegan Paul, 1979); Irving Horowitz and James Katz, *Social Science and Public Policy in the United States* (New York: Praeger, 1975). Charles Lindblom and David Cohen, *Usable Knowledge: Social Science and Social Problem Solving* (New Haven, CT: Yale, 1979); and Carol Weiss (ed.), *Using Social Research in Public Policy Making* (Lexington, MA: Lexington-Heath, 1977).

TABLE 10-2
RELATIONS BETWEEN UTILIZATION AND ADOPTION

	Utilization *(Referred to by policymakers* *or other evaluators)*	
	No	*Yes*
Adoption *(Recommendations* *adopted, regardless* *whether referred to)* **Yes**	A Middle (#2)	B Best (#1)
No	C Worst (#4)	D Middle (#3)

nullified by a chief executive or a high court. A policy is also more meaningfully adopted if a bigger appropriation or enforcement/administrative apparatus is provided along with the adoption. For the sake of discussion, however, we can talk in terms of the presence of adoption as meaning the proposed policy was officially adopted by some governmental body. Adoption of a policy, of course, does not necessarily mean successful implementation.

Given those definitions of utilization and adoption, it is possible to be yes on both (Cell B), no on both (Cell C), or yes on utilization in the sense of being cited, but no on adoption in the sense of not being adopted (Cell D). It is also possible to be no on utilization in not being referred to, but yet the bottom-line recommendation was adoption in spite of (rather than because of) the research project, or the adoption and the research project were unrelated (Cell A).

One can treat Table 10-2 not just as a four-cell table that shows four alternative ways of combining two dichotomous variables. The table can also be treated as a payoff matrix, in which we indicate the relative net benefits of each outcome. The best outcome from the perspective of a policy research is to have one's work cited and to have one's recommendations adopted. The worst outcome is to not be cited and to not have one's recommendations adopted. In between, one could say that Cell A is more desirable than Cell B because getting one's recommendations adopted should be more important than being cited, especially if one is working directly or indirectly for a governmental agency or interest group. Thus, a no on utilization accompanied by a yes on adoption should be worth more than a yes on utilization accompanied by a no on adoption.

A four-cell table can have at least three purposes. One purpose is to show how the categories on two variables can be combined together. That is the main purpose of Table 10-2. Such a four-cell table can be referred to as a combinations matrix. They generally only have letters or words in the cells, like yes-yes or yes-no. A second purpose is to show for each combination its relative or absolute value in comparison to the other combinations. That kind of table is referred to as a payoff matrix. They have numbers in the cells that indicate rank orders, relative values on a zero to 100 scale, dollar values, or other evaluations of the four outcomes. The third purpose is to show for each combination how often it occurs out of a set of possibilities. That kind of table is referred to as a cross-tabulation matrix. Table 10-3 is such a table. It involves a sample of 100 hypothetical (but realistic) policy-research studies. In each study there was a key policy proposed for adoption or a key policy that had been adopted.

TABLE 10-3
CROSS-TABULATING THE VALUES OF
POLICY EVALUATION AND POLICY-MAKERS

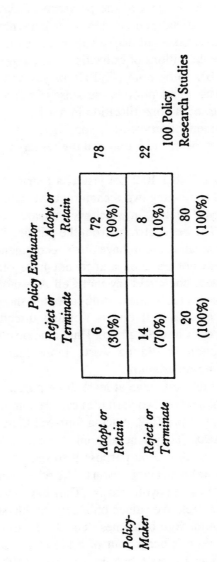

Of the 100 studies, the policy evaluators concluded in 80 instances that the policy should be adopted or should be retained. In 20 instances, they concluded the policy should be rejected or terminated. Of those 80 instances, the policy-makers voted to adopt or retain 90 percent of the time and voted contrary to the evaluations 10 percent of the time. Of the 20 instances of the negative evaluations, the policy-makers voted to adopt or retain 30 percent of the time, and voted in accordance with those evaluations 70 percent of the time. Those hypothetical findings could be converted into a regression equation of the form $M = .30 + .60(E)$. That equation means that when the evaluator moves from a zero score of reject to a 1 score of adopt, then the probability of the policy-maker adopting moves from a base of .30 up to .90. The reason for the close relation, however, is probably because both the policy evaluators and the policy-makers are responding to the same stimuli or social forces, and not because the policy evaluators are causing the policy makers to adopt when they otherwise would reject.[9]

VALIDITY

Table 10-4 shows the relation between the concepts of policy-research utilization and policy-research validity. The utilization concept has the same meaning as in Table 10-2. There are four key elements in policy-evaluation research which lead to four aspects of policy-research validity. The four elements are:

1. Goals to be achieved, including normative constraints and relative weights for the goals.
2. Policies, programs, projects, decisions, options, means, or other alternatives that are available for achieving the goals.
3. Relations between the policies and the goals, including relations that are established by intuition, authority, statistics, observation, deduction, guesses, or other means.
4. Drawing a conclusion as to which policy or combination of policies is best to adopt in light of the goals, policies, and relations.

---

[9]On the adoption of proposed public policies, see James Anderson, *Public Policy-Making* (New York: Holt, Rinehart and Winston, 1979); Robert Eyestone, *From Social Issues to Public Policy* (New York: Wiley. 1978); Charles Jones, *An Introduction to the Study of Public Policy* (N. Scituate, MA: Duxbury. 1977); Charles Lindblom, *The Policy-Making Process* (New Haven, CT: Yale, 1980); and Judith May and Aaron Wildavsky (eds.), *The Policy Cycle* (Beverly Hills, CA: Sage, 1978).

TABLE 10-4

RELATIONS BETWEEN UTILIZATION AND VALIDITY

	Utilization	
	No	Yes
Validity (More Important) **Yes**	A Middle (#2)	B Best (#1)
No	C Middle (#3)	D Worst (#4)

Validity in general refers to being accurate. In the context of policy-evaluation research and its key elements, validity refers to:

1. The internal consistency of logically drawing a conclusion that follows from the goals, policies, and relations.
2. The external consistency with empirical reality in describing the relations between the alternative policies and the goals.
3. The policies being considered should encompass the total set of feasible alternatives and only feasible alternatives. Feasibility in this context refers to being capable of being adopted and implemented by the relevant policy-makers and policy-appliers.
4. The listed goals include all the major goals and only the goals of the relevant policy-makers in this context.

Validity (like adoption and utilization) can occur in degrees, or at least invalidity can. A valid study meets all four of the above requirements. An invalid study fails to meet at least one of the four requirements. A study is even more invalid if it fails to meet more than one of the requirements, or fails to meet a requirement by a large margin. Validity in policy evaluation is thus like equity where equity is defined as providing a minimum benefits level for all relevant persons, groups, or places. Thus, if that minimum level is met, equity is present although equality may not be present. There can, however, be degrees of inequity depending on the size of the individual deviations from that minimum level and the number of people involved, as is the case with non-validity.

In relating utilization to validity, there are four possible combinations when utilization and validity are both dichotomized. The best possibility is for a study to be both utilized and valid. If validity is more important than utilization as it should be, then the next best possibility is for one's research to be valid even if it is not utilized. The yes row on validity thus dominates the no row on validity in Table 10-4, just as the yes row on adoption dominates the no row on adoption in Table 10-2. Unlike Table 10-2, however, it is better to be no on both variables in Table 10-4 than it is to be yes on utilization and no on validity. This is so because the worst combination is to have an invalid study utilized in view of the harm that such a study could have if utilized. In other words, utilizing invalid studies worsens the situation, rather than improves it.

One could create a table like Table 10-4 in which adoption rather than utilization is related to validity. The relative value of the cells would be the same since utilization and adoption are associated by virtue of the fact that adoption is sometimes a high degree of utilization, although one's policy recommendations can be adopted without one's research being utilized or referred to. The absolute value and disvalue of the cells, however, would be different with adoption substituted for utilization. Cell D would still be the worst cell, but the harm might be even greater since one can get a yes on utilization by merely being cited, but a yes on adoption means the proposed policy has become an actual or promulgated policy. One should, however, distinguish between the validity of the research study and the validity of the proposed policy. The research study may be invalid for any one of the four reasons mentioned above. The policy might nevertheless be valid in the sense of being capable of achieving the desired goals, even though the research study involved faulty deductive logic in drawing a conclusion and/or faulty inductive statistical inference in determining the relations between the policies and the goals.[10]

IMPORTANCE

Table 10-5 shows the relation between the concepts of policy-research utilization and policy-research importance. The concept of importance can be defined in two ways:

1. Does the research deal with issues in which there are big societal benefits minus societal costs being analyzed? Thus research on avoiding nuclear war is more important than research on whether the city of Champaign should have a strong mayor form of government or a city manager.
2. Does the research deal with a subject matter or a set of causal hypotheses that potentially have broad explanatory power? This is theoretical importance, as contrasted to policy importance.

There can be degrees of policy importance depending on the product of the total benefits times the total costs that are at stake. That benefits-

---

[10]On validity in policy evaluation methods, see Michael Carley, *Rational Techniques in Policy Analysis* (London: Heinemann, 1980); William Dunn, *Public Policy Analysis* (Englewood Cliffs, NJ: Prentice-Hall, 1981); Duncan MacRae and James Wilde, *Policy Analysis for Public Decisions* (N. Scituate, MA: Duxbury. 1979); Edward Quade, *Analysis for Public Decisions* (Amsterdam: North Holland, 1982); Edith Stokey and Richard Zeckhauser, *A Primer for Policy Analysis* (New York: Norton, 1978); and S. Nagel, *Public Policy: Goals, Means, and Methods* (New York: St. Martins, 1983).

TABLE 10-5

RELATIONS BETWEEN UTILIZATION AND IMPORTANCE

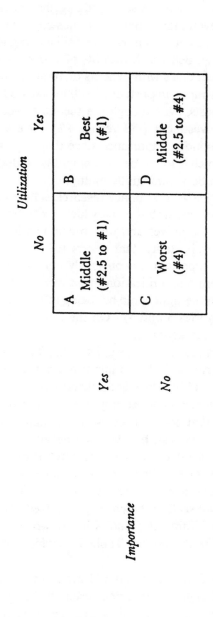

	Utilization	
Importance	*No*	*Yes*
Yes	A Middle (#2.5 to #1)	B Best (#1)
No	C Worst (#4)	D Middle (#2.5 to #4)

times-costs criterion make sense in judging the relative importance of two research projects even though benefits-minus-costs is the criterion for judging which of two investments or alternative policies to adopt. In other words, if one research project deals with benefits of 100 units and costs of 150 units, and a second project deals with benefits of 10 units and costs of 8 units, then the first project is more important (15,000 versus 80) given the size of the benefits and the costs, even though the second project would be a better or more profitable investment (-50 versus +2). We would not want to add benefits to costs to judge importance since they are likely to be measured in different units which cannot be meaningfully added, but in this context, different units can be meaningfully multiplied.

Table 10-5 shows that policy research is best which is both important and utilized. Policy research is worst which is neither important nor utilized. In the middle are the no-yes and yes-no combinations. We could also have a middle row on importance that covers the gray area of research that is neither obviously important nor obviously unimportant. We could likewise have a middle column on utilization that covers "just being cited" (category 2 in Table 10-1). On the right could be "being influential" regardless of whether one is cited (categories 3 and 4). On the left could be "being both uncited and uninfluential" (category 1).

Some policy researchers would say that it is better for one's feelings of satisfaction to do research that is important but not utilized, than it is to do research that is trivial but does get utilized. Other policy researchers would say that research which is not so important (meaning small societal benefits minus costs), but that gets utilized is better than research on achieving the ultimate societal happiness, but does not get utilized for anything. In other words, they would say that unutilized research is useless, just as a tree falling in Siberia with no one to hear or see it makes no noise or visual display. Given the differences of opinion on the relative value (at least to the researcher) of small scale research that is utilized versus large scale research that is not utilized, Table 10-5 shows those two middling positions as being close to tied, unlike the related Table 10-2 which deals with utilization and adoption.

In spite of that, one could still argue that doing important research should be valued higher than doing research that gets utilized because the important research might get utilized and then have a far greater payoff. We therefore change the numbers to show that being in Cell A is worth more than being in Cell D, and that importance does dominate utilization. In light of that reasoning, one might also say importance dominates adoption as well.

In other words, unused research could be viewed narrowly as being of no value, regardless whether (1) the recommendations get adopted, (2) the research is valid, or (3) the subject matter is important. On the other hand, one could emphasize that unused research could have been used or could even still be used. It is thus worth doing for its expected value, which is the value that it would have if it were used, discounted by the probability of its being used as of the present time or as of when the research was being done. One could also emphasize that unused research has value in itself to policy researchers as a satisfying activity, at least when the research is validly done on an important subject.[11]

COMBINING CONCEPTS

Table 10-6 shows there are 16 possible situations which combine the presence or absence of validity, importance, adoption, and utilization. A plus sign shows the characteristic is absent. A question mark shows that it does not make any difference whether the characteristic is present or absent for the purpose of calculating the total value of the situation. In light of the previous discussion, we can rank order the policy research characteristics as being validity, importance, adoption, and utilization in terms of their relative value. We can thus give them rank scores of 4, 3, 2, and 1 respectively.

Situation 1 has the highest total value since all four characteristics are present. The total value is shown as being a 10 by summing the four rank scores. Situation 2 has the next to highest total value since it is only missing utilization. As discussed previously, it is possible for one's recommendations to be adopted, even though one's study is uncited and unknown. Situation 3 is the opposite in the sense that there is utilization, but not adoption. It has a total value of 8 points by summing the rank scores of the characteristics that are present. Likewise, one can proceed through the first eight situations. They all have validity. They are arranged in descending order of their total values.

Situations 9 through 16 lack validity. Validity can be considered a con-

---

[11]On the concept of importance or value in policy analysis research, see William Dunn (ed.), *Values, Ethics, and the Practice of Policy Analysis* (Lexington, MA: Lexington-Heath, 19831; Joel Fleishman and Bruce Payne, *Ethical Dilemmas and the Education of Policy-Makers* (Hastings-on-Hudson, NY: Hastings Center, 1981); Fred Frohock, *Public Policy: Scope and Logic* (Englewood Cliffs, NJ: Prentice-Hall, 1979); Wayne Leys, *Ethics for Policy Decisions: The Art of Asking Deliberative Questions* (Englewood Cliffs, NJ: Prentice-Hall, 1952); and Duncan MacRae, *The Social Function of Social Science* (New Haven, CT: Yale, 1976).

TABLE 10-6
COMBINING VALIDITY, IMPORTANCE,
ADOPTION AND UTILIZATION

Situation	4 Validity	3 Importance	2 Adoption	1 Utilization	Total Value
1	+	+	+	+	10
2	+	+	+	−	9
3	+	+	−	+	8
4	+	+	−	−	7
5	+	−	+	+	7
6	+	−	+	−	6
7	+	−	−	+	5
8	+	−	−	−	4
9 to 16	−	?	?	?	0

+ = Present
− = Absent
? = Could be present or absent

straint in that it must be met for the research study to have any value from the perspective of a professional policy evaluator. Validity is not a variable that can be traded for combinations of other variables, or for higher degrees of importance, adoption, and/or utilization. Thus, situations 9 through 16 all have a total value of zero, regardless how well they score on importance, adoption, or utilization. This brings out the importance of doing valid research as an ethical obligation in policy evaluation. One should also seek to do important research whose recommendations are adopted and utilized, but those are variables in an objective function to be achieved, rather than constraints to which the objective function is subject.

Perhaps one can define a good policy evaluation as one that had validity plus importance, regardless whether it is referred to or its recommendations are adopted. One could also include within a definition of a good policy evaluation a criterion that relates to whether one agrees with what the policy research recommends. That, however, is getting away from criteria that relate to methodology las validity does) or substance (as importance does). It involves getting into the direction of the recommendations, which is within the criteria of normative philosophy and being a good citizen, but outside the criteria of technical policy evaluation. Policy evaluators can concern themselves with such questions in their roles as political activists, but those roles should be kept separate from the role of objective policy evaluator. One's policy recommendations will have more credibility if the policy research of which they are a part is done from an objective perspective, rather than an advocacy perspective. An objective perspective seeks to determine the policy or combination that is best for achieving a given set of goals in light of the relations between the policies and the goals. An advocacy perspective seeks to justify why a policy or combination should be adopted and avoids providing support for any other policy. It is like the difference between a judge (trying to determine the law and the facts) and a lawyer (trying to argue as to how the law and the facts should be interpreted).

In defining good policy evaluation, one should add as a criterion the concept of originality to the concepts of validity, social/theoretical importance, and utilization/adoption. Originality can be measured in degrees since all research differs to some extent from previous research unless an exact plagiarism is involved. Even highly original research builds on and synthesizes prior research. Feasibility is an additional criterion for judging proposed policy research, as contrasted to completed policy research. Feasibility is concerned with how easily the research can be implemented given the limited time, expertise, interests, funds, and other resources of the researcher.

CONCLUSIONS

Conceptualizing the field of policy analysis or policy evaluation emphasizes the key elements of goals, policies, relations between the policies and goals, and drawing a conclusion as to which policy or combination of policies is best. That basic four-part framework can be crossed with four categories that relate to the source of those elements. Those sources include authority, statistical observation, deduction, and sensitivity analysis. Rationality in this context means using procedures for deriving goals, policies, relations, and conclusions in a way that will maximize benefits minus costs if one has adequate information and average luck. Such procedures are possible in spite of the subjectivity of goals, missing information, the multiplicity of goals, and the alleged complexity of rational policy evaluation. There have been many recent improvements in dealing with these key elements of goals, policies, relations, and conclusions in policy evaluation.

Conceptualizing a specific policy analysis project emphasize the nature of the conclusion-drawing and what is done with the conclusions. Conclusion-drawing may involve deciding on an optimum choice with mutually exclusive alternatives or allowing combinations, with or without probabilistic risks. It may also involve finding an optimum level where doing too much or too little is undesirable, or finding an optimum mix of scarce resources across activities or places. The conclusions may have potential usefulness mainly for making, influencing, or predicting decisions. They may have actual usefulness in the sense of being referred to by others. The ideas recommended may or may not be adopted. More important than actual utilization or adoption is internal consistency or logical validity, and external consistency or empirical validity. Also important are conclusions that have societal importance in terms of benefits minus costs, or theoretical importance in terms of explanatory power. Other desirable characteristics of policy analysis projects include originality and feasibility. It is hoped that this analysis of basic concepts in public policy analysis will add to the conceptual framework that is being built by many people in this relatively new, useful, and important field of study.

11

POLICY ANALYSIS WITH MICROCOMPUTERS

The essence of decision-aiding software is that it is designed to process a set of:
1. Goals to be achieved,
2. Alternatives for achieving them and
3. Relations between goals and alternatives,

in order to choose the best alternative, combination, or resource allocation in light of the goals, alternatives, and relations.

The main benefits of decision-aiding software are in accurately and quickly handling five key methodological problems in decision-making. They are:

1. Multiple dimensions on multiple goals. This is the apples and oranges program.
2. Multiple missing information.
3. Multiple alternatives that are too many to be able to determine the effects of each one.
4. Multiple and possibly conflicting constraints.
5. The need for simplicity in drawing and presenting conclusions in spite of all that multiplicity.[1]

---

[1]For further details on optimizing analysis in terms of goals, policies, relations, and conclusions, see S. Nagel, *Public Policy: Goals, Means, and Methods* (St. Martin's, 1984) and

ADDING APPLES AND ORANGES

Decision-making problems often involve multiple goals measured on a variety of different dimensions, such as miles, hours, dollars, 1-5 attitude scales, yes-no dichotomies, etc.

Some of the ways in which multiple dimensions are handled are:

1. Multiply the apples by two if you like each apple twice as much as each orange. Then everything will be expressed in orange units.
2. Ask whether the gain in apples from choosing one alternative is worth more or less than the gain in oranges from choosing a second alternative.
3. Convert the apple units into percentages by dividing the raw scores on the apple goal by the sum of the apples, and convert the orange units into percentages by dividing the raw scores on the oranges goal by the sum of the oranges.
4. Ask the relevant decision-makers a series of questions designed to determine what sum of money is the satisfaction equivalent of one nonmonetary unit. With that information and knowing that $0 equals zero nonmonetary units, one can generate a diminishing returns curve connecting those points. The curve is expressed by an equation of the form $\$Y = (N)^b$, where $\$Y$ is money, N is the nonmonetary unit, and b is the translation coefficient generated by a computer or calculator using nonlinear regression analysis.

These methods become clearer with the concrete illustrative example of choosing between two affirmative action programs for a medical school. One program produces a lot of minority students, but treats few patients. The other program produces few minority students, but treats a lot of patients. The example is shown in Table 11-1.[2]

Edward Quade, *Analysis for Public Decisions* (North Holland, 1982). These two books could be referred to for any of the eight principles. The first book uses numerous legal examples. Other books that take an optimizing perspective toward law include Richard Posner, *Economic Analysis of Law* (Little, Brown, 1977); and Gordon Tullock, *The Logic of the Law* (Basic Books, 1971).

[2]On dealing with non-monetary benefits and costs, see Mark Thompson, *Benefit-Cost Analysis for Program Evaluation* (Sage, 1980); and Edward Gramlich, *Benefit-Cost Analysis of Government Programs* (Prentice-Hall, 1981), although they may overemphasize monetizing non-monetary variables, rather than working with them in their original form or close to it. Also see S. Nagel, "Nonmonetary Variables in Benefit-Cost Evaluation," 7 *Evaluation Review* 37-64 (1983) and S. Nagel, "Economic Transformations of Nonmonetary Benefits in Program

TABLE 11-1
FOUR METHODS FOR DEALING WITH
MULTIDIMENSIONAL TRADEOFFS

POLICY	RAW SCORE INCREMENTS		PART/WHOLE PERCENTAGING			
	Students Trained(S)	Patients Treated(P)	Students Trained $w=1$	Patients Treated $w=2$	Unweighted Sum	Weighted Sum
Policy A (X_1)	30	10	60%	36%	96%	132%
Policy B (X_2)	20	18	40%	64%	104%	168%
Total(Whole)	50	28	100%	100%	100%	100%
Difference (Increment)	$+10S$ >> $-8P?$					
Threshold				$W60+36+W40+64W^* = 1.40$		

POLICY	PAIRED-COMPARISON MONETIZING			WEIGHTED RAW SCORES		
	Students Trained $\$Y=(S)^{.92}$	Patients Treated $\$Y=(P)^{.90}$	SUM	Students (Expressed in Terms of Patients) $w=2$	Patients	Sum
Policy A (X_1)	$22.85	$ 7.94	$30.79	60	10	20
Policy B (X_2)	$15.74	$13.48	$29.22	40	18	58
Total	$38.59	$21.42	$60.01	100	28	128
Threshold				$W30+10+W20+18W^* = .80$		

NOTES:

1. Incremental analysis has the advantage of simplicity, especially where there are only a few policies and goals. It is also applicable to variables that are nonquantitative. It involves a minimum of transforming of the raw data. It reduces the value judgment to determining whether the incremental gain of one policy is preferred over the incremental gain of

Evaluation" in James Catterall (ed.), *Economic Evaluation of Public Programs* (Jossey-Bass, 1985).

a second policy.

2. Percentaging analysis has the advantage of being applicable where there are many policies and goals. It reduces the value judgment to determining the relative weight of the goals.

3. Paired-comparison monetizing tends to consider all the values of the relevant decision-makers, although their values are not disaggregated into separate components. Working with monetized variables may also be more comfortable for many people. Paired-comparison monetizing reduces the value judgments to determining at what point a set of nonmonetary benefits is equal to a quantity of dollars.

4. Weighted raw scores have the advantage of being relatively easy to apply where all the goals have tangible units like students or patients, rather than intangible units like scores on a 1-9 attitude scale, where part/whole percentaging tends to be easier to handle.

MISSING INFORMATION

We often do not know relation scores of each alternative on each goal, and we often do not know the relative weights of the goals. The key way in which missing information is handled is to allow the user to quickly and accurately determine the effects of inserting various values for the missing information. More specific techniques include:

1. What-if analysis, whereby the computer shows what would happen if we make changes in the goals, alternatives, and/or relations.
2. Threshold analysis, whereby the computer shows for each relation-score and goal-weight the value which would cause a tie between the second-place alternative and the first place alternative.
3. Convergence analysis, whereby the computer shows for each goal weight at what magnitude the goal tends to dominate the other goals such that nothing is to be gained by increasing the weight further.
4. Best-worst analysis, whereby the computer shows what the conclusion would be using values that most favor a given alternative, and then values that least favor a given alternative. The two conclusions are then averaged.

The important method of threshold analysis becomes clearer with the concrete illustrative example of deciding between nuclear energy and solar energy in light of their long-term value and cost, as is shown in Table 11-2.[3] On a 1-5 scale, a 5 usually means highly conducive to the goal; a 4 means mildly conducive; a 3 means neither conducive nor adverse; a 2 means mildly adverse; and a 1 means highly adverse. With that scoring, nuclear receives a winning total score of 7 points, and solar receives a losing total score of 6 points. The gap is 1 point. The threshold value of cell a is thus 3. That means if the score of 4 were to drop 1 point, there would be a tie. Likewise, the threshold value of cell b is a 2. If cell c were to rise from 5 to 6, there would be a tie, or if cell d were to rise from 1 to 2.

The threshold weight for long-term value is 2. This means that if long-term value were twice as important as low cost, there would be a tie between

---

[3]On dealing with missing information without having to gather additional information, see Mark Thompson, *Decision Analysis for Program Evaluation* (Ballinger, 1982); and Clifford Harris, *The Break-Even Handbook* (Prentice-Hall, 1978). Also see S. Nagel, "Dealing with Unknown Variables in Policy/Program Evaluation" 6 *Evaluation and Program Planning* 7-18 (1983), and S. Nagel, "New Varieties of Sensitivity Analysis," 9 *Evaluation Review* 772-779 (1985).

TABLE 11-2
THRESHOLD VALUES, INSENSITIVITY RANGES,
AND CHANGE SLOPES

GOALS POLICIES	Long-Term Value (Y_1)	Low Cost (Y_2)	WEIGHTED SUM
Nuclear (X_a)	a_1 +1 4 (3 to ∞)	a_2 +1 3 (2 to ∞)	7
Solar (X_b)	b_1 -1 5 (-∞ to 6)	b_2 -1 1 (-∞ to 2)	6
Weights	W_1 -1 1 (-∞ to 2)	W_2 +2 1 (.5 to ∞)	

NOTES:

1. The symbol in the upper left-hand corner of each cell shows (1) the identifying symbol of each relation, with the letter indicating the goal; (2) the identifying symbol of each weight, with the subscript indicating the goal to which the weight refers.
2. The number in the middle of each cell shows (1) the value of the relation on a 1 to 5 scale; (2) the value of the weight, with the least important goal having a weight of 1.
3. The number in the upper right-hand corner of each cell shows by how much the gap changes between the two alternatives being compared if the input increases by one unit.
4. The number other than infinity in parentheses in each cell is the threshold value for each input. At that value, there will be a tie in the weighted sum of the two alternatives being compared.
5. The range in parentheses in each cell is the insensitivity range. That range shows how far down and up each input can go without affecting which alternative is the winner.

TABLE 11-3
ALLOCATING CASES TO METHODS OF RESOLVING

A. THE RAW DATA

	Delay (Days)	Respect (0-10 Scale)
Trials	120	6
Pleas	30	2
	150	8

B. THE TRANSFORMED RAW DATA

	Speed (1/Days)	Respect (-5 to +5)
Trials	1/120 or .00833	+1
Pleas	1/30 or .03333	-3
	5/120 or .04166	-2

C. THE PART/WHOLE PERCENTAGES

	Speed P/W%	Respect P/W%	Aggregate P/W%	Allocation %
Trials	20%	100%	120%	60%
Pleas	80%	0%	80%	40%
	100%	100%	200%	100%

D. THE WEIGHTED P/W%'s

	Speed w=1	Respect w=2	Aggregate P/W%	Allocation %
Trials	20%	200%	220%	73%
Pleas	80%	0%	80%	27%
	100%	200%	300%	100%

nuclear and solar. That would mean doubling the 4 and the 5 in the long-term value column. The result would be that nuclear would have an overall score of twice 4 plus 3, or 11. Likewise, solar would have an overall score of twice 5 plus 1, or 11. If the relative importance of long-term value to low cost were a key missing information item, then all one would have to decide is whether long-term value is more than twice as important as low cost or less than twice as important.

The bottom of cell a shows that any score from 3 to infinity in cell a would make nuclear a winner. That is thus an insensitivity range where any score within that range does not change the initial winner. Likewise, the insensitivity range for cell c is any score from negative infinity up to 6. This means any score within that range will not change the initial winner. Those insensitivity ranges show that there is generally a log of room for error in this kind of analysis.

The upper right-hand corner of cell a shows a plus 1. This means if the score of 4 in that cell goes up by 1 point, then the winning gap also goes up by 1 point. Those change slopes are useful for indicating what changes have the most leverage for increasing or decreasing the winning gap.

ALLOCATING RESOURCES

Decision-aiding software can help in allocating resources, as contrasted to the generally easier problem of just finding a best alternative or combination.

A good way of allocating resources is to convert into percentages the raw merit scores of the objects to which the resources are to be allocated. One can then apply the percentages to the grand total available to be allocated. A good way to convert the raw scores into percentages is by dividing them by their total within the same goal in order to get part/whole percentages. Those percentages can then be summed across the goals, using a weighted sum where the goals have different weights.

Table 11-3A shows how the P/G% software can be used in an allocation problem where the bottom line consists of allocation percentages. The alternative methods shown are trials and plea bargains. Additional alternatives could be added such as diversions or dismissals. The goals shown are to reduce delay and to increase respect for the legal system. Additional goals could be added such as reducing expense and increasing the probability of innocent defendants being acquitted.

The raw data shows that in our hypothetical court system, the averagetrial takes 120 days, and the average plea bargain takes 30 days from arrest to disposition. The data also shows that the trials alternative receives a respect score of 6 on a 0-10 scale in a rough survey of attorneys, and pleas receives a score of only a 2. It would not be meaningful to add 120 days to a respect score of 6 to get an overall score for trials because (1) delay is measured in days, and respect is measured on a 0-10 scale necessitating a common measure in order to be able to add these scores, (2) delay is a negative goal where high scores are undesirable, and (3) a score of 2 on respect may be a negative score such that each additional plea bargain decreases respect for the system.

To deal with those problems, we do the following:

1. The delay scores are converted into part/whole percentages by dividing each score by the sum of the delay column, but after inverting for the negative goal.
2. The inversion is done by working with the reciprocals of the delay scores. That means working with 1/120 and 1/30 rather than 120 and 30. Doing so preserves the fact that trials are four times as bad as pleas on the goal of delay, while making the pleas score higher than the trials score. We are then working with speed rather than delay as a goal. Speed should be given a weight of +1 if delay has previously been given a weight of -1.
3. The respect scores are also converted into part/whole percentages by dividing each score by the sum of the respect column, but after adjusting for the fact that pleas may have a negative score.
4. That means determining the value of a true zero on the 0-10 scale and subtracting that value from the 0-10 scores. Thus, if a 5 is the separation point between positive scores and negative scores, then a 6 is the equivalent of a +1, and a 2 is the equivalent of a -3. Those transformed numbers are shown in Table 11-3B.

Table 11-3C converts the transformed data into part/whole percentages. Pleas is given 0% on respect because one would not want to allocate anything more than the minimum possible if pleas has a negative score and if more respect were the only criterion. We can now add across the percentages and obtain an aggregate percent of 120% for trials and 80% for pleas. We then divide by 2 to bring the sum of those percentages down to 100% because we cannot allocate more than 100%.

Table 11-3D takes into consideration that respect is considered to be twice as important as speed. That means multiplying the percentages in the respect column by 2. The new aggregate percentages are then 220% and 80%. We then divide by 3 or the sum of the weights to obtain the allocation percentages of 73% and 27%. Not all allocation problems involve multiple dimensions, negative goals, or negative scores. If, however, one can follow the allocation analysis of Table 11-3, then one can deal with simpler allocation problems.[4]

ADJUSTING FOR CONSTRAINTS

Decision-aiding software can help in dealing with constraints that require minimums or maximums on the alternatives or the goals or other conditions that must be met, regardless how high the scores are of an alternative on the goals.

The main ways in which constraints are handled are:

1. The constraints can be met before one allocates scarce resources or determines the relation scores. Doing so tends to result in giving an alternative more than it is entitled where it only deserves the minimum. That result cannot occur if adjustments are made after allocating so as to bring alternatives up to their minimums.
2. The best way of resolving conflicting constraints is to expand the total benefits available or reduce the total costs to be imposed so that all the constraints can be satisfied simultaneously. If that is not possible, then resolve conflicting constraints by developing compromises that satisfy each constraint in proportion to its importance. Other less desirable alternatives involve partially satisfying all constraints equally, or fully satisfying certain constraints in the order of their priority.

Adjusting for constraints is illustrated with the same problem as allocating a budget to police and courts in light of crime reduction and fair procedure. The constraints specify minimum amounts to the police and the

---

[4]On diverse methods for dealing with the multiplicity of alternatives in allocation problems, see Philip Kotler, *Marketing Decision Making: A Model Building Approach* (Holt, 1971) (calculus and statistical analysis); Claude McMillan, *Mathematical Programming: An Introduction to the Design and Application of Optimal Decision Machines* (Wiley, 1970) (reiterative guessing and operations research); and S. Nagel, *Policy Evaluation: Making Optimum Decisions* (Praeger, 1982) (variations on part/whole percentaging in chapters 10-13). Also see S. Nagel, "Optimally Allocating Federal Money to Cities," 5 *Public Budgeting and Finance* 39-50 (1985).

courts, but those minimums may add to more than the total budget available.

A good way to adjust to satisfy the equity constraints with two, three, and four budget categories is as follows:

1. With two budget categories, suppose category A is below its minimum and category B is above its minimum. After allocating in proportion to their aggregate scores, then give category A its minimum. Give the rest of the total budget to category B.
2. With three budget categories, suppose A is below its minimum and B and C are above their minimums. Then give A its minimum. Divide the rest of the total budget between B and C in proportion to their aggregate scores.
3. With four or more budget categories, one can reason by analogy to the three category situation. No matter how many budget categories are below their minimum in the initial optimizing, give them their minimums and then remove them from further allocating. The remainder of the total budget then gets divided proportionately among the other budget categories.[5]

SIMPLICITY OF ANALYSIS

Decision-aiding software that is based on multi-criteria decision-making can greatly simplify the analysis of a variety of decision-aiding problems that have traditionally used more complicated and often less valid methods, such as arrow diagrams, payoff matrices, decision trees, optimum level curves, indifference curves, functional curves, and multi-objective programming. The essence of MCDM software is that it works with a table, matrix, or spreadsheet with alternatives on the rows, evaluative criteria on the columns, relation scores in the cells, and a summation column at the right showing the overall score or allocation percent of each alternative.

A good illustration of the simplicity of MCDM and P/G% software is the decision whether to take away or leave an abused child with the child's

---

[5]On dealing with constraints in public policy analysis in general, see S. Nagel, *Public Policy: Goals, Means, and Methods* (St. Martin's, 1984), especially the chapters on equity, effectiveness, human rights, discretion, economic structure, government structure, political feasibility, and ethical constraints. On quantitative constraints in allocation problems, see "Allocation Logic" in S. Nagel, *Policy Evaluation: Making Optimum Decisions* (Praeger, 1982), where the problem of allocating to police, courts, and corrections is also discussed.

TABLE 11-4

DATA FOR ILLUSTRATING EQUITY CONSTRAINTS AND ADJUSTMENTS TO SATISFY THEM

ALLOCATION CRITERIA / BUDGET CATEGORIES	RAW SCORES		TRANSFORMED SCORES			ALLOCATION RESULTS				
	Crime Reduction (1)	Fair Procedure (2)	Aggregate Scores (3)	Allocation Percentages 2-way (4a)	3-way (4b)	Optimum Allocation 2-way (5a)	3-way (5b)	Minimums (6)	Adjusted Allocations 2-way (7a)	3-way (7b)
POLICE	2.00	1.00	3.00	43%	39%	$214	$195	$240	$240 (Min.)	$240 (Min.)
COURTS	1.00	3.00	4.00 ----- 7.00	57%	51%	$286	$255	$ 80	$260 (100% of $260)	$218 (84% of $260)
CORREC-TIONS	.50	.25	.75	N/A		10% N/A		$ 50	$ 40 N/A	$ 42 (16% of $260)
TOTALS	—	—	7.75	100%	100%	$500	$500	$360	$500	$500

NOTES:

1. Optimizing can be done first, and then adjustments are made to satisfy the constraints if they have not been satisfied already. In other words, if we optimally allocate without considering the minimums, we obtain what is shown in column 5a (for two budget categories) and column 5b (for three budget categories). If we then consider the minimums, we obtain what is shown in columns 7a and 7b.

2. There is $500 available to be allocated this year. There was $450 available to be allocated last year. N/A = Not Applicable.

3. The minimums in column 6 are equal to 80% of last year's budget. Last year, the police received $300, the courts received $100, and corrections received $50.

4. The numbers in columns 1 and 2 are based on a rough survey of a small sample of some people who are knowledgeable about the criminal justice system.

5. The formulas for the numbers in the other columns are: (3) = (1) + (2); (4a) = (3)/7.00; (4b) = (3)/7.75; (5a) = (4a) ($500); (5b) = (4b) ($500); (6) = 80% of last year's allocation.

6. The best way to make the adjusted allocations of 7a and 7b is to give any budget category its minimum (from column 6). If its optimum (from column 5a or 5b) falls below its minimum, then divide the residue among the other budget categories in proportion to their aggregate scores (from column 3).

family. Table 11-5 shows the problem analyzed with a traditional payoff matrix, and Table 11-5B shows the problem analyzed with a P/G% spreadsheet table. Both approaches show the alternatives on the rows. The payoff matrix shows contingent events and possibly their probabilities on the columns, whereas the P/G% approach shows goals and their relative weights on the columns. The payoff matrix shows relative payoffs in the cells, whereas the P/G% approach shows relation scores on a 1-5 scale in the cells between the alternatives and the goals. The payoff matrix shows benefits minus costs on the right side with each element discounted by the probability of its occurring, whereas the P/G% approach shows the weighted summation scores for each alternative at the right side.

Both approaches are applied to the same empirical situation in Table 11-5. The payoff matrix tends to lead to a decision to take the child away because the probability of severe abuse is likely to be greater than the threshold probability. The P/G% approach leads to a closer decision because it emphasizes multiple criteria of avoiding abuse, preserving family love, and saving the taxpayer cost. One could argue that those three criteria are taken into consideration in the relative payoffs in the cells of the payoff matrix. However, by lumping all three criteria together, their separate existences and sensitivity values get overwhelmed by the criterion of avoiding abuse. The payoff matrix may thus lead to results that are less valid in terms of the decision-maker's goals than the P/G% approach.

The advantages of the P/G% approach over a payoff matrix include:
1. P/G% can explicitly consider any number of criteria such as the three shown above.
2. P/G% can explicitly consider any number of alternatives such as, take away to an institution, take away to a foster home, take away to a relative's home, leave with counselling, or leave without counselling.
3. Being able to consider multiple criteria and multiple alternatives makes the P/G% approach more validly in conformity with reality, and not just a simplistic abstraction.
4. P/G% is also simpler with its 1-5 scales, weighted criteria, computerized threshold analysis, and logical way of analyzing a problem in terms of alternatives, criteria, and relations.[6]

---

[6]On the matter of simplicity in drawing and presenting conclusions in evaluation analysis, see S. Nagel, "Comparing Multi-Criteria Decision Making and P/G% with Traditional Optimizing," in Yoshikazu Sawaragi (ed.), *Multiple-Criteria Decision Making* (Springer-Verlag, 1987) and "Simplifying Basic Methods" in S. Nagel, *Public Policy: Goals, Means, and Methods*

TABLE 11-5
COMPARING A PAYOFF MATRIX WITH P/G% ON
DECISION-MAKING UNDER CONDITIONS OF RISK
(Eg., Deciding Whether to Take Away or Leave an Abused Child)

A. THE PAYOFF MATRIX

SEVERE SUBSEQUENT ABUSE

	Would Not Occur	Would Occur	Benefits	Costs
TAKE AWAY	a -50	b -100	(P)(100) - (1-P)(50)	
LEAVE	c +50	d -100		

B. THE P/G% APPROACH

GOALS ／ POLICY	Avoid Abuse (w=2)	Preserve Family Love (w=1)	Save Taxpayer Cost (w=1)	Weighted Sum
TAKEAWAY	4	2	2	12
LEAVE	2	4	4	12

(St. Martin's, 1984). On the subject of taking away abused children, see "Neglect" in George Cooper, et al., *Law and Poverty: Cases and Materials* (West, 1973).

NOTES:

1. The cell entries in Table 11-5A are arrived at by asking the decision-makers the following questions:
   (1) Of the four possible occurrences, which ones are desirable (marked plus), and which ones are undesirable (marked minus)?
   (2) Of the undesirable occurrences, which one is the most undesirable (marked minus 100)?
   (3) How much more undesirable is the most undesirable occurrence in comparison to the less undesirable occurrence (marked minus 50 to show that cell d is twice as bad as cell a)?
2. With that information, one can determine the threshold probability as follows:
   (1) At the threshold, the discounted benefits equal the discounted costs (i.e., $100P = 50$ minus $50P$).
   (2) The solution for P in that equation is $P^* = d/(a + d)$ or $P^* = 100/(50 + 100) = .33$.
   (3) That means that if the probability is greater than .33 that there will be severe subsequent abuse, then the child should be taken away.
3. The scoring of each alternative in Table 11-5B on each criterion is on a 1-5 scale, where 5 = highly conducive to the goal, 4 = mildly conducive, 3 = neither conductive nor adverse, 2 = mildly adverse to the goal, and 1 =

SOME CONCLUSIONS

As mentioned at the beginning of this chapter, the main benefits of the decision-aiding software are its accuracy and speed in handling the five key methodological problems in evaluation analysis. To fully appreciate the relevance of the software, it is necessary to actually use it. We can, however, briefly describe how the software applies to each problem.

On the matter of multiple dimensions on multiple goals:

1. In comparing any two alternatives, one can show for each goal the incremental gain of the better alternative over the other alternative. This can be more easily done by putting the goals on the rows and the two alternatives on the columns since the software subtracts across the rows. One can then pick the alternative that has the more desired set of increments.
2. One can specify the importance of each goal relative to the least important goal. Those weights can consider both importance and the nature of the measurement units where raw scores are used.
3. The software is capable of working with the relations either as raw scores or part/whole percentages by exercising an option on the data management menu.

On the matter of missing information:

1. The software can do what-if analysis by allowing the user to change any of the inputs and quickly see how those changes affect the bottom-line conclusion.
2. The main menu gives the user an option to do a threshold analysis or a convergence analysis to determine the critical values for relation scores or goal weights, above which one alternative would be better and below which another alternative would be better.
3. In specifying the criteria, one can divide each criterion into a best version and a worst version, such as the best possible cost on each alternative and the worst possible cost. The computer can then show the overall best score, the overall worst score, and the midpoint for each alternative.
4. The software can also draw indifference curves or threshold curves showing the combination of scores on two or more variables which would lead to a tie between any two alternatives.

On the matter of allocating resources:

1. The user can specify the grand total available to be allocated. The program will multiply that grand total by the allocation percentages for each alternative or budget category.
2. The allocation percentages are calculated by obtaining an overall score for each alternative and then dividing each overall score by the sum of the scores in order to obtain part/whole allocation percentages.
3. The program can transform the raw scores by determining their reciprocals where negative goals are involved, or by subtracting the value of absolute zero from each raw score where negative scores are involved. Those transformations may, however, be easier to do with a calculator and then just enter the results into the data matrix.

On the matter of adjusting for constraints:

1. The user can enter minimum constraints for each alternative, and the program can guarantee they will be met in whatever allocation is done. A better approach though would be to optimize ignoring the constraints. and then make adjustments for any alternative or criterion that violates its minimum or maximum.
2. The ease of doing what-if analysis facilitates resolving conflicting constraints and conflicting decision-makers by enabling both sides or a mediator to try different alternatives, criteria, weights, constraints, relations, and other inputs until a mutually satisfying solution is found.

On the matter of simplicity:

1. The essence of the software is the idea of putting alternatives on the rows of a spreadsheet matrix, criteria and weights on the columns, relations in the cells, and overall scores for the alternatives in the right-hand column.
2. That system is in conformity with a great deal of systematic decision making, as indicated by the popularity of spreadsheet software, payoff matrices, decision trees, and other formats that can be reduced to a decision matrix.

This kind of evaluation analysis could be done with pencil and paper or even implicitly in one's mind. The analysis is, however, substantially facilitated by the availability of the software and microcomputers. The software encourages thinking more explicitly about evaluation problems without confining the user to quantitatively measured variables. It facilitates creativity by allowing changes to be so easily made. We may be at the advent of new ways of thinking about program evaluation, policy analysis, and decision-making to the benefit of the decision-makers and those who are affected by their decisions.[7]

---

[7]On Policy/Goal Percentaging and the P/G% software, see Benjamin Radcliff, "Multi-Criteria Decision Making: A Survey of Software" 4 *Social Science Microcomputer Review* 38-55 (1986); S. Nagel, "P/G% Analysis: An Evaluating Aiding Program," 9 *Evaluation Review* 209-214 (1985); and S. Nagel, "A Microcomputer Program for Dealing with Evaluation Problems" 9 *Evaluation and Program Planning* (1987). On the applicability of P/G% to all five analytic problems, see S. Nagel, *Evaluation Analysis with Microcomputers* (Sage, 1987).

SECTION F:

DECISION AIDS IN LAW

12

DECISION-AIDING SOFTWARE
AND THE LAW

The purpose of this chapter is to describe the nature, classifications, and literature of the new decision-aiding software which relates to law practice and the legal process. Most of what is included in this chapter is also applicable to decision-aiding software for other fields of knowledge. The law field, however, is one in which there is a lot of decision-making, and it especially lends itself to experimenting with decision-aiding software.

THE SOFTWARE

DEFINITIONS AND CLASSIFICATIONS

The essence of decision-aiding software is the ability of the software to process a set of (1) law-related alternatives to choose among, (2) relevant criteria, goals, or rules for determining which alternative or alternatives are most appropriate or most likely to be chosen, and (3) the relations between each alternative and each criteria.

Any software can be helpful to making decisions such as information retrieval software like Westlaw and Lexis which provide relevant citations and excerpts. We are now also seeing information-retrieval software that emphasizes trial court decisions, especially in damages cases such as

SettleMate and a forthcoming on-line version of the reports of the Jury Verdict Research Corporation. Even office practice software such as word processing, file management, and bookkeeping software can be helpful in making decisions by providing relevant reports. To qualify as decision-aiding software, though, the software should deal with the five essential elements of alternatives, criteria, relations, tentative conclusions, and what-if analysis, either for prescribing what decisions ought to be reached or for predicting what decisions will be reached.

EXAMPLES AND REFERENCES

There are at least eight different kinds of decision-aiding software. Those categories include decision trees, linear programming, statistical software, spreadsheets, rule-based software, multi-criteria decision-making, substantive software, and idea generators. They are discussed below in roughly random order. First, there is decision tree software for making decisions under conditions of risk such as whether to go to trial or accept a settlement. A decision tree is usually pictured as looking like a tree on its side with branches and sub-branches. The branches generally represent alternative possibilities that depend on the occurrence or non-occurrence of probabilistic events. Decision tree software includes the Arborist, SuperTree, Clarence, Ondine, StrataTree, and RiskCalc. For an analysis of decision trees applied to law, see Morris Raker, "The Application of Decision Analysis and Computer Modeling to the Settlement of Complex Litigation," *Symposium on Computer Models and Modeling for Negotiation Management* (Massachusetts Institute of Technology, 1987); and S. Nagel, "Microcomputers, Risk Analysis, and Litigation Strategy," 19 *Akron Law Review* 35-80 (1985).

Second, there is linear programming software for allocating money, time, people, or other scarce resources to activities, places, tasks, or other objects to which the resources are to be allocated. In terms of form rather than function, linear programming involves maximizing or minimizing an objective function or algebraic expression subject to constraints generally in the form of inequalities like greater than or less than. Linear programming and related software includes Erikson-Hall, Lee-Shim, IFPS, Holden-Day, LP Master, Burns-Austin, LP Professional, and Vino-Gino-Lindo. A good comparative analysis of linear programming and related packages is Ramesh Sharda, et al., "Mathematical Programming Software for Microcomputers" in Saul Gass, et al. (eds.), *Impacts of Microcomputers on Operations Research* (North-Holland, 1986).

Third, there is statistical software for predicting how a future case is likely to be decided regarding liability, damages, guilt, sentence, or other judgement in light of past cases or expert opinions. Statistical software generally involves calculating averages or predictive equations in which decisions or other outcomes are related to legal or factual inputs. Statistical software include StatPal, Hall-Adelman, ABC, Stat, EpiStat, PsychoStats, Crosstats, Chao, SPSS, SAS, BDM, StatFast, and StatPac. A good comparative analysis of statistics packages is Dennis Lezotte, "Statistical Software for Micro-computers" in the Saul Gass book cited above.

Fourth, there is spreadsheet-based software in which the alternatives tend to be on the rows, the criteria on the columns, relations in the cells, overall scores for each alternative in a column at the far right, and a capability for determining what it would take to bring a second-place or other-place alternative up to first place. Spreadsheet software (especially if based on Lotus 1-2-3) includes Best Choice, What's Best, 1-2-Tree, Minitab, 1-2-3 Breakeven, PG Lotus, and GoalSeeker. For an analysis of some aspects of decision-aiding spreadsheet software, see Deepak Bammi and Loren Padelford, "Using Spreadsheets for Decision Analysis" in the Saul Gass book cited above. Also S. Nagel, "Using Spreadsheets to Choose Among Alternatives," *Ashton-Tate Quarterly* (1990).

Fifth, there is rule-based software which contains a set of rules for dealing with a narrow or broad field of law. The user gives the computer a set of facts, and the computer applies the rules to the facts in order to determine which alternative decision is likely to be decided. Such software is sometimes referred to as artificial intelligence or expert systems, but the other forms of decision-aiding software also have characteristics associated with AI and expert systems. Rule-based software for prediction or prescribing decisions could include Teknowledge, Expert87, ExSys, ESCA-DSS, MicroExpert, Ashton-Tate, and Texas Instruments. For a good comparative review of rule-based expert systems software, see Carl Grafton and Anne Permaloff, "Expert System Development Programs and Their Alternatives," 4 *Social Science Microcomputer Review*, 165-180 (1986). Rule-based software that is specifically related to legal rules include Judith, DataLex, Rubric, Hypo, Lex, Default, Oblog -2, Esplex, and LexVision. Many of those law-related programs are described in *Proceedings of the First International Conference on Artificial Intelligence and Law* (Northeastern University, 1987).

Sixth, there is other decision-aiding software that does not fit into the above categories but that does process alternatives, criteria, and relations to arrive at a prescription-evaluation or a prediction-explanation. This software is often referred to as multi-criteria decision-making (MCDM) software because it emphasizes multiple criteria, although it may also work with multiple alternatives. The miscellaneous MCDM software includes such names as Lightyear, Confidence Factor, Decision Analyst, Expert Choice, Prefcalc, DecAid, Electre, Policy PC, P/G%, DecisionMaker, Decision, PG Plato, Seriatim, Decision Making, Decide, Pairs, MASS, MOLP, MAUD, and MIDAS. For comparisons of MCDM software, see Patrick Humphreys and Ayleen Wisudha, *Methods and Tools for Structuring and Analyzing Decision Problems* (London School of Economics and Political Science, 1987); Benjamin Radcliff, "Multi-Criteria Decision Making: A Survey of Software," 4 *Social Science Microcomputer Review* 38-55 (1986); B. Golden, et al., "Decision Insight Systems for Microcomputers," in the Saul Gass book cited above. Some of the software fits into more than one category, such as Best Choice or P/G%, which can perform the functions in all six categories, although it is mainly classified as spreadsheet-based software.

Seventh, there is decision-aiding software that focuses on a specific field of law, as contrasted to the above software, which cuts across all fields of law. The fields of law in which specialized decision-aiding software seems to be most developing are personal injury law, estate planning, and taxation. Relevant substantive legal software includes Determining Damages, Legal Analytics, SettleMate, InValue, ComproWise, TaxCalc, Aardvark, TaxMan, and Meldman.

Eighth, there is software that is useful for generating alternatives, goals, or relations, but that does not process those elements in order to draw a conclusion. Software that can help in generating alternatives includes the Idea Generator, the Brainstormer, and Trigger. Software that helps generate relations such as the probability of an alternative achieving a goal includes SPAT. Statistical software can also sometimes be used for generating relations, such as regression co-efficients or average scores of an alternative on a criterion.

As for evaluations of the different kinds of decision-aiding software, useful comparative evaluations can be found in the articles that are cited above. Other relevant literature compares methodologies rather than software packages. That literature includes Ching-Lai Hwang and Kwangsun Yoon, *Multiple Attribute Decision Making: Methods and Applications* (Springer-Verlag, 1981); Harvey Brightman, *Problem Solving: A Logical and Creative Approach* (Georgia State University, 1980); and S. Nagel, *Evaluation Analysis with Microcomputers* (JAI Press, 1989). The category that is most versatile and user-friendly is probably the spreadsheet category, especially variations on Lotus 1-2-3. It can do most kinds of risk analysis, allocation analysis, and prediction analysis easier than decision tree, linear programming routines, or a statistical package.

ACTUAL AND POTENTIAL BENEFITS

As for the actual and potential benefits of decision-aiding software, they depend to some extent on the kind of software to which we are referring, but there are a number of cross-cutting benefits (as well as costs) worth mentioning. They include:

FRAMING THE ALTERNATIVES, GOALS, AND RELATIONS

Encouraging lawyers to be more explicit about goals they are seeking to achieve, alternatives available for achieving them, and relations between goals and alternatives. Being more explicit can generate an interesting ethical cost that Jim Sprowl has raised, namely that it forces lawyers to think more clearly about the goals they should be pursuing. That could be considered a benefit to improving the legal profession, even if it creates dilemmas for individual lawyers.

In listing some alternatives, criteria, and relations, the lawyer's creativity may be stimulated regarding the development of new alternatives. Decision-aiding software also stimulates creativity in the development of criteria and determining relations.

Working with multiple criteria can facilitate the adoption of alternatives or solutions in which one side comes out ahead on some criteria, and the other sides come out ahead on other criteria. Thus, a multiple-criterion perspective can more easily lead to solutions in which one side wins and the other side loses. Decision-aiding software can facilitate making changes in alternatives, criteria, relations, and other inputs in order to determine the effects of those changes on the tentative conclusions.

OVERCOMING ANALYTIC PROBLEMS

Such software can be helpful in dealing with missing information by indicating how high a damage award, settlement offer, or other input has to be in order to bring a tentative second-place or other-place alternative up to first place. The software can thus change a question as to the numerical value of an item into the easier questions of whether the numerical value is likely to be above or below a threshold, breakeven, or critical value. The software can be helpful in dealing with problems of how to combine goals or criteria that are measured on different dimensions.

The software can be helpful in making choices in mutually exclusive situations or in situations that allow for combinations of alternatives. In addition to choosing among alternatives, the software can also aid in allocating scarce resources to the alternatives or budget categories with or without a variety of constraints that need to be satisfied. The software can simplify complicated problems by asking the user to supply only enough information to deal with the problem, and then outputting only enough information for the user to make a decision. This is without subjecting the user to the complicated processing which might occur between the input and the output unless the user wants it.

DIVERSE USERS AND USES

Decision-aiding software is not only beneficial to practicing lawyers, it can be used by legal policy-makers to help evaluate alternative legal policies in light of various criteria. The software can also be beneficial to legal scholars in obtaining a better understanding of why decisions are reached the way they are, and a better understanding of what decisions ought to be reached on a high level of generality.

Decision-aiding software has been applied with concrete examples to all fields of law, including contracts, property, torts, family law, constitutional law, economic regulation, criminal law, international law, civil procedure, and criminal procedure. Decision-aiding software has been applied to all types of legal skills, including counseling clients, negotiating with the opposition, advocating a position in court, mediating disputes, generalizing from a set of cases, generalizing from a set of facts, evaluating alternative legal policies, assigning people to tasks, deciding the best order in which to process cases, and group decision-making.

Decision-aiding software can be useful in teaching law, since it can facilitate role playing with regard to how to handle and develop alternatives, criteria, and relations in order to arrive at decisions.

GENERAL BENEFITS

Decision-aiding software decreases the possibility of making clerical errors in keeping track of the inputs, doing arithmetic, and manipulating data. Some decision-aiding software provides the benefit of encouraging users to inject their knowledge of the subject matter into the process, rather than have substance imposed on them. Some users, though, may prefer decision-aiding software in which they do not have to inject any substantial knowledge, although such software may not sufficiently consider specific situations.

Decision-aiding software can stimulate lawyers to become more receptive to doing systematic decision analysis even when the software is not available. A cost involved in using decision-aiding software is the need to learn how to use it. That investment of time may be highly worthwhile in terms of the above-mentioned future benefits. The amount of time needed to learn decision-aiding software is becoming less as the software becomes more user-friendly and the documentation is improved.

In general, the benefits of decision-aiding software do seem to substantially outweigh the costs, especially if the software is considered to be a supplement to traditional perspectives rather than a substitute.

RELEVANT TRENDS

There are a number of trends which indicate that the time is appropriate for the adoption of decision-aiding software by law firms. These trends include:

JOURNALS AND BOOKS

An increasing mention of decision-aiding software in journals for practicing lawyers, as, for example, the lead article entitled "Decision Analysis: Using Computers to Make Better Choices" from the February, 1988 *Attorney's Computer Report*. The article says, "The decision-making technique known as decision analysis can be a powerful tool for the lawyer familiar with its nature and use."

An increasing mention of decision-aiding software in the scholarly law reviews, as for example, an article entitled "Computer-Aided Legal Decisions" from the Summer, 1987 *Akron Law Review*. It is the third article on that subject which the *Akron Law Review* has published in the last few years. The other two deal with judicial prediction and litigation strategy.

An increasing mention of decision-aiding software in the journals for judges, as, for example, an article entitled "Can Computers Aid in Dispute Resolution?" from the February-March issue of *Judicature*. This is also the third article that Judicature has published on decision-aiding software in the last few years. The other two deal with sequencing cases and assigning judges to tasks.

An increasing publication of whole books devoted to decision-aiding software for lawyers including David Johnson and Paul Mode, *Improving Law Firm Productivity by Encouraging Lawyers' Use of Personal Computers* (Harcourt Brace Jovanovich, 1985), and S. Nagel, *Microcomputers as Decision-Aids in Law Practice* (Greenwood-Quorum, 1987).

OTHER INDICATORS

Increasing publication of relevant software such as "Determining Damages" by Shepard's McGraw-Hill, "SettleMate" by Lawyers Technology, Inc., "The Art of Negotiation" by Experience in Software, Inc., and "Best Choice" by Decision Aids, Inc.   Increasing mention by law firms of the use of decision-aiding software. This can be seen by comparing the Chicago-Kent surveys of the top 500 law firms in 1985 and 1986. They reveal a substantial increase in the use of spreadsheets for modeling purposes in that recent one-year period.

Increasing presentations of relevant papers at scholarly meetings and bar association meetings, including world-wide conferences like the Fourth Annual World Congress on "Law and Computers" held in Rome in 1988. Increasing inclusion of decision-aiding software in training courses and job descriptions for paraprofessionals, legal administrators, and related personnel, as indicated by journals like the *Legal Administrator* and *Legal Assistant Today*. Increasing occurrence of relevant training institutes for continuing legal education programs as indicated by the ALI-ABA short courses on "Applying Decision Science to Law Practice" and "Using Personal Computers for Decision-Making in Law Practice."

What may be needed is the establishment of an appropriate committee within the American Bar Association. It could perform such functions as (1) making lawyers more aware of what decision-aiding software is, (2) stimulating the development of new and better decision-aiding software for lawyers, and (3) evaluating existing and future programs and packages designed to aid lawyers in reaching decisions from alternatives, criteria, and relations.   Decision-aiding software does have a lot to offer in terms of making law practice more effective, efficient, and equitable. It is good to see law practice benefit as much as possible from new technology developments, including decision-aiding software.

Thinking more broadly, decision-aiding software has a lot to offer all fields of decision-making. It is good to see that other fields and decision analysis in general are developing relevant software for important decision-making. On decision-making software in general see Patrick Humphreys and Ayleen Wisudha, *Methods and Tools for Structuring and Analyzing Decision Problems* (London: London School of Economics and Political Science, 1987); Gautam Mitra (ed.), *Computer Assisted Decision Making: Expert Systems, Decision Analysis, Mathematical Programming* (Amsterdam: North Holland, 1986); and the forthcoming comparative report by Charles Vlek of the University of Groningen in the Netherlands.

13

COMPUTER-AIDED LAW DECISIONS

The purpose of this chapter is to describe how microcomputers can aid in making law decisions, including decisions that relate to the judicial process, law practice, and law management.

Those three kinds of law decisions are subdivided into eight examples. The material on the judicial process deals with computer-aided (1) case synthesizing, (2) fact synthesizing, and (3) law evaluation. The law practice material deals with computer-aided (4) counseling, (5) negotiation, and (6) advocacy. The law management material deals with (7) judicial administration, and (8) legal administration. Each of those eight types of computer-aided law decisions is described along with a concrete example and an illustrative visual aid.

The idea of computer-aided law decisions is a law variation on computer-aided manufacturing (CAM) and computer-aided design (CAD), which are becoming increasingly important in the American economy. Computer-aided law decisions have in common a systematic procedure for processing a set of (1) goals to be achieved or predictive criteria, (2) alternatives for achieving the goals or alternative situations, and (3) relations between criteria and alternatives in order to choose a best alternative, combination, allocation, or predictive decision-rule.[1]

---

[1]For general materials on multi-criteria decision-making applied to the legal process, see S. Nagel, *Using Personal Computers for Decision-Making in Law Practice* (Westport, CT: Greenwood-Quorum Press, 1986). An earlier version is available from the Committee on

Computer-aided decisions thus differ substantially from computer-aided clerical work like word processing, file management, litigation support, document drafting, citation access, or law office bookkeeping.[2] At the other extreme, computer-aided decisions differ from the idea of computers making decisions in place of appellate judges, trial judges, legislators, legal counselors, law negotiators, lawyer advocates, judicial administrators, or law firm administrators.[3] Computerized clerical work is highly possible and useful, but it is not lawyer work. Computers as decision-makers without judges, lawyers, and other legal personnel is probably not possible and of questionable value if it were possible.

Microcomputers can be helpful in processing goals, alternatives, and relations, especially for indicating what it would take to bring a second-place alternative up to first place, or what it would take to improve a predictive decision-rule. The microcomputer software described in this chapter belongs in the general categories of multi-criteria decision-making, expert systems, and artificial intelligence. The specific software is called Policy/Goal Percentaging (abbreviated P/G%) because it relates policies or decisions to goals or criteria, and it uses part/whole percentaging to deal with the goals being measured in different ways.

COMPUTER-AIDED JUDICIAL PROCESS (CAJP)

COMPUTER-AIDED CASE SYNTHESIS (CACS)

Table 13-1 provides an example of synthesizing a set of appellate cases using

---

Continuing Professional Education of the American Law Institute and the American Bar Association. On the general methodology, see S. Nagel, *Microcomputers and Evaluation Problems* (Beverly Hills, CA: Sage Publications, 1986), and the "Policy/Goal Percentaging" program, Decision Aids, Inc., 361 Lincoln Hall, University of Illinois, Urbana, IL 61801.

[2]For discussions of computer-aided clerical work, see Mary Ann Mason, *An Introduction to Using Computers in the Law* (St. Paul, MN: West, 1984); and Daniel Remer, *Computer Power for Your Law Office* (Berkeley, CA: Sybex, 1983). Relevant software includes "WordStar" (word processing), "DBase II" (File management), "Evidence Master" (litigation support), Matthew Bender (document drafting), "WestLaw" and Lexis" (access to citations and case excerpts), and "Data Law" (billing and bookkeeping).

[3]For articles that optimistically, pessimistically, or jokingly view computers as partly replacing judges and lawyers, see Paul Bartholomew, "Supreme Court and Modern Objectivity," 33 *New York State Bar Journal* 157-164 (1961); Hugh Gibbons, "Using Computers to Analyze Legal Questions," in Thomas Rasmusson (ed.), *System Science and Jurisprudence* (Lansing, MI: Spartan Press, 1986); and Reed Lawlor, "Stare Decisis and Electronic Computers," in Glendon Schubert (ed.), *Judicial Behavior: A Reader in Theory and Research* (Chicago, IL: Rand McNally, 1964).

TABLE 13-1. SYNTHESIZING APPELLATE CASES: LEGISLATIVE REDISTRICTING

Criteria / Cases	Equality Requirement W = 1 (or 2)	State Legislature W = 1	Equality Violation W = 1	Federal Court W = 1	SUM (Weighted)	OUTCOME Winner.	Award
Colegrove	1 (2)	1	1	2	5 (6)	D	$0
Grills	2 (4)	2	1	1	6 (8)	A	2
Maryland	1 (2)	2	2	1	6 (7)	D	0
Scholle	1 (2)	2	2	1	6 (7)	D	0
WMCA	1 (2)	2	1	2	6 (7)	D	0
Asbury	2 (4)	2	2	1	7 (9)	A	6
Dyer	2 (4)	1	2	2	7 (9)	A	8
Baker	2 (4)	2	2	2	8 (10)	A	9
Magraw	2 (4)	2	2	2	8 (10)	A	10

NOTES:

1. A 1 in columns 1 to 4 means No. A 2 means Yes. An "A" in the outcome column means that the attacker wins. A "D" means that the defender wins.
2. The decision rule that the above data initially generates is the following:
   (1) If a redistricting case during the time period covered has a summation score of 7 or above, the attacker wins.
   (2) With a summation score of 6 or below, the defender wins.
3. That decision rule generates one inconsistent case. The inconsistency can be eliminated by (1) changing the decision rule to say that a summation score of 6 leads to an unclear outcome; (2) giving the first variable a weight of 2, which would be consistent with the importance of requiring equality; (3) adding a fifth variable called "Deciding after the Maryland Case;" (4) eliminating the Grills case, but that does not seem justifiable; (5) changing the measurement on the first variable from no-yes to a 1-3 scale and giving Grills a score of 3; (6) finding that Grills really deserves a relation score of 2 on the third of the four variables.
4. Each predicted criterion is initially given an equal weight of 1. If the equality requirement is given a weight of 2 in view of its substantive importance, then the Grills case would no longer be an inconsistently low-scoring case in which the attacker won. The new predictive decision rule would be the following:
   (1) If a redistricting case has a weighted summation score of 8 or above, the attacker wins.
   (2) If the weighted summation score is 7 or below, the attacker loses.
5. The dollar amounts in the last column represent hypothetical data showing how many thousands of dollars the successful attacker received in the form of damages. That information is useful for illustrating how the methodology can predict a continuum outcome as contrasted to a dichotomous outcome of winning versus losing.

the P/G% software. The appellate cases consist of nine cases dealing with legislative redistricting from *Colegrove v. Green* in 1948 to *Baker v. Carr* in 1962. Each case is scored yes with a 2 and no with a 1 on each of the four predictive criteria. The criteria include (1) whether equality is explicitly required by the relevant federal or state constitution, (2) whether a state or federal legislature is involved, (3) whether the degree of equality violation is big or little, and (4) whether a federal or state court is involved. The yes answer is the one that favors a decision for the side that is attacking the existing redistricting system.

The last column shows how each case was decided in terms of whether the winner was the defender or the attacker of the existing redistricting system. The second-to-last column shows the sum of the raw scores. It leads to a decision rule that says, "if there is a total raw score of 7 or above, then the attacker wins; and if there is a total raw score of 6 or below, then the defender wins." That decision rule, however, has one inconsistency. It is the Grills case, in which there were only 6 points, but the attacker still won.

To eliminate such inconsistencies, one can do a variety of legitimate things, as indicated in the notes below the table. The most meaningful approach is generally to give the predictive criteria different weights to indicate their relative importance. In this context, the most important criteria are the first criterion (which deals with the nature of the law) and the third criterion (which deals with the key facts). Of the two, the equality requirement is the most important since the degree of equality violation would mean little if there is no equality requirement. Giving the equality requirement a weight of 2 doubles all the numbers in the first column. Doing so changes the summation scores. The new weighted summation scores now lead to a decision rule that says, "if there is a total raw score of 8 or above, then the attacker wins; and if there is a total raw score of 7 or below, then the defender wins." That new decision rule results in no inconsistencies. The set of cases have thus been synthesized into a meaningful decision rule.[4]

---

[4]On applying multi-criteria decision-making to synthesizing sets of appellate cases, see S. Nagel, "Using Microcomputers and P/G% to Predict Court Cases," 18 *Akron Law Review* 541-574 (1985); S. Nagel, "Case Prediction by Staircase Tables and Percentaging," 25 *Jurimetrics Journal* 169-196 (1985); and S. Nagel, *Causation, Prediction, and Legal Analysis* (Westport, CT: Greenwood Press, 1986). Also see Karl Llewelleyn, *The Common Law Tradition: Deciding Appeals* (Boston, MA: Little, Brown, 1960). Relevant software for inductively synthesizing appellate cases could include statistical analysis software, such as "SPSS-PC" 444 N. Michigan Avenue, Chicago, IL 60611.

COMPUTER-AIDED FACT SYNTHESIS (CAFS)

Table 13-2 provides an example of synthesizing a set of facts in a trial decision using the P/G% software. This is a criminal case in which the key question is whether the defendant is guilty or not. For the sake of simplicity, there are two pieces of evidence. One is a defense witness who offers an alibi for the defendant. That witness has an 80% probability of telling the truth, which would favor the defendant being found not guilty. The second piece of evidence is a prosecution witness who claims to have seen the defendant at the scene of the crime. There is a 70% probability that the witness is telling the truth when one just analyzes that witness alone without considering the testimony of related witnesses.

Not all witnesses or pieces of evidence are of equal importance. An alibi witness is more important than a witness who saw the defendant at the scene of the crime. If the alibi witness is telling the truth, then the defendant cannot be guilty. If the crime-scene witness is telling the truth, then the defendant could still be innocent, since being at the scene of the crime does not mean that the defendant committed the crime. Therefore, give the alibi statement a weight of 2 or a multiple of 2.

The synthesizing then involves adding .40 to .70 in order to obtain a weighted sum for the alternative that the defendant is not guilty. Those two weighted sums should then be divided by the sum of the weights (which are 2 and 1) in order to obtain probabilities that add to 1.00. The bottom line thus shows there is a .37 probability that the defendant is guilty in light of the analysis and a .63 probability that the defendant is not guilty. It would therefore be appropriate to acquit the defendant since the probability of guilt should be higher than about .90 in order to justify a conviction.[5]

COMPUTER-AIDED LAW EVALUATION (CALE)

Table 13-3 provides an example of using the P/G% software to arrive at a conclusion as to what policy ought to be adopted in light of a set of goals to be achieved. The subject matter is how should illegally obtained evidence be treated by the courts in criminal cases. The four alternatives listed consist of

---

[5]On systematic synthesizing of facts in trial decisions, see Jerome Frank, *Court on Trial: Myth and Reality in American Justice* (Princeton, NJ: Princeton University Press, 1950); Bruce Sales (ed.), *The Trial Process* (New York: Plenum Press); and Norbert Kerr and Robert Bray (eds.), *The Psychology of the Courtroom* (New York: Academic Press, 1982). Relevant software for calculating probabilities includes the Bayesian probabilities program in the package called "Computer Models for Management Science," Addison-Wesley, Reading, MA.

TABLE 13-2
SYNTHESIZING TRIAL FACTS: A CRIMINAL CASE

Criteria Alternatives	(1) Defense Statement (Alibi) $W_1 = 2$	(2) Prosecution Statement (Scene of Crime) $W_2 = 1$	(3) SUM (1)+(22)	(4) SUM N (3)/2	(5) Weighted Sum (1.5)+(2)	(6) Weighted Sum Sum of Weights (5)/3
Defendant is Guilty	.20 (.40)	.70	.90	.45	1.10	.37
Defendant is Not Guilty	.80 (1.60)	.30	1.10	.55	1.90	.63
	1.00 (2.00)	1.00	2.00	1.00	3.00	1.00

NOTES:

1. The numbers in columns 1 and 2 are probabilities. They indicate the degree of accuracy or truth associated with the statements in the direction of establishing the defendant's guilt. Thus, the .20 probability means that there is a .80 probability that the defense statement is true, and the .20 complement is in the direction of establishing the defendant's guilt. These are probabilities of truth, not probabilities of guilt.

2. The weights indicate the degree of importance of the evidence items. Thus an alibi statement is quite important (if true) in establishing innocence. A statement saying the defendant was at the scene of the crime is less important because even if it is true, it does not establish the defendant's guilt. The numbers in parentheses in column 1 are weighted probabilities.

3. The numbers in column 3 are the sum of the two unweighted probabilities. The numbers in column 5 are the sums of the two weighted probabilities.

4. The numbers in column 4 are unweighted average probabilities. The numbers in column 5 are weighted average probabilities. The numbers in column 6 are an approximation of Bayesian conditional probabilities especially when one only has probabilities of truthfulness and degrees of importance to work with.

5. If the probability in the upper right hand corner is greater than .90, then the judge, juror, or other perceiver of these two items of evidence should vote to convict assume (1) .90 is accepted as the threshold probability interpretation of beyond a reasonable doubt, and (2) these are the only items of evidence. If the starred probability is .90 or less, then one should vote to acquit.

6. With two alibi witnesses, each might receive a weight of 1.5 if one witness receives a 2. They do not both receive a 2 because they partly reinforce each other.

7. No set of weights will cause the weighted average to exceed .90 with probabilities of .20 and .70. Thus, there is no threshold value for either W1 or W2.

8. The difficulty of obtaining a set of evidence items across the prosecution and the defense that average better than a .90 probability may indicate that jurors and judges generally operate below the .90 threshold, even though judges and commentators say that .90 is roughly the probability translation of "beyond a reasonable doubt."

(1) the good-faith exception to excluding the evidence, (2) the suspension-dismissal exception to excluding the evidence, (3) the prevailing rule of excluding illegally seized evidence from criminal proceedings, and (4) the previous emphasis on the possibility of damage suits and prosecution to deter illegal searches. The goals to be achieved include (1) decreasing illegal police searches, (2) not encouraging lying by the police, (3) decreasing crime occurrence, and (4) feasibility in being capable of being adopted.

Table 13-3 also shows how each alternative is scored on each criterion using a 1-3 scale, where 3 = relatively high on the goal, 2 = middling on the goal, and 1 = relatively low on the goal. On the goal of decreasing illegal police searches, the alternatives of suspensions-dismissals and damages-prosecution are the strongest deterrents if applied. On not encouraging lying, the good-faith exception does not do so well compared to the other alternatives. On decreasing crime occurrence, the good-faith exception scores highest because it allows the police the freest hand. On the matter of feasibility, the good-faith exception may be questionable as to its constitutionality. Suspensions-dismissals lacks legislative feasibility, and damages-prosecution lacks judicial feasibility.

If one adds across each alternative without giving different weights to the goals, then the scores of the alternatives are 5 for the good-faith exceptions and a three-way tie for the other three alternatives. Even with different weights for the goals to consider the liberal, neutral, and conservative positions, there is still a three-way tie between suspension-dismissal, the exclusionary rule, and damages-prosecution. The bottom line conclusion is that the exclusionary rule is the best of the tied alternatives because it is the only one that passes the feasibility constraint.

It is feasible in the sense that it has been widely adopted across the 50 states. The other three alternatives have not been widely adopted, and there is considerable doubt as to whether they ever could be.[6]

---

[6]On legal policy evaluation, see Richard Posner, *Economic Analysis of Law* (Boston, MA: Little, Brown, 1977); Lawrence Friedman and Stewart Macaulay (eds.), *Law and the Behavioral Sciences* (Indianapolis, IN: Bobbs-Merrill, 1977); S. Nagel, *Policy Evaluation: Making Optimum Decisions* (New York: Praeger, 1982); and S. Nagel, *Law, Policy, and Optimizing Analysis* (Westport, CT: Greenwood-Quorum Press, 1986). Relevant software for evaluating policies in light of given goals includes those packages discussed in Benjamin Radcliff, "Multi-Criteria Decision Making: A Survey of Software," 4 *Social Science Microcomputer Review* 38-55 (1986), such as "Expert Choice," Decision Support Software, 1300 Vincent Place, McLean, VA 22101.

TABLE 13-3
LAW EVALUATION: EVIDENCE ILLEGALLY OBTAINED

| | GOALS TO BE ACHIEVED | | | | OVERALL SCORES | | | | | | | |
	Decrease Illegal Police Searches (L)	Not Encourage Lying by Police (N)	Decrease Crime Occurrence (C)	Feasibility	Liberal Score B	Liberal Score A	Neutral Score B	Neutral Score A	Conservative Score B	Conservative Score A	Total B	Total A
1. Good Faith Exception	1	1	3	1	8	11	10	13	12	15	30	39
2. Suspension-Dismissal	3	2	2	1	15	18	14	17	13	16	42	51
3. Exclude Evidence	2	2	1	3	11	20	10	19	9	18	30	57
4. Damages-Prosecution	3	2	2	1	15	18	14	17	13	16	42	51

NOTES:

1. The four alternatives are (1) allow the evidence in if the policy testify they did not intend to engage in illegal behavior, (2) allow the evidence in if the state adopts a system of suspensions on the first offense and dismissal on the second offense, (3) exclude illegally seized evidence from criminal proceedings, and (4) emphasize damage suits and prosecution to deter illegal searches.

2. Conservatives are considered as giving the relatively conservative goals a weight of 3, neutral goals a weight of 2, and liberal goals a weight of 1. Liberals are considered as giving the conservative goals a weight of 1, neutral goals a weight of 2, and liberal goals a weight of 3. Neutrals are considered as giving all the goals a weight of 2. Feasibility is assumed to be worth a weight of 3 in view of its importance.

3. The scoring of the alternatives on the goals is done on a 1-3 scale. A 3 means conducive to the goal. A 2 means neither conducive nor adverse. A 1 means adverse to the goal.

4. An overall score is calculated by summing the products of the relation scores multiplied by the weights across each row or policy. for example, the liberal score of 8 is arrived at by summing (1 times 3) plus (1 times 2) plus (3 times 1), or 3 + 2 + 3 = 8.

5. The liberal, neutral, conservative, and total scores are shown before (B) and after (A) adding the feasibility criterion. Without that criterion, the exclusionary rule comes out third or fourth out of the four alternatives. With that criterion, the exclusionary rules comes out first on all four value systems.

6. The other three alternatives are relatively lacking in feasibility because (1) the good-faith exception has questionable constitutionality, since it may provide too little deterrence against illegal search and seizure; (2) a system of suspensions and dismissals would require approval by state legislators or police administrative boards, which is unlikely; (3) prosecution of police officers for illegal searches without physical violence is unlikely, and the probabilities are quite low of an innocent or guilty person suing for damages, winning, and collecting anything substantial.

COMPUTER-AIDED LAW PRACTICE (CALP)

COMPUTER-AIDED COUNSELING (CAC)

Table 13-4 provides an example of computer-aided counseling in the field of will drafting. There are computer programs available that will convert decisions concerning estate allocation into the proper legal form to serve as a valid will, such as the WillWriter program. Those programs, however, are not for helping the testator decide how to divide his or her estate. They assume such decisions have already been made. They are useful in providing checklists as to what decisions should have been made or need to be made.

In this example, the testator is trying to decide among three possible beneficiaries, namely his son, daughter, and wife. In using the P/G% program to aid in making such decisions, the lawyer and the testator together can list the possible beneficiaries. The testator with the aid of the lawyer can tentatively decide on a set of criteria for evaluating the potential beneficiaries. In this case, there are two criteria. One is need, and the other is deservingness.

Need is scored on a 1-5 scale. A 5 in this context means highly needy, and a 4 means mildly needy. At the other extreme, a 1 means highly well-off or the opposite of highly needy, and a 2 means mildly well-off or the opposite of mildly needy. A 3 thus means neither needy nor well-off, but somewhere in the middle. On such a scale, the wife scores a 5. The daughter scores a 4, and the son scores a 2. Deservingness is also scored on a 1-5 scale. A 5 in this context means highly deserving; a 4 means mildly deserving; a 3 means neither deserving nor undeserving; a 2 means mildly undeserving; and a 1 means highly undeserving. Deservingness can especially refer to how nice the potential beneficiary has been to the testator, or refer to the good the beneficiary might do with the bequest, although those could be two separate criteria. On the deservingness scale, the son scores a 4. The wife scores a 3, and the daughter scores a 2.

The object now is to use that jointly-determined information to derive meaningful allocation percentages for each of the three beneficiaries. A simple way to do that is to add each person's two scores in order to arrive at an overall score for each person. Doing so gives the wife an overall score of 8. Both the son and the daughter receive overall scores of 6 apiece. The sum of those three scores is 6 + 6 + 8, or 20. With a total evaluative pie of 20, the son and daughter should logically receive 6/20 or 30% apiece. The wife should receive 8/20, or 40%.

Those allocations, however, are only tentative. They represent a first

TABLE 13-4
COMPUTER-AIDED COUNSELING: ESTATE ALLOCATION

A. Scoring the Beneficiaries on Need and Deservingness

	Need	Deservingness
Son	2.00	4.00
Daughter	4.00	2.00
Spouse	5.00	3.00

NOTE: Table 4A shows that the alternative beneficiaries are a son, a daughter, and a spouse. The criteria for allocating are need and deservingness. Each beneficiary is scored on each criterion on a 1-5 scale. A 5 means highly conducive to the criterion. A 4 means mildly conducive. A 3 means neither conducive nor adverse. A 2 means mildly adverse, and a 1 means highly adverse.

B. Allocating in Proportion to How Well the Beneficiaries Score on Each Criterion

	Need	Deservingness
Son	18.18	44.44
Daughter	36.36	22.22
Spouse	45.45	33.33

NOTE: Table 4B shows in the first column how the estate would be allocated if only need were considered. The son then receives 2/11 or 18%, the daughter 4/11 or 36%, and the spouse 5/11 or 45%. Likewise with the second column on deservingness.

C. Averaging the Separate Allocations to Determine the Overall Allocations

	Alloc.	P/W%
Son	$313.13	31.31
Daughter	$292.93	29.29
Spouse	$393.94	39.39

NOTE: Table 4C averages the allocations based on need and deservingness to determine an overall allocation. Thus, the son gets 31% overall which is the average between 18% on need and 44% on deservingness. Likewise with the daughter and the spouse. The averages in Table 4C are based on treating need and deservingness as having equal weight or importance. One could

TABLE 13-4. COMPUTER-AIDED COUNSELING:
ESTATE ALLOCATION (Continued)

arrive at a weighted average for each beneficiary if the criteria had different weights or degrees of relative importance. One can also specify minimum allocations for each beneficiary. If a beneficiary fails to receive the minimum percentage in step 4C, then give the beneficiary that minimum and reallocate the remainder to the other beneficiaries.

D. What it Would Take to Bring a Second Place Alternative Up to First Place

	Son	Spouse	Weight
Need	3.60	3.00	0.407
Deservingness	6.00	1.86	2.455

NOTE: Table 4D shows the scores the son or spouse would have to receive on each criterion to justify the son receiving the same allocation as the spouse. It also shows that there would be a tie in the allocation if the weight of need were cut more than half from 1.00 to .41, or if deservingness were more than doubled from 1.00 to 2.46. A similar table could be generated for the daughter and spouse or for the son and spouse. Table 4D can be helpful to someone who is advocating an increased percentage to one of the beneficiaries. It can also be helpful to the will-maker in deciding whether he or she really wants a certain beneficiary to have more or less than another beneficiary.

E. The Weights at Which Each Criterion Dominates the Other Criteria

	Weight	
Need	5.00	Stopping difference set at
Deservingness	5.00	5.1 percentage points

NOTE: Table 4E shows that if the weight of need is raised from 1 to 5, then the allocation percentages in Table 4C will be within 5 percentage points of the percentages on the left side of Table 4B. Likewise if the weight of deservingness is raised from 1 to 5, then the allocation percentages in Table 4C will be within 5 percentage points of the percentages on the right side of Table 4B.

cut or initial analysis, subject to change depending on what is revealed as a result of making changes in the inputs. An appropriate change to experiment with might involve additional beneficiaries, such as other relatives, friends, or charities. Doing so might suggest additional criteria, such as the extent to which the bequest might be appreciated, or might result in the testator receiving favorable publicity. One might also experiment with other ways of measuring need or deservingness besides a 1-5 scale, although the methodology changes if the two criteria are measured on two different scales.

An especially useful tool for analyzing the effects of changes in the scores is the threshold analysis shown in Table 13-4C. It shows the changes in the scores that would have to occur to bring the son or daughter up to the allocation level of the wife, or to bring the wife down to the level of the son or daughter. This is useful where the testator is having doubts as to whether the beneficiaries should receive equal or different amounts. Table 13-4C shows that for the son to share equally with the wife, one of four scores or a combination would have to change, namely (1) the son's 2 on need would have to be a 4, (2) the son's 4 on deservingness would have to be 6 which is impossible on a 1-5 scale, (3) the wife's 5 on need would have to drop to a 3 or be mis-estimated by that much, or (4) the wife's deservingness would have to be a 1 instead of a 3. If all those possibilities seem unrealistic, then one can feel more confident in giving the extra allocation to one's wife. The analysis also shows that the son should be given the same allocation as the wife if the testator values deservingness as being 3 times as important as need, or if need is considered 1/3 as important as deservingness. The same kind of analysis can be applied in determining what it would take to bring the daughter up to the same allocation as the wife.

The P/G% program has other useful features for estate allocation or for any kind of allocation. It can deal with negative criteria such as keeping administrative costs down. It can work with 1-5 scales, dollars, percentages, years of service, or other measurement dimensions. It can show at what weight a criterion becomes strong enough that the bottom-line allocations are within five percentage points of what the allocations would be if that were the only criterion. The program can be used to help allocate partnership profits among the members of a law firm, to allocate time or money to various activities or places, and to allocate taxes to various governmental programs.[7]

---

[7]On allocating money or other resources to activities, places, or people, see S. Nagel, "Optimally Allocating Money to Places and Activities," in P. Humphreys and J. Vecsenyi (eds.), *High Level Decision Support: Lessons from Case Studies* (1986). Microcomputer programs

COMPUTER-AIDED NEGOTIATION (CAN)

Table 13-5 provides the data for an example of computer-aided negotiation in a damages case. The alternatives basically are either to go to trial or to settle out of court. This example is presented from a plaintiff's perspective although it could have also been presented from a defense perspective. The example involves a contingency fee arrangement, although it could have been shown with an hourly rate or a flat fee. Table 13-5B shows the criteria for deciding between trial and settlement from both the lawyer's perspective (L) and the client's perspective (C). The lawyer here happens to be a female, and the client is a male. The criteria can also be classified as those which involve benefits (positive weights) and those which involve costs (negative weights). They can also be classified in terms of whether the criteria relate to the trial alternative (1-4) or the settlement alternative (5-8).

The weights in Table 13-5B indicate the following:

1. The .22 shows that there is an estimated .65 probability of winning and that the lawyer gets .33 of what is won. That probability could also be discounted for time, using the time-discounting provisions of the P/G% program.
2. The .43 shows there is an estimated .65 probability of winning, and the client gets .67 of what is won.
3. The $30 indicates the lawyer feels her litigation hours are worth $30 an hour to her.
4. The -1 shows the client has litigation costs that are figured as a lump amount, not by the hour.
5. The .20 indicates the lawyer retains 20% of the settlement.
6. The .80 indicates the client retains 80% of the settlement.
7. The $20 indicates the lawyer feels her settlement hours are worth $20 an hour to her.
8. The -1 shows the client has settlement costs (if any) that are figured as a lump amount, not by the hour.

Table 13-5C and 13-5D show how each alternative scores on each criterion as follows:

---

relevant to estate allocation inlude "WillWriter" of Nolo Press, 950 Parker St., Berkeley, CA 94710; "Fiduciary Accountant" of the Institute of Para-legal Training, 1926 Arch Street, Philadelphia, PA 19103; and "Estate Tax Planner," of Aardvark-McGraw-Hill, 1020 North Broadway, Milwaukee, WI 53202. None of the three specifically deal with how to divide an estate. The first one converts allocation decisions into a will. The second aids in probating and admnistering a will. The third makes tax calculations for various decisions.

TABLE 13-5
COMPUTER-AIDED NEGOTIATION: A DAMAGES CASE

A. The Alternatives of Trial Versus Settlement
Alternative
1. Go to Trial
2. Settle

B. The Criteria and Weights of the Benefits and Costs

Criterion	Meas. Unit	Weight
1.(L)Dams.if Won	$	0.22
2 (C)Dams.if Won		0.43
3 (L)Lit.Hours		-30.00
4 (C)Lit.Costs		-1.00
5 (L)Set.Offer		0.20
6 (C)Set.Offer		0.80
7 (L)Set.Hours		-20.00
8 (C)Set.Costs		-1.00

C. Scoring the Alternatives on the Criteria for Trial

	(L)Dams.	(C)Dams.	(L)Lit.H.	(C)Lit.C
Go To Trial	3000.00	3000.00	20.00	400.00
Settle	0.00	0.00	0.00	0.00

D. Scoring the Alternatives on the Criteria for Settlement

	(L)Set.O	(C)Set.O	(L)Set.H	(C)Set.C
Go to Trial	0.00	0.00	0.00	0.00
Settle	1000.00	1000.00	5.00	0.00

E. The Overall Results from the Lawyer's Perspective

	(L)Dams.	(L)Lit.H	(L)Set.O	(L)Set.H	Combined Rawscores
Go to Trial	650.00	-600.00	0.00	-0.00	50.00
Settle	0.00	-0.00	200.00	-100.00	100.00

F. The Overall Results from the Client's Perspective

	(C)Dams.	(C)Lit.C	(C)Set.O	(C)Set.C	Combined Rawscores
Go to Trial	1300.00	-400.00	0.00	-0.00	900.00
Settle	0.00	-0.00	800.00	-0.00	800.00

G. What It Would Take to Get the Client to Settle

	Go to Trial	Settle	Weight
(C)Dams. If Won	2769.23		0.400
(C)Lit. Costs	500.00		
(C)Set.Offer		1125.00	0.900
(C)Set.Costs		-100.00	

H. What It Would Take to Get the Lawyer to Trial

	Go to Trial	Settle	Weight
(L)Dams. If Won	3230.77		0.233
(L) Lit.Hours	18.33		-27.500
(L)Set.Offer		750.00	0.150
(L)Set.Hours		7.50	-30.000

1. The damages if won are estimated at $3,000.
2. The lawyer's litigation hours are estimated at 20 hours.
3. The client's litigation costs are estimated at $400.
4. The settlement offer thus far is $1,000.
5. The lawyer's settlement hours are estimated at 5.
6. The client's settlement costs are nothing.

In light of the above data, Table 13-5E shows the lawyer would do better to settle, rather than go to trial. For the lawyer, the $3,000 damages income (discounted by the .65 probability of victory and the .33 contingency fee rate) becomes $650. If she subtracts $600 in litigation costs ($30 times 20 hours). there is a net profit of $50. On the other hand, a $1,000 settlement means $200 income at 20%. If she subtracts $100 in settlement costs ($20 times 5 hours), there is a net profit of $100 for settling. Table 13-5F however, shows the client would be better off going to trial, rather than settling. For the client, the $3,000 damages income (discounted by the .65 probability and the .67 complement of the contingency fee rate) is $1,300. If he subtracts $400 in litigation costs, there is a net profit of $900. On the other hand, a $1,000 settlement means $800 income at 80%. If he subtracts nothing in settlement costs, there is a net profit for settling that is $100 less than the estimated trial net profit.

The P/G% program is especially useful for computer-aided negotiation because it can so conveniently indicate what it would take to bring a second-place alternative up to first place. Table 13-5G, for example, shows that settlement would become more profitable to both the client and the lawyer than going to trial if the lawyer can get the insurance company to raise its offer from $1,000 to anything higher than $1,125. If the insurance company is unwilling to go higher than $1,125, then the lawyer has an ethical obligation to go to trial, assuming the estimated inputs are reasonably accurate. If, however, the estimated damages amount is as low as $2,769, then the lawyer should settle in the client's best interests, or if the client's litigation costs are more than $500. The lawyer should also accept the $1,000 settlement if the combination of victory probability and contingency complement are as low as .40 rather than .43, or if the client is allowed to keep 90% of the settlement rather than 80%, although then the lawyer may not be so enthusiastic about settling.

Table 13-5H shows from the lawyer's perspective what it would take to make going to trial more profitable than settling. There are eight answers plus combinations of them, as indicated by the eight breakeven values shown in Table 13-5H. If any of the original scores change to the scores shown in

Table 13-5H, then going to trial becomes more profitable. Those changes include increased damages, decreased litigation hours, decreased settlement, increased settlement hours, increased probability of victory, increased contingency fee, decreased litigation hourly rate, decreased settlement percentage, or increased settlement hourly rate. The table shows exactly what increase or decrease will generate a tie between the profitability of going to trial and the profitability of settling.

With that kind of information, the lawyer can negotiate better with the insurance company over the settlement offer and possibly with the client over the contingency fee. The lawyer can also see from these figures what margin of error there is on the estimates. Thus, if it is better for the client's interests to go to trial with an estimated damages higher than $2,769, then the lawyer need not anguish over whether the damages are likely to be $3,000 or $5,000, since either figure is over $2,769, and likewise with the other estimates.[8]

COMPUTER-AIDED ADVOCACY (CAA)

Table 13-6 provides an example of a case brief using the P/G% software. The case is *San Antonio v. Rodriquez*, 411 U.S. Supreme Court 1 (1973). The case dealt with the extent to which a state is required to help equalize expenditures per student across school districts within the state. The first part of the brief shows that the Supreme Court was faced with the four basic alternatives of (1) no equality required, (2) equal expenditures per student, (3) a minimum amount of expenditures per student, but otherwise allowing for inequality, or (4) a requirement of equality but at a high level. The first part of the brief also shows that the court answered yes to the first alternative, but no to the others.

The second part of the brief shows that there are about six relevant

---

[8]The data for the above example comes mainly from S. Nagel, "Applying Decision Science to the Practice of Law," 30 *Practical Lawyer* 13-22 (April, 1984). On computer-aided negotiation, see S. Nagel and M. Mills, "Microcomputers, P/G% and Dispute Resolution," (Paper presented at the annual meeting of the Society for Professionals Involved in Dispute Resolution, 1986); S. Nagel, "Microcomputers, Risk Analysis, and Litigation Strategy," 19 *Akron Law Review* 35-80 (1985); and S. Nagel, "Lawyer Decision-Making and Threshold Analysis," 36 *University of Miami Law Review* 615-642 (1983). Microcomputer programs relevant to litigation negotiation include "The Art of Negotiating," Experience in Software, Inc., 2039 Shattuck Avenue, Suite 401, Berkeley, CA 94704; and "SettleMate," Lawyers Technology Inc., 339 15th Street, #200, Oakland, CA 94612. The first one is basically a checklist of suggestions for improving one's negotiating skills, although it leaves out systematically comparing the benefits minus costs of settling. The second program is useful for determining the value of different types of injuries.

TABLE 13-6
COMPUTER-AIDED ADVOCACY: SAN ANTONIO V. RODRIGUEZ

A. THE ALTERNATIVES AND THE CRITERIA

Alternative	Previous Outcome	Criterion	Meas.Unit	Weight
NO EQUALITY REQD.	YES	1 EDUCATED POPL	1-3	1.00
= $ PER STUDENT	NO	2 -DISCONTENT		1.00
MIN. $ PER STUDENT	NO	3 -DOWNGRADING		1.00
HIGH $ PER STUDENT	NO	4 ADMIN.EASE		1.00
OTHER	?	5 CONST.W/CASES		1.00
		6 -EXPENSE		1.00

B. THE SCORES OF THE ALTERNATIVES ON THE CRITERIA

	EDUCATE	-DISCON	-DOWNGR	ADMIN.EA	CONSIST.	EXPENSE
NO EQUALITY REQD.	1.00	1.00	3.00	3.00	2.00	3.00
= $ PER STUDENT	2.00	2.00	1.00	1.00	2.00	2.00
MIN. $ PER STUDENT	2.00	2.00	2.00	1.00	2.00	1.50
HIGH $ PER STUDENT	3.00	3.00	2.00	1.00	1.00	1.00

C. THE TOAL SCORES OF THE ALTERNATIVES

Alternative	Combined Rawscores	Previous Outcome
NO EQUALITY REQD.	13.00	YES
= $ PER STUDENT	10.00	NO
MIN. $ PER STUDENT	10.50	NO
HIGH $ PER STUDENT	11.00	NO

D. WHAT IT WOULD TAKE TO BRING THE SECOND PLACE ALTERNATIVE UP TO FIRST PLACE

	NO EQUALIT	MIN. $ PER	Weight
EDUCATED POP.	-1.50	4.50	3.500
- DISCONTENT	-1.50	4.50	3.500
- DOWNGRADING	0.50	4.50	-1.500
ADMIN.EASE	0.50	3.50	-0.250
CONSIST.W/CASES	-0.50	4.50	??
- EXPENSE	0.50	4.00	-0.667

criteria including (1) having an educated population, (2) decreasing discontent due to educational disparities, (3) avoiding the downgrading of affluent schools, (4) administrative ease, (5) consistency with prior cases, and (6) avoiding heavy taxpayer expense. The third part of the brief shows how each alternative scores on each criterion using a simple 1-3 scale, where 3 = highly conducive to the goal, 2 = neither conducive nor adverse, and 1 = adverse to the goal. The fourth part of the brief shows the combined raw scores for each alternative using the apparent scoring of the Supreme Court. The alternative with the highest combined raw score is "no equality required," which is the alternative that the Supreme Court adopted.

The fifth part of the brief is the threshold analysis. It shows what it would take to bring the second-place alternative up to first place. There was a gap of 2.50 points between first and second place on the combined raw scores. That gap would be eliminated if the "no equality" alternative were to drop by 2.50 points on any of the six criteria. That would be too big a drop on any one criterion since the criteria cannot go below 1.00. The gap would also be eliminated if the second place alternative of having a "minimum number of dollars per student" were to increase by 2.50 points on any of the six criteria. That would be too big an increase on any one criterion since the criteria cannot go above 3.00. The gap would also be eliminated if the Supreme Court were to place substantially more weight on having an educated population or on decreasing discontent due to educational inequalities. Those are two areas which the advocates of a minimum-dollars position should emphasize. The gap would be eliminated if the other criteria were given negative weights which is unlikely. Changing the weight would not help with regard to consistency with prior cases, since both alternatives scored the same on that criterion.[9]

---

[9]On systematic case briefing, see Harry Jones, et al. (eds.), *Legal Method: Cases and Text Materials* (Mineola, NY: Foundation, 1980); William Statsky and John Wernet, *Case Analysis and Fundamentals of Legal Writing* (St. Paul, MN: West, 1977); and Wayne Thode, et al. (eds.), *Introduction to the Study of Law: Cases and Materials* (Mineola, NY: Foundation, 1970). Relevant software includes programs designed to teach law students how to analyze cases, as described in Russell Burris, Robert Keeton, Carolyn Landis, and Roger Park, *Teaching Law with Computers: A Collection of Essays* (Denver, CO: Westview Press, 1979).

COMPUTER-AIDED LAW MANAGEMENT (CALM)

COMPUTER-AIDED JUDICIAL ADMINISTRATION (CAJA)

Table 13-7 shows how one can systematically view the problem of assigning judges to case types. This hypothetical problem involves two judges named Fox and Wolf. It involves the case types of criminal and civil cases. Each judge is expected to spend 10 hours in trial in an average week. In such a week, there are about 8 criminal hours and 12 civil hours of trial work.

Judge Fox received a score of 4 for criminal cases on a 1-5 scale, and Judge Wolf a 2. On civil cases, they both received a score of 3. The scoring was done by having each judge or all the judges in the system anonymously score each other. Each judge also scored himself or herself on degree of interest in the case types on a 1-5 scale. The ability scores and interest scores were averaged to give the scores of 4, 2, 3, and 3. What is the best allocation of these two judges to these two case types?

"Best" in this context means an allocation or assignment that will result in as large an overall quality score as possible within the row and column constraints. The overall quality score is the sum of each product of a judge's quality score times the hours assigned for a given case type. In this context the overall quality score is equal to $4a + 2c + 3b + 3d$. The object is to solve for a, b, c, and d so as to maximize that overall score while satisfying the constraints. The best way to proceed if one does not have a computer is to give as few hours as possible to those cells which have quality scores of 1 or 2, and as many hours as possible to those cells which have quality scores of 5 or 4, while satisfying the constraints. Doing so results in an allocation of 0 hours to c, 8 hours to a, 2 hours to b, and 10 hours to d.

That method can be meaningful for a substantial number of judges and case types. One can, however, solve big judicial assignments faster and with more accuracy by using a linear programming routine. Such routines are easy to use on microcomputers. One simply informs the computer of the row totals, the column totals, and the quality scores. The computer then generates the optimum allocations. The program will also indicate (1) how much each quality score can vary without affecting the optimum result, (2) how much each row total and column total can vary, and (3) how much of a change in the overall quality score would occur as a result of a 1-unit change in the

TABLE 13-7
JUDICIAL ADMINISTRATION:
ASSIGNING JUDGES TO TYPES OF CASES

| CASES | CRIMINAL | | CIVIL | | |
JUDGE	Quality Score	Hours Assigned	Quality Score	Hours Assigned	Hours per Judge
FOX	4	a	3	b	10
WOLF	2	c	3	e	10
Hours per Casetype		8		12	20

NOTES:

1. The allocation system is shown in its simplest form with two judges and two casetypes. Each judge is expected to put in ten hours a week to satisfy the average weekly total of 20 hours of trial time. Criminal cases constitute 40% of the total or 8 hours, and civil cases constitute 60% or 12 hours. Judge 1 receives scores of 4 and 3 on the two casetypes, and Judge 2 receives scores of 2 and 3.
2. A logical way to resolve the optimum allocation with this relatively simple example is to reason as follows:
    (1) Judge Wolf does a bad job on criminal cases. Therefore, give Judge Wolf 0 criminal hours. That means Judge Wolf gets 10 civil hours to add across to 10. Judge Fox must then get 8 criminal hours to add down to 8. Judge Fox must also get 2 civil hours to add across to 10 and down to 12.
    (2) Judge Fox does a good job on criminal cases. Therefore, give Judge Fox as many hours as possible on criminal cases which is 8. That means Judge Wolf gets 0 criminal hours to add down to 8. Judge Wolf must then get 10 civil hours to add across to 10. Judge Fox must also get 2 civil hours to add across to 10 and down to 12.
3. On a more general level, resolve the optimum allocation by reasoning as follows:
    (1) Pick out all the quality scores that are 1's or 2's. Give those cells as few hours as possible.
    (2) Pick out all the quality scores that are 5's or 4's. Give those cells as many hours as possible.
    (3) Make logical adjustments so that all the columns add down to what they should, and all the rows add across to what they should.
    (4) Also try to minimize the number of casetypes per judge rather than have every judge do at least a little bit of everything.
4. The optimum allocation is defined as allocating the total number of hours to each cell so as to satisfy the row constraints, the column constraints, and any cell constraints, while at the same maximizing the sum of the products of the quality score times the hours assigned for each cell. A cell includes a quality score of a judge on a casetype and a quantity of hours assigned to a judge on a casetype.

hours assigned or in any of the inputs.[10]

COMPUTER-AIDED LEGAL ADMINISTRATION (CALA)

Table 13-8 shows an example of computer-aided legal administration in the field of optimum sequencing of law cases. The illustrative problem is, "What is the best order in which to handle three cases that involve an estimated 10, 20, and 30 hours and that are predicted to generate $21, $61, and $80 in billing?" For the sake of simplicity, assume we have a one-lawyer firm who works a 40-hour week. With three cases labeled A, B, and C, there are six ways in which they can be ordered consisting of ABC, ACB, BAC, BCA, CAB, and CBA. Which is the best order?

A more general way to view the problem is in terms of five different methods that are frequently proposed for ordering cases in a law firm, a government agency, or elsewhere. Those alternative methods arranged randomly are:

1. Take the cases in the order of the highest benefits first. That means CBA.
2. Look to the cases with the lowest costs first. That means ABC.
3. Take them first come, first served. That also means ABC.
4. Prefer the most profitable first, meaning the ones with the highest benefits minus costs. That means C ($80-30), B ($61-20), and then A ($21-10).
5. Take them in the order of their benefit/cost ratios. That means B ($61/20, or 3.05), C ($80/30, or 2.67), and then A ($21/10, or 2.10). We want to pick the best ordering criterion in terms of maximizing the profits of the law firm, while operating within ethical constraints. At first glance, one might think the order of the cases will make no difference in the profit that can be made from these three cases. The cases are going to consume a total of 60 hours regardless of the order in which they are handled. Likewise, the order will not affect the fact that they will collectively bring in $162 in billings. If we assume that one hour is worth $1 or one monetary unit, then their net profit will be $162 minus $60, or $102

---

[10]Assigning judges to casetypes is briefly discussed in Task Force on the Administration of Justice, *The Courts* (Washington, DC: President's Commission on Law Enforcement and Administration of Justice, 1967), 88-90 and 165-67; and the ABA Commission on Standards of Judicial Administration, *Standards Relating to Trial Courts* (Chicago, IL: American Bar Association, 1976), 86-93. Also see the more general literature and software on assigning people to tasks, such as Warren Erikson and Owen Hall, *Computer Models for Management Science* (Reading, MA: Addison-Wesley, 1983). On assigning lawyers to case types, see S. Nagel and M. Mills, "Allocating Attorneys to Casetypes," *Capital University Law Review* (1986).

TABLE 13-8
LAW FIRM ADMINISTRATION: SEQUENCING CASES
(PROBLEM: What is the best order to handle three cases that involve
10, 20, and 30, hours and that generate $21, $61, and $80 in billing?)

A. *The Alternatives: Five Sequencing Methods*
   Alternative
   1 Highest B's First
   2 Lowest C's First
   3 1st Come, 1st Serv
   4 Highest B-C First
   5 Highest B/C First

B. *The Criteria: Two Weeks of Profit*

Criterion	Meas. Unit	Weight
1 1st Week Profit	$	2.00
2 2nd Week Profit	$	1.00

C. *The Profit Obtained by Each Alternative for Each Week*

Alternative/Criteria Scoring	1st Week	2nd Week
Highest B's Fir	70.50	31.50
Lowest C's Firs	68.67	33.33
1st Come, 1st S	68.67	33.33
Highest B-C Fir	70.50	31.50
Highest B/C Fir	74.33	·27.67

D. *The Overall Score for Each Sequencing Method*

Alternative	Combined Rawscores
1 Highest B's First	172.50
2 Lowest C's First	170.67
3 1st Come, 1st Serve	170.67
4 Highest B-C First	172.50
5 Highest B/C First	176.33

NOTES:

1. The above computer printout shows that by taking the first three cases in the order of the highest benefit/cost ratio first, one thereby maximizes overall benefits minus costs.
2. This is so because the B/C order results in more profit being earned earlier, and that profit is thus available to draw interest or to be reinvested more so than if it earned later.
3. In the above example profit from the first week is given twice the weight or importance as profit of the second week. An alternative approach would be to weight the weeks equally, but to time-discount the second week more so than the first week.
4. The reasonable assumption is that the 60 hours of work involved in doing the first three cases means 40 hours in the first week and 20 hours in the second week. The assumption is also that there is billing every week, not just at the end of the cases, and that the bills are paid promptly.

regardless of the order in which they are processed.

At second glance, however, we realize that one method may bring in more money earlier than another method. The method that brings in the most money as early as possible is the most profitable because that early money can be invested in the firm or elsewhere, thereby drawing interest which might otherwise be a missed opportunity. Table 13-8B shows that the criterion for judging these methods should be how much profit they generate in the first week, the second week, and so on, with more weight given to the profit of the first week than the second week.

Table 13-8C shows for each method how profitable it is in terms of the separate weekly profits, rather than the overall profit which is the same $102 for all the methods. The winning method is taking the cases in the order of their benefit/cost ratios. That method generates $74.33 in the first week, which is about $4 higher than its nearest competitor. If we assume that these numbers are $1,000 units, then by not taking the cases in their B/C order, the firm may be losing the interest that could have been made on $4,000 invested for one week. If that kind of loss is multiplied by 52 weeks and 30 cases rather than three cases, then a lot of money may be needlessly lost.

The $74.33 is calculated by noting that case B has the highest B/C ratio, and thus comes first. Case B takes 20 hours and generates a net profit of $41. We then go to case C, which has the second best B/C ratio. It takes 30 hours, but we only have 20 hours left in the week. We therefore do 2/3 of the case, and thus earn 2/3 of the $50 profit which is $33.33. If we add that to $41, the first week generates $74.33 profit. The second week brings $27.67 in profit, or the remainder of the $102.

One can contrast that optimally profitable sequencing with any of the other less profitable methods. For example, if the cases are processed in terms of their individual profitability, we would take case C first, rather than case B. Doing so would consume 30 hours for a profit of $50. We would then have time for only 10 of 20 hours of case B, which is the next most profitable case. That would earn half of the $41 profit, or $20.50. If we add $50 to $20.50, then we get only $70.50, or $70,500, rather than $74.33, or $74,333.

To be more exact we could time discount the profits of the second week using the time-discounting provisions of the P/G% program. That would give a more accurate overall score than giving the first week's profits a weight of 2. The time discounting, however, would not change the rank order as to which is the best sequencing method.

A computer can aid in implementing the B/C sequencing method by questioning the relevant lawyers as the cases come in as to their estimates of the expenses and income for each case. The computer can then arrange the cases each week in the order of the B/C ratios, and then display that order to aid in deciding which case to take next. To prevent cases with a low B/C ratio from being unreasonably delayed, the computer can flag cases for immediate processing in time to meet the statute of limitations, other deadlines, or an ethical constraint that says no case should have to wait more than a given time to reach a certain stage.

By following such procedures, the law firm administration will not only be maximizing the law firm's profits, but it will also be maximizing the happiness of the clients collectively. This is so if we assume that $1 in billing activity generates the equivalent of one happiness unit. That way the B/C method thus generates more client happiness earlier than the alternative methods do. The estimated total happiness units per week can be calculated by adding 40 to the numbers given in the first column of Table 13-8C and adding 20 to the numbers in the second column. The B/C method thus generates 114.33 happiness units, which is higher than any of the other methods. It is pleasing when law-firm administrative methods can be found that maximize both the interests of the law firm and the interests of the clients.[11]

SOME CONCLUSIONS

The essence of computer-aided decision making is the processing of goals, alternatives, and relations between goals and alternatives in order to choose a best alternative. This is the basic model or methodology. The essence of law decisions is judging, lawyering, and the administration of judging and lawyering. This is the basic substance.

What are the benefits of using computer-aided decision-making which

---

[11]On computer-aided sequencing of law firm cases and other jobs, see S. Nagel, "Sequencing and Allocating Attorney Time to Cases," 13 *Pepperdine Law Review* 1021-1039 (1986); and S. Nagel, Mark Beeman, and John Reed, "Optimum Sequencing of Court Cases to Reduce Delay," *Alabama Law Review* (1986). Also see the more general literature on efficient sequencing, such as Richard Conway, et al., *Theory of Scheduling* (Reading, MA: Addison-Wesley, 1967). On allocating time per case regardless of the order of the cases, see S. Nagel, "Attorney Time Per Case: Finding an Optimum Level," 32 *University of Florida Law Review* 424-441 (1980). The software that is most relevant to optimum sequencing is probably docketing software such as "Docket" by Micro-Craft, 2007 Whitesburg Drive, Huntsville, AL 35801.

justifies their general use in law decisions?   The benefits include the following:

1. Working with the basic model encourages being more explicit about goals to be achieved, alternatives for achieving them, and relations between goals and alternatives.
2. The model leads to choosing the alternative, combination, or allocation that is best in light of the goals, alternatives, and relations.
3. The model leads to choosing predictive decision rules that are capable of separating the past cases into winners and losers in light of their characteristics.   That separation is relevant to accurately predicting or explaining future cases.
4. The model facilitates making changes in order to determine the effects on the bottom line of different goals, alternatives, relations, and other inputs.
5. The model informs the users what it would take in order to bring second-place alternatives or other alternatives up to first place.
6. The model allows and encourages the users to inject their knowledge of the subject matter, rather than impose substance on the users.
7. The model lends itself to being used with microcomputers in order to simplify arithmetic, record keeping, and manipulation of the data.
8. The model stimulates new insights into causal and normative relations that might otherwise be overlooked.

Costs involved in obtaining these benefits are mainly a willingness to think differently and more explicitly about the judicial process and lawyering than one may be accustomed to.   The benefits do seem to substantially outweigh these costs, especially if these models are considered supplements to traditional perspectives, rather than substitutes.   What is especially needed is to spread an awareness of these decision-aiding methods and applications, because to know them is to find them useful.   It is hoped that this chapter will facilitate that purpose of making these models better known, so they can be made even more useful.

FURTHER EXAMPLES OF COMPUTER-AIDED LAW DECISIONS

The purpose of this brief addendum is to provide three specific examples of lawyers who have made use of the P/G% software to aid in arriving at lawyer-like decisions.   The first example is E. Fremont Magee, a partner in the firm of Piper and Marbury of Baltimore, Maryland.   He says in a

February 19, 1985, letter: "I regularly make use of P/G% for the selection of candidates for arbitration panels in medical malpractice claims here in Maryland. Before a medical malpractice matter can be tried in court in Maryland, it must first be submitted to a statutory three member arbitration panel. Each side is given sketchy resumes of five potential candidates to serve as panel chairmen. Each of these is an attorney. In addition, there are five candidates to serve as the lay member and five health care providers to serve as the health care provider member. Each side has the opportunity to strike two candidates from each list. Generally, the biographical information of the lawyers includes date of birth, year of admission to the bar, undergraduate school, graduate school, trial frequency, number of years of litigation experience, medical malpractice experience, arbitration experience, association with health providers, nature of practice and related matters. I use the program to rank the five potential candidates based on the various values I assign to these various criteria."

The second example is C. Howard Thomas, Jr., a partner in the firm of Saul, Ewing, Remick, and Saul of Philadelphia. He presented two interesting uses of P/G% made by his law firm at the Legal Tech '86 Conference in Philadelphia. One use involved deciding where to move the offices of the firm. The firm had to move because it needed larger quarters. There were about five key places to choose among. There was considerable emotion in arguing over the five places. The partners decided to be explicit on the criteria the firm was seeking to achieve and how each place scored on each of those criteria. By doing that, the emotional subject could be handled more rationally. The analysis showed a certain place to be the tentative winner. A sensitivity analysis was then performed to see what changes in the relative weights of the criteria and in the scores of the alternatives on the criteria would be necessary to bring each other place up to the same desirability level as the first place alternative. It was decided that all of the needed changes were unreasonable. The partners then felt pleased they had made the right choice as to where to move the law firm. The firm has also made use of P/G% in deciding whether to litigate or settle out of court. The analysis in at least one big case was shared with the client to convince the client that accepting the settlement was a wise decision.

The third example is Karen S. Dickson and John Finan of the Akron University Law School. They analyzed a dozen key cases which involved the issue of whether a worker is an employee or an independent contractor. The analysis involved scoring each case on seven criteria as to whether the criterion was present or absent. Each case was given a summation score by adding its points on the criteria. The cases in which the total points were nine or more consistently found the worker to be an employee. The cases in which the total points were eight or less consistently found the worker to be an independent contractor. That consistent pattern was established after noting the need to give extra weight to whether the principal has control of the details of the agent's work, as compared to the other criteria. Dickson and Finan thus used the P/G% prediction methodology to inductively operationalize the concepts of employee and independent contractor more clearly than the courts had previously verbalized those concepts.

PART FOUR:

THE SOCIAL SCIENCE OF SUPER-OPTIMUM SOLUTIONS

14

SUPER-OPTIMUM SOLUTIONS
IN PUBLIC CONTROVERSIES

Super-optimum solutions in public controversies are solutions that simultaneously exceed the best expectations of both liberals and conservatives. One example is using well-placed subsidies and tax breaks to increase the GNP enough that the tax revenue to the government increases even if the tax rate decreases. Doing so would provide for a lowering of taxes instead of trying to choose between liberal and conservative ways of raising them. It would also provide for increasing domestic and defense expenditures instead of having to choose between the two.

Ways of arriving at super-optimum solutions include (1) redefining goals to be higher than what is traditionally considered the best, but still realistic, (2) finding items that will provide large benefits to one side but only small costs to the other side, (3) arranging for an outside benefactor such as a government agency that will offer substantial benefits to both sides in order to facilitate a super-optimum settlement, (4) developing a package of items some of which achieve relatively liberal goals and some of which achieve relatively conservative goals, (5) combining the conservative and liberal alternatives where they are not mutually exclusive, and (6) removing the source of the conflict, rather than trying to synthesize the liberal and conservative alternatives. Other facilitators relate to the use of decision aiding software, the role of mediators, the stimulation of creativity. and the importance of realistic positive thinking.

One of the most exciting waves of the future in human interaction is the movement that relates to alternative dispute resolution. That movement began with the rather mundane purpose of decreasing delay in resolving disputes. It has now shifted toward the more important purpose of resolving disputes in mutually beneficial ways, or even in ways in which all sides come out ahead of their best expectations.

To put the subject into a broader historical context, one might note that human beings have been having and resolving disputes since prehistoric times. The traditional method of resolving disputes (as with other primates and mammals) is for one side to dominate the other either by brute force, or by verbal argument. A higher form of dispute resolution is to arrive at a compromise whereby there is a splitting of the difference between the two sides either with or without the aid of a neutral third party. Compromising is considered to be a more civilized form of human interaction, at least where it does not involve retreating from fundamental principles.

In recent times, there has been a growing literature advocating dispute resolution in which all sides come out ahead. Such solutions are associated with the concept of settlement through mediation or through win-win negotiation, as contrasted to the adversary determination of who is right and who is wrong. Win-win negotiation, however, may merely involve each side coming out ahead of their worst expectations.

The concept of super-optimum solutions goes beyond settlement mediation and win-win negotiation by emphasizing the possibility and desirability of each side in a dispute coming out ahead of their best expectations. That kind of dispute resolution partly stems from new philosophies that relate to supply-side economics, industrial policy, and other forms of expansionist thinking, rather than zero-sum or fixed pie thinking.

The purpose of this chapter is to discuss the new, almost futuristic concept of achieving super-optimum solutions in public controversies. The discussion covers (1) the essence of super-optimum solutions, (2) examples from dispute resolution, (3) examples from policy making, (4) contrasts with other types of solutions, (5) procedures for arriving at super-optimum solutions, (6) the helpfulness of decision-aiding software, (7) the generic super-optimum solution from a spreadsheet perspective, (8) classifying super-optimum solutions, and (9) streams of relevant ideas and literature.

In addition to discussing super-optimum solutions, this chapter also helps add to the bridge-building between futures research and policy studies.

Futures research tends to emphasize describing what the future is likely to be. Policy studies emphasizes the development of public policies for achieving a desired future. Both futures research and policy studies are currently undergoing change in the direction of becoming more global geographically, more long-term in the time dimension, and more interdisciplinary or cross-cutting regarding traditional fields of knowledge.

THE ESSENCE OF SUPER-OPTIMUM SOLUTIONS

In general terms, a super-optimum solution is a solution to a decision-making problem where the solution is considered to be objectively better than what has traditionally been considered to be the best possible solution to that type of problem.

One type of super-optimum solution is a solution that achieves a super-optimum goal. A super-optimum goal is one that is far higher than is traditionally considered to be the best attainable. An example would be doing better than 0% unemployment by simultaneously eliminating or reducing traditional unemployment and greatly increasing job opportunities for those who are willing and able to work more, but who were formerly considered outside the labor force or formerly considered fully employed.

A second type of super-optimum solution occurs in resolving public policy disputes. It is a solution that provides a way of satisfying liberals and conservatives in a policy dispute so that both the liberals and the conservatives consider the solution to be better than their original best expectations by their own respective goals and priorities. The attached minimum wage policy dispute is an example.

A third type occurs in resolving adjudicative or rule-applying controversies, rather than policy-making disputes. It is a solution that provides a way of satisfying the disputants that is better than their respective best expectations. An example is where a plaintiff demands $900,000, the defendant refuses to pay more than $300,000, and they agree that the defendant will turn over merchandise which the defendant manufactures that is worth more than $1,000,000 to the plaintiff, but whose variable cost is worth less than $200,000 to the defendant.

A fourth type enables all sides in a dispute to add substantially to their original net worth. An example would be in the same litigation dispute where the defendant agrees to give the plaintiff a franchise for selling the defendant's products and the franchise brings in a net of $1,000,000 a year, with $500,000 a year for the plaintiff and $500,000 a year for the defendant. This type of expanded-sum solution would still be met if the total net worth of all participants substantially increased even if the net worth of some of the participants slightly decreased, provided that the decrease did not cause those participants to go below a minimum level of satisfaction.

Whatever solution is reached, it should not only be optimum in one or more of the above four ways, but should also enable affected outsiders to come out ahead who are not parties to the dispute or the negotiations. That excludes an agreement which greatly benefits the immediate parties, but at the substantial expense of others.

AN EXAMPLE FROM DISPUTE RESOLUTION

THE SITUATION

A good example from the field of resolving litigation disputes is where the plaintiff (or one side) demands $800 as a minimum to avoid going to trial or resorting to other non-settlement action. The defendant (or the other side) insists that it will not part with more than $200. So long as the dispute remains on that single dimension, there is no way that both sides can come out truly ahead. Whatever the plaintiff gains, the defendant loses, and vice versa. A traditional compromise would involve splitting the difference to settle for $500, or else going to trial. The plaintiff might console himself by saying that it could have been worse if liability were rejected at trial, since the plaintiff would then get $0. The defendant might console himself by saying that it could have been worse if liability were established at trial, since the defendant might then wind up paying $800 or more. In reality, the plaintiff has lost $300 if he really thought that $800 is what he deserved to get, and the defendant also lost $300 if he really thought that $200 is what he deserved to pay.

THE SOLUTION OF SMALL COSTS AND BIG BENEFITS

The same problem might be approached from a multi-criteria perspective by adding one or more additional criteria to the plaintiff's goal of maximizing dollars paid. The additional criteria could include products of the defendant. Those products might include insurance annuities, manufactured goods, or free transportation. Those criteria have in common that they cost relatively little per incremental unit for the defendant to produce if he is already in the business of producing them. They, however, may have considerable value to the plaintiff in view of their market price, even with liberal discounts.

For example, in the case just mentioned, suppose the defendant manufactures electronic equipment, including television sets or other electronic equipment worth over $800 to the plaintiff. The same equipment might be worth less than $200 to the defendant since the equipment has already been manufactured by the defendant. An exchange of a product like that is possible, maybe along with some cash to pay the plaintiff's attorney. It could result in the plaintiff gaining more than $800 in terms of the plaintiff's values and the defendant losing less than $200 in terms of the defendant's values. That is a multi-criteria dispute resolution in a litigation or rule-applying situation with mutually beneficial results. The best expectation of the plaintiff in the litigation example was probably to collect $800 since the plaintiff's initial demand tends to reflect an exaggerated high starting point. Likewise, the best expectation of the defendant was probably to have to pay only $200 since the defendant's initial offer also tends to reflect an exaggerated low starting point. Solutions like these can be referred to as super-optimum solutions because they are above the optimum or best that each side was initially expecting to achieve. This example is summarized in Table 1.

EXAMPLES FROM POLICY-MAKING

THE OUTSIDE OFFER

The minimum wage dispute could be used as an example of a potential super-optimum solution. The liberals in Congress are arguing for a minimum wage of approximately $4.50 an hour. The conservatives are arguing for approximately $4.00 an hour. A traditional compromise would be $4.25 an hour. That might be greeted as a victory by liberals since it is $0.90 more than the current $3.35. It might be greeted as a victory by conservatives since it is $.25 less than what the liberals are seeking.

A wage of $4.25 an hour, though, could be considered a loss for both sides. It is a loss to liberals if $4.50 an hour is necessary for minimum food, shelter, clothing. and other necessities for an average family of four. The $4.25 is a loss to conservatives if $4.00 an hour is the maximum that business firms can afford to pay to minimum-wage employees and thus anything higher than $4.00 an hour will mean laying off workers who will thereby suffer a lack of minimum food, shelter, clothing, and other necessities.

TABLE 14-1
A SUPER-OPTIMUM SOLUTION TO SETTLING VERSUS
GOING TO TRIAL

1A. FROM THE PLAINTIFF'S PERSPECTIVE

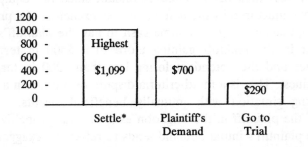

1B. FROM THE DEFENDANT'S PERSPECTIVE

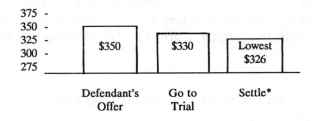

NOTES TO TABLE 14-1A:
1. The expected value of settling from the plaintiff's perspective is $1,099,000, as described in the text (the first bar).
2. The middle bar shows that the plaintiff's first demand or best expectation was $700,000.
3. The expected value of going to trial from the plaintiff's perspective is only $290,000, as described in the text (the third bar).

NOTES TO TABLE 14-1B:
1. The defendant's first offer or best expectation is $350,000 (the first bar).
2. The expected value of going to trial from the defendant's perspective is $330,000 (the second bar).
3. The expected value of settling from the defendant's perspective is only $326,000 (the third bar).
4. Note that the settlement is lower and thus better than the defendant's best expectation from the defendant's perspective.
5. The $326,000 settlement figure could be substantially lower and still bring the plaintiff to a settlement in view of the big gap between the settlement value and the trial value from the plaintiff's perspective, their children and grandchildren who might otherwise be caught in a cycle of unemployment, public aid, criminal activity, and lack of productivity.

A super-optimum solution might involve the minimum wage being raised to $4.75 an hour in terms of what each worker would receive, but simultaneously requiring each employer to pay only $3.75 an hour. The $1.00 difference would be paid by the government for every minimum-wage worker who would otherwise be unemployed either because the firm could not afford to hire the worker, or because the worker would not be sufficiently inspired to take the job at less than the increased minimum wage.

Under such an arrangement the liberals come out ahead of their initial bargaining position of $4.50 and probably ahead of their best expectations. Likewise the conservatives come out ahead of their initial bargaining position of $4.00 and probably ahead of their best expectations.

The government and the taxpayers might especially come out ahead by virtue of (1) the money saved in terms of public aid, public housing, Medicaid, and unemployment compensation, (2) the decreased cost of anti-social behavior associated with people who are embittered by unemployment or who resort to criminal sources of income, (3) the increase in the GNP as a result of the product these people produce and the accompanying increase in the taxes they pay, and (4) the better role models they now provide for their children and grandchildren who might otherwise be caught in a cycle of unemployment, public aid, criminal activity, and lack of productivity.

As an additional requirement for a business firm to be eligible to pay only $3.75 an hour, the firm would be expected to provide on-the-job training so the workers would become even more productive to the firm, the economy, and themselves. One thing to especially point out regarding this example is that by getting off the single track of the exchange of dollars between an employer and an employee, one can not only arrive at mutually beneficial solutions, but also at solutions that exceed the initial best expectations of both sides.

This example is summarized in Table 14-2. Table 14-2A shows the liberal, neutral, and conservative alternatives, as well as the super-optimum solution. Table 14-2B shows six criteria for judging among the alternatives, although the emphasis in the subsequent analysis for the sake of simplicity is just on the first two criteria. Table 14-2B also shows that liberals place a relatively high weight on paying a decent wage compared to conservatives. On the other hand, conservatives place a relatively high weight on avoiding overpayment compared to liberals. The other criteria are given middling weights on a 1-3 weighting scale for the criteria, where a 3 means relatively big importance, 2 means middling importance, and 1 means relatively low importance.

Table 14-2C shows how each alternative is scored on each criterion using

TABLE 14-2.   MINIMUM WAGES AS AN SOS POLICY EXAMPLE
INVOLVING A THIRD PARTY OFFER

2A. THE ALTERNATIVES

Alternative
1 SOS WAGE SUPP.	($4.75)	(To Workers)
2 +SUBSTANTIAL	($4.50)	(Liberal)
3 COMPROMISE	($4.25)	(Neutral)
4 +SLIGHT	($4.00)	(Conservative)
5 SOS WAGE SUPP.	($3.75)	(From Employers)

2B. THE CRITERIA

Criterion	Meas. Unit	Liberal Weights	Neutral Weights	Conserv. Weights
1 PAY DECENT WAGE	1-5 Scale	3.00	2.00	1.00
2 AVOID OVERPAYMENT		1.00	2.00	3.00
3 SAVE TAXES		2.00	2.00	2.00
4 EMPLOY UNEMPLOYED		2.00	2.00	2.00
5 ON-JOB TRAINING		2.00	2.00	2.00
6 +ROLE MODELS		2.00	2.00	2.00

2C. SCORES OF ALTERNATIVES ON CRITERIA

	Pay Decent	Avoid Over	Save Taxes	Employ Unemp	On-Job Train	+Role Model
+SUBSTANTIAL	4.00	3.00	3.00	2.00	2.00	2.00
COMPROMISE	3.50	3.50	3.00	2.50	2.50	2.50
+SLIGHT	3.00	4.00	3.00	3.00	3.00	3.00
SOS WAGE SUPP.	5.00	5.00	4.00	4.00	4.00	4.00

2D.   INITIAL ANALYSES

Alternative	Liberal Combined Rawscores	Neutral Combined Rawscores	Conserv. Combined Rawscores
1 +SUBSTANTIAL	15.00	14.00	13.00
2 COMPROMISE	14.00	14.00	14.00
3 +SLIGHT	13.00	14.00	15.00
4 SOS WAGE SUPP.	20.00	20.00	20.00

NOTES ON HOW THE WAGE SUPPLEMENT OPERATES:

1. The minimum wage gets raised to $4.75 per hour.
2. Employers need pay only $3.75 per hour for workers who were otherwise unemployed and who are provided with on-the-job training.
3. Those workers receive a wage supplement of $1 per hour from the government, bringing their total wage up to the $4.75 per hour new minimum wage.
4. The government provides the $1 per hour supplement to the employer to cover the minimum wage as an incentive to get the employer to hire an unemployed worker and to provide on-the-job training.
5. The government provides the $1 per hour supplement to the worker to cover the minimum wage as an incentive to get the worker to accept the job and to provide the worker with a decent wage to cover necessities.
6. The government provides the $1 per hour supplement which helps both the employer and the worker partly because
   (1) It relieves the taxpayer from various welfare burdens such as Medicaid, Medicare, food stamps, unemployment compensation, public housing, aid to dependent children, social security, disability aid, etc.
   (2) It facilitates better role models thereby relieving the taxpayer of the welfare burdens of future generations.
   (3) The new employment lessens costly anti-social behavior and attitudes such as crime, drugs, vice, bitterness, and depression.
   (4) The employment adds to the gross national product, helps create jobs for others, and adds to the tax base.

NOTES ON THE GENERAL ANALYSIS:

1. The alternatives can be generalized into the four basic alternatives of liberal, neutral, conservative, and super-optimum alternatives. (Table 2A)
2. The dollar amounts of $4.75, $4.50, $4.25, $4.00, and $3.75 are approximations partly to facilitate easy arithmetic. They do, however, approximate the actual minimum wage amounts over which liberals and conservatives are arguing in Congress as of 1989. (Table 2A)
3. Liberals and conservatives both place a positive weight on paying a decent wage and avoiding overpayment. They differ, however, in the relative weights which they are likely to assign to those two key criteria. (Table 2B)
4. The alternatives are scored on the criteria using a 1-5 scale where 5 means highly conducive to the goal, 4 means mildly conducive, 3 means neither conducive nor adverse, 2 means mildly adverse, and 1 means highly adverse to the goal. (Table 2C)
5. Liberals and conservatives tend to be roughly in agreement on the scores relating the alternatives to the criteria even though they disagree on the relative importance of the key criteria. (Table 2C)
6. The combined raw scores are determined by adding the weighted relation scores together. For example, a substantial increase receives 15 points in the liberal total by adding (3 times 4) to (1 times 3). For the sake of simplicity in this introductory analysis, only the two key criteria are used of paying a decent wage and avoiding overpayment. (Table 2D)
7. The wage supplement comes out so far ahead of the second-place alternative on each of the three totals that the only way the second-place alternative could be a winner is (1) if one or more of the goals were to be given a negative weight, or (2) if one or more of the relation scores were to go above 5, below 1, or otherwise be unreasonable. (Table 2D)

a 1-5 scoring scale for the relations. A 5 means the alternative is highly conducive to the goal relatively speaking, a 4 means mildly conducive, a 3 means neither conducive nor adverse, a 2 means mildly adverse, and a 1 means highly adverse. Thus the liberal solution has at least a mildly conducive effect on paying a decent wage, but a rather neutral effect on avoiding overpayment. The conservative solution is rather neutral on paying a decent wage, but mildly conducive on avoiding overpayment.

Table 14-2D shows the total scores for the liberal, neutral, and conservative alternatives. The first total column involves the liberal weights or multipliers of a 3 for paying a decent wage and a 1 for avoiding overpayment. With those weights the liberal alternative gets a total score of 15, which is 3 x 4 plus 1 x 3. The conservative alternative gets a total score of 13, which is 3 x 3 plus 1 x 4. The second total column involves the neutral weights of a middling 2 for each goal. With those weights, the liberal alternative gets a total score of 14, which is 2 x 4 plus 2 x 3. The third total column involves the conservative weights of a 1 for paying a decent wage and a 3 for avoiding overpayment. With those weights, the liberal alternative gets a relatively low score of 13, which is 1 x 4 plus 3 x 3.

COMBINING ALTERNATIVES INTO A CREATIVE SYNTHESIS

The kind of dispute resolution with which this chapter is especially concerned is disputes over public policies for dealing with various social problems. For example, in the controversy over how to provide legal services for the poor, liberals and Congress advocate salaried government lawyers by way of the Legal Services Corporation. Conservatives and the Reagan White House advocate a program of volunteer lawyers serving the poor. Both sides agree that the key criteria for deciding among the alternative delivery systems are (1) inexpensiveness, (2) accessibility, (3) political feasibility, and (4) competence. There is also rough agreement that volunteers are better on inexpensiveness and political feasibility, whereas salaried government lawyers are better on accessibility and competence. The big dispute as to the inputs for arriving at a conclusion is over the relative weights of the goals. The liberals place a higher weight on accessibility and competence, whereas the conservatives place a higher weight on inexpensiveness and political feasibility.

Perhaps the best way to resolve disputes over the relative weights of the goals (or for that matter over any disputed policy problem) is to try to find a new alternative that will please both sides in light of their differing weights, goals, perceptions, constraints, or other inputs. An example is working with the existing Legal Services Corporation, but requiring all Legal Services

Agencies to use 10% of their budgets to improve the accessibility and competence of volunteer lawyers. Accessibility can be improved by bringing the volunteer lawyers to the agency offices to meet with relevant clients. Competence can be improved through training manuals, training workshops, and matching specialist lawyers with clients who relate to their specialties. Such a 10% system may be better than a pure Legal Services Corporation even for those with liberal weights, because it provides a better benefit/cost ratio and greater political feasibility without decreasing accessibility or competence. Such a system is also better than the existing Legal Services Corporation from a perspective with conservative weights because it represents an improvement on all four goals over the existing system. Also if volunteering becomes mandatory for license renewal, then the volunteers are likely to dominate the system.

Computer output for the legal service example is given in Table 14-3. The first part of the Table shows how the two original alternatives and the new alternative score on the four criteria on a scale of 1-2, corresponding to "relatively no" and "relatively yes." The second part of the Table shows the same data, but with the scores on inexpensiveness and political feasibility doubled to reflect conservative values. The third part shows the same data as the first part, but with the scores doubled on accessibility and competence to reflect the liberal emphasis. The key item to note is that the optimizing compromise scores better than the favored alternative of either side using each side's own value system. Finding such optimizing compromises is facilitated by this kind of analysis.

CONTRASTED WITH OTHER TYPES OF SOLUTIONS

Disputes in adjudication or policymaking can take various forms. Perhaps the most basic form relates to the winning and losing dimension. In that regard, the solutions to disputes can be classified as follows:

1. Super-optimum solutions in which all sides come out ahead of their initial best expectations, as described above. At the opposite extreme is a super-malimum solution in which all sides come out worse than their initial worst expectations. That can be the case in a mutually destructive war, labor strike, or highly expensive litigation.
2. Pareto optimum solutions in which nobody comes out worse off and at least one side comes out better off. That is not a very favorable solution compared to a super-optimum solution. A Pareto malimum solution would

TABLE 14-3. AN EXAMPLE OF COMPUTER-AIDED MEDIATION

	Inexpen- siveness	Accessibility	Political Feasibility	Competence
3A. WITH UNWEIGHTED CRITERIA				
Volunteer	2.00	1.00	2.00	1.00
Salaried	1.00	2.00	1.00	2.00
SOS	1.50	2.00	2.00	2.00
3B. WITH CONSERVATIVE VALUES				
Volunteer	4.00	1.00	4.00	1.00
Salaried	2.00	2.00	2.00	2.00
SOS	3.00	2.00	4.00	2.00
3C. WITH LIBERAL VALUES				
Volunteer	2.00	2.00	2.00	2.00
Salaried	1.00	4.00	1.00	4.00
SOS	1.50	4.00	2.00	4.00

NOTES:

1. The alternative ways of providing legal counsel to the poor include:
   (1) Volunteer attorneys, favored by the White House
   (2) Salaried government attorneys, favored by the Congress
   (3) A compromise that involves continuing the salaried system, but requiring that 10 percent of its funding go to making volunteers more accessible and competent. (Table rows)
2. The criteria are inexpensiveness, accessibility, political feasibility, and competence. Each alternative is scored on each criterion on a scale from 1.00 to 2.00. (Table columns and cells)
3. Conservative values involve giving a weight of 2 to inexpensiveness and political feasibility when the other criteria receive a weight of 1. (Table 3B) Liberal values involve giving a weight of 2 to accessibility and competence when the other criteria receive a weight of 1. (Table 3C)
4. With conservative values, the volunteer system wins over the salaried system 10 points to 8. The compromise is an overall winner with 11 1/2 points. (Table 3B)
5. With liberal values, the salaried system wins over the volunteer system 10 points to 8. The compromise is an overall winner with 11 1/2 points. (Table 3C)
6. The "10 percent compromise" is thus a super winner in being better than the original best solution of both the conservatives and the liberals. (The third row in tables 3A, 3B, and 3C)

be one in which nobody is better off and at least one side is worse off.

3. A win-lose solution where what one side wins the other side loses. The net effect is zero when the losses are subtracted from the gains. This is the typical litigation dispute when one ignores the litigation costs.

4. A lose-lose solution where both sides are worse off than they were beforethe dispute began. This may often be the typical litigation dispute, or close to it when one includes litigation costs. Those costs are often so high that the so-called winner is also a loser. That is also often the case in labor-management disputes that result in a strike, and even more so in international disputes that result in going to war.

5. The so-called win-win solution. At first glance this sounds like a solution where everybody comes out ahead. What it typically refers to though is an illusion since the parties are only coming out ahead relative to their worst expectations. In this sense, the plaintiff is a winner no matter what the settlement is because the plaintiff could have won nothing if liability had been rejected at trial. Likewise, the defendant is a winner no matter what the settlement is because the defendant could have lost everything the plaintiff was asking for if liability had been established at trial. The parties are only fooling themselves in the same sense that someone who is obviously a loser tells himself he won because he could have done worse.

Another common way of classifying dispute resolutions is in terms of whether there is a third party present. In that sense, adjudication, arbitration, and mediation are frequently referred to as forms of three-party dispute resolution, and negotiation refers to two-party dispute resolution. Adjudication tends to mean a court or administrative agency that resolves disputes usually in a win-lose way. Arbitration tends to involve an ad hoc third party who is hired or obtained just for the immediate dispute, but who also tends to operate from a win-lose perspective. A mediator, like an arbitrator, tends to be ad hoc but seeks to have both sides arrive at mutually beneficial settlements which could be win-win, Pareto optimum, or even super-optimum, but not win-lose, or lose-lose. That distinction between three-party and two-party dispute resolution may be undesirable because it encourages two-party negotiation to go for a win-lose solution. It is possible when two negotiators are present for one or both of them to have a mediation perspective in the sense of seeking to truly bring about a super-optimum or Pareto optimum solution.

Another way of classifying dispute resolutions or policy solutions is in terms of the substance or subject matter. That can include such categories as disputes involving family members, neighbors, merchant-consumer situations, management-labor situations, litigation or rule-applying, legislation or rule-making, and international disputes. Those categories are meaningful in the sense that it is possible to tell a family dispute from an international dispute. Emphasizing those distinctions, however, may be undesirable because the same underlying principles may apply regardless of the subject matter. Those principles include (1) the desirability of getting off a single dimension into multiple criteria, (2) the desirability of generally seeking super-optimum solutions where all sides including society come out ahead of their best expectations, and (3) the usefulness of decision-aiding software for dealing with multi-criteria dispute resolution toward achieving super-optimum solutions.

Still another way of classifying solutions to policy controversies is in terms of the directions in which benefits and costs move. In a super-optimum solution, the benefits go up, and the costs go down. In a traditional solutions, the benefits may go up, but at the expense of increased costs; or the costs may go down, but at the expense of decreased benefits. In a super-malimum solution, both the benefits go down and the costs go up, which is the opposite of a super-optimum solution. Drug crackdowns can have that effect by being highly expensive, and yet encouraging more suppliers to enter the market by raising the sales price of drugs.

PROCEDURES FOR ARRIVING AT SUPER-OPTIMUM SOLUTIONS

NEW ALTERNATIVES

One procedure for arriving at super-optimum solutions is to think in terms of what is in the conservative alternative that liberals might like. And likewise, what is in the liberal alternative that conservatives might like. Then think whether it is possible to make a new alternative that will emphasize those two aspects.

Another technique is to emphasize the opposite. It involves saying what is in a conservative alternative that liberals especially dislike. What is in the liberal alternative that conservatives especially dislike. Then think about making a new alternative that eliminates those two aspects.

In arriving at super-optimum solutions in litigation settlements, one should especially try to find something that the defendant can give to the plaintiff that is not worth so much to the defendant but is worth a lot to the plaintiff. This may relate to a product that the defendant manufactures or sells which has a low variable cost to the defendant but a high market value to the plaintiff. An example is the defendant insurance company giving a valuable annuity to the plaintiff. Another example is the defendant manufacturer giving manufactured products to the plaintiff which the plaintiff can use. That kind of trade can be generalized to policy-making situations as well as litigation situations.

NEW GOALS

Another technique is not to concentrate on the alternatives as the above procedures do, but instead to concentrate on the goals. One way of doing that is to ask what goals are especially important to liberals, and what goals are especially important to conservatives. Then try to find alternatives that can simultaneously satisfy both of those goals. This technique could be illustrated by the minimum wage example where the goals do not change at all. Conservatives endorse the goal of low wages, and liberals endorse the goal of high wages. Or to put it differently, conservatives endorse the goal of providing a stimulating environment for business, liberals endorse the goal of preventing abuse of workers. The minimum wage supplement allows business to pay as low as $.40 per hour while the worker receives $1.40 per hour as a result of the voucher supplement.

A variation on that is to add new goals. The usual procedure starts with the conservative goals as givens in light of how they justify their current best alternative, and it starts with the liberal goals as givens in light of how they justify their current best alternative. This technique says to think about the goals conservatives tend to endorse that are not currently involved in the controversy, but that could be brought in to justify a new alternative. Likewise, what goals do liberals tend to endorse that are not currently involved in the controversy, but that could also be brought in. For this technique, a good example is the free speech controversy where liberals want virtually unrestricted free speech in order to stimulate creativity and conservatives want restrictions on free speech in order to have more order in the legal system. However, liberals also like due process, equal protection, and right to privacy. That raises questions as to whether it might be permissible to restrict free speech in order to satisfy those constitutional rights, where the restrictions are not so great, but the jeopardy of those other rights might be great. Likewise, conservatives like policies that are good for business. They might therefore readily endorse permissive free speech that relates to advertising, to trying to convince workers that they should not join unions or that relates to lobbying.

COMBINING ALTERNATIVES

An important technique is to find a policy that in effect combines two policies into one. On the first policy, liberals receive a lot, but conservatives give up relatively little. On the second policy, conservatives receive a lot but liberals give up relatively little.

BRINGING IN A THIRD PARTY

In the minimum wage example, conservatives get more than what they want, and liberals also get more than what they want. The important thing is that conservatives do not get by taking it from liberals, and liberals do not get by taking from conservatives. Instead, at least on the surface, they are both taking from a third party. In this context the third party in the short run is the federal government and the American taxpayer. In the long run, though, the taxpayer benefits if subsidizing the minimum wage results in putting to work people who otherwise would be receiving public aid or would be engaging in anti-social or possibly criminal behavior. The taxpayer especially benefits if combined with that minimum wage is an on-the-job training requirement that upgrades the skills of the workers so they substantially add to national productivity.

GETTING THE SOLUTION ADOPTED

One problem with super-optimum solutions is that they look so good that they may cause some people to think they might be some kind of a trap. An example is the Camp David Accords. That example is a classic super-optimum solution where Israel, Egypt, the United States, and everybody involved came out ahead of their original best expectations. According to the New York Times for March 26, 1989, however, Israeli intelligence at least at first opposed Anwar Sadat's visit to Israel and the Camp David Accords until close to the signing on the grounds that it all sounded so good, it must be a trap. The Israeli intelligence felt that Israel was being set up for a variation on the Yom Kippur war whereby Israel got into big trouble by relaxing its guard due to the holidays. They viewed this as an attempt to get them to relax their guard again, and that any minute the attack would begin. They were on a more intense alert at the time of the Camp David negotiations than they were at any other time during Israel's history. That nicely illustrates how super-optimum solutions can easily be viewed by people as a trap because they look so good that they are unbelievable. Traditional solutions are not so likely to be viewed as traps, and they are taken more at their face value, which is generally not much.

THE HELPFULNESS OF DECISION-AIDING SOFTWARE

Super-optimum solutions are not only facilitated by multi-criteria thinking, but also by decision-aiding software that is based on multi-criteria spreadsheets. A spreadsheet is nothing more than a table, matrix, or chart that has rows, columns, and cells which can be subject to manipulation in various ways.

In that context, the goals of each side are put on the columns. The alternatives available to them are put on the rows. The cells show how each alternative scores on each goal. A column at the far right shows the total scores for each alternative when adding across to take into consideration that the goals may be measured in different ways. The whole system is subject to what-if analysis, which can be especially useful for dealing with missing information.

Each side has its own spreadsheet perspective on the dispute that needs to be resolved. A super-optimum solution has been achieved if settling becomes the most desired alternative on each of those spreadsheets, and if such settling results in more net benefit to each side than its original favored alternative.

THE GENERIC SUPER-OPTIMUM SOLUTION FROM A SPREADSHEET PERSPECTIVE

From the examples that have thus far been given (especially Tables 14-1, 14-2, and 14-3), one can talk about the generic super-optimum solution from a spreadsheet perspective. Table 14-4 is designed to achieve that purpose. It shows the alternatives, criteria, scores of the alternatives on the criteria, and the initial analyses using general language. The alternatives are referred to as the conservative, compromise, liberal, or super-optimum alternatives. The criteria are referred to as the conservative, liberal, or neutral goals.

Each goal has a conservative weight and a liberal weight, since the conservatives and liberals especially differ in terms of the relative weights they assign to goals. The scores are expressed on a 1-5 scale to bring out the relations more clearly. The initial analysis shows how well each alternative scores overall in terms of the conservative weights and then in terms of the liberal weights.

Among the three basic alternatives, the conservative alternative is the winner using the conservative weights, as expected. The liberal alternative is

TABLE 14-4
THE GENERIC SOS SOLUTION
FROM A SPREADSHEET PERSPECTIVE

4A. THE ALTERNATIVES

Alternatives
1 CONSERVATIVE ALT.
2 COMPROMISE
3 LIBERAL ALT.
4 SOS1 (Dominating SOS)
5 SOS2 (Non-Dominating SOS)
6 SOS3 (New-Goal SOS)

4B. THE CRITERIA

Criterion	Meas. Unit	Conserv. Weights	Liberal Weights
1*CONSERVATIVE GOAL	1-5 Scale	3.00	1.00
2*LIBERAL GOAL		1.00	3.00
3 NEUTRAL GOAL		2.00	2.00

4C. SCORES OF ALTERNATIVES ON CRITERIA

	CONS.GOAL	LIB.GOAL	NEUT.GOAL
CONSERVATIVE ALT.	5.00	1.00	3.00
COMPROMISE	3.10	3.10	3.00
LIBERAL ALT.	1.00	5.00	3.00
SOS1	5.10	5.10	3.10
SOS2	4.50	4.50	2.90
SOS3	4.00	4.00	4.00

4D. INITIAL ANALYSES

Alternative	Conserv. Combined Raw Scores	Liberal Combined Raw Scores
1 CONSERVATIVE ALT.	16.00	8.00
2 COMPROMISE	12.40	12.40
3 LIBERAL ALT.	8.00	16.00
4 SOS1	20.40	20.40
5 SOS2	18.00	18.00
6 SOS3	16.00	16.00

NOTES TO THE ALTERNATIVES:

1. The conservative alternative is shown first because it tends to be the current alternative on which we would like to improve. The conservative alternative or set of alternatives in a policy problem tends to differ from the liberal alternatives in the relative extent to which it favors those who are relatively well off in a society, whereas the liberal alternative tends to favor those who are not so relatively well off.

2. The first super-optimum solution (and the most difficult to achieve) is to find an alternative that is better than the conservative, liberal, and compromise alternatives on all the goals. The second super-optimum solution is an alternative that is not better on all the goals than the other alternatives, but it is better on the overall or combined score adding across the goals. The third super-optimum solution is not better on all the goals and is not better on the overall score with the initial goals, but it is better on the overall score than the non-SOS alternatives when another goal is added.

NOTES TO THE CRITERIA:

3. The conservative goal or goals in this context are by definition goals that conservatives disproportionately favor, as indicated by the fact that those goals are given relatively high weight by conservatives. The liberal goals are likewise given relatively high weight by liberals. Note however that in a typical policy problem, conservatives tend to give positive weight to liberal goals (although relatively less weight than to conservative goals), and vice versa with liberals.

4. The scores of the alternatives on the criteria are based on a 1-5 scale for the sake of simplicity, although that does not have to be. Under a 1-5 scale, 5 means highly conducive to the goal, 4 means mildly conducive, 3 means neither conducive nor adverse, 2 means mildly adverse, and 1 means the alternative is highly adverse to the goal.

NOTES TO THE RELATION SCORES:

5. The conservative alternatives logically score high on the conservative goals and low on the liberal goals, and vice versa for the liberal alternatives. The compromise alternative scores slightly above the middle on each goal. That avoids ties in this analysis, and that is the general nature of compromises.

6. The scores of the super-optimum solutions on the conservative, liberal, and neutral goals are consistent with their definitions. Likewise the scores of

the alternatives on the neutral goal are consistent with the definition of the neutral goal as being between the conservative goal and the liberal goal in its normative direction.

NOTES TO THE INITIAL ANALYSES:

7. The combined raw scores are determined by adding the weighted relation scores together. For example, the conservative alternative receives 16 points using the conservative weights by adding (3 times 5) to (1 times 1). Using the liberal weights, the conservative alternative receives only 8 points by adding (1 times 5) to (3 times 1). For the sake of simplicity in this generic analysis, only the conservative goal and the liberal goal are used. The neutral goal has to be activated to enable the "New Goal SOS" to be a super-optimum solution.

8. Using the conservative weights, the conservative alternative logically comes out ahead of the liberal alternative, and vice versa using the liberal weights. The compromise alternative is the winner among those three alternatives with an aggregate score of 24.80 versus 24.00 for either the conservative or the liberal alternative, but the compromise alternative is only the second choice of both groups.

9. The three super-optimum alternatives all do better than the traditional compromise. What is more important, the three super-optimum alternatives all simultaneously do better than the conservative alternative using the conservative weights and they do better than the liberal alternative using the liberal weights. That is the essential characteristics of a super-optimum alternative. It is the new first choice of both groups.

10. Even the worst of the three super-optimum solutions comes out so far ahead of the traditional compromise that the only way the traditional compromise could be a winner is (1) if one or more of the goals were to be given a negative weight, or (2) if one or more of the relation scores were to go above 5, below 1, or otherwise be unreasonable.

then the loser, with the compromise in between. The opposite is true using the liberal weights. The super-optimum solution does better than any of the three basic alternatives using the conservative weights. It also does better than any of the three alternatives using the liberal weights. That is the essence of a super-optimum solution.

Three different types of super-optimum solutions are presented, but they all have that essential characteristic of being simultaneously better than the conservative first choice in light of the conservative goals and better than the liberal first choice in light of the liberal goals. Further details are given in the notes to the table corresponding to the sections of the table dealing with the alternatives, the criteria, the relation scores, and the initial analyses.

CLASSIFYING SUPER-OPTIMUM SOLUTIONS

Dimensions for classifying super-optimum solutions:

1. Whether or not super-optimum goals are involved.
2. Whether we are talking about dispute resolution or policy making.
3. Whether we are talking about all sides coming out ahead of their best expectations, or coming out ahead in a more absolute sense.
4. A typology that emphasizes the ways of arriving at super-optimum solutions, including:
   (1) An alternative that involves small costs to one side and big benefits to the other.
   (2) The outside offer.
   (3) The combination alternative that does well on everybody's goals.
   (4) A package of items that does not simply involve combining the liberal and conservative alternatives into a new synthesis. An example would be the Vera system for dealing with pre-trial release so as to simultaneously increase the probability of released defendants showing up without committing crimes (in order to please conservatives) while increasing the percentages of defendants who are released prior to trial (in order to please liberals). The Vera package of items includes screening for good risks, having released defendants report to the courthouse periodically prior to trial, notification immediately prior to trial, prosecution of no-shows, and reduction of delay between arrest and trial.
   (5) A super-optimum solution which involves removing the problem rather than trying to synthesize the liberal and conservative solutions. An

example would be better birth-control to deal with the abortion problem.

5. Whether or not a third party is present as a mediator, arbitrator, or adjudicator.
6. The situation can be classified by the substance or subject matter.
7. Whether or not decision-aiding software is present.
8. Ways of arriving at super-optimum solutions in terms of concentrating on the alternatives, the goals, or a better subclassification might be:
   (1) Developing a new alternative that is not a combination of the old alternatives.
   (2) Developing a new alternative that is a combination of the old alternatives.
   (3) Bringing in a new goal, which enables an old or new alternative to become super-optimum which it would not be without the new goal.
9. Classifying the super-optimum solutions in terms of:
   (1) Whether the solution is better or at least as good on all goals as the original alternatives.   This is a solution that is dominating.
   (2) Whether the solution is better than all the original alternatives on the summation score but not necessarily on every criterion.   This is the non-dominating super-optimum solution.
   (3) The non-dominating super-optimum solution that requires an additional goal to receive the highest summation score.

MUTUALLY BENEFICIAL TRENDS

Table 14-5 summarizes some of the trends in specific policy fields. The overall idea is that there have been increased benefits for people who had few rights as of the base years of 1910, 1930, or 1950. These people have been the immediate beneficiaries of the policy changes. It is, however, unduly narrow to limit the analysis to those immediate effects. The longer-term and broader effects have also been to benefit the dominant groups and the total society.

This is shown, for example, on the top row. Labor has benefitted from better wages, shorter hours, better working conditions, the ending of child labor, and the lessening of race and sex discrimination. Also highly important is the stimulus those labor policies have had on encouraging the development and adoption of labor-saving technology. The United States as of 1980 might still be using slave labor or cheap immigrant labor and be a backward low-technology country if it had not been for the successful efforts of labor unions

TABLE 14-5
SOME TRENDS IN SPECIFIC POLICY FIELDS

POLICY FIELDS	BENEFITS FOR THE HAVE NOTES	BENEFITS FOR THE HAVES OR ALL
ECONOMIC POLICY		
Labor	Better wages, hours, working conditions. No child labor. Less discrimination.	Stimulus to labor-saving technology. Happier and more productive workers.
Consumer	More rights concerning product liability.	Stimulus to providing better products & greater sales.
POLITICAL-LEGAL POLICY		
Free Speech	More rights in politics, art, and commerce	Stimulus to creativity.
Due process & criminal justice	More rights to counsel, notice, hearings.	More respect for the law.
Equal treatment	More rights to blacks, women, & the poor on voting, criminal justice, schools, employment, housing, & consumer.	More equality of opportunity and allocation on the basis of merit.
Government reform	Less corruption, intimidation, & incompetence.	More effectiveness & efficiency.
World peace & trade	Increased standards of living for developing countries.	Uplifted countries become good trading partners.

TABLE 14-5
SOME TRENDS IN SPECIFIC POLICY FIELDS (Continued)

POLICY FIELDS	BENEFITS FOR THE HAVE NOTES	BENEFITS FOR THE HAVES OR ALL
SOCIAL POLICY		
Poverty	More rights as employees, consumers, tenants, welfare recipients, & family members.	The same rights apply to middle-class employees, consumers, tenants, & family members.
Education	More access to more education.	More efficient economy from better training. Less welfare.
SCIENCE POLICY		
Environmnt	More rights to cleaner air, water, solid waste, noise, radiation, and conservation.	The same rights are important to all people.
Health	More access to medical help.	That includes catastrophic help from which even the rich benefit.

and working class people to increase the cost of their labor. A third-level result is that the labor-saving technology has made labor more productive and more skilled. This has the effect of increasing wages still further, thereby stimulating greater consumption and the creation of jobs, especially in service fields.

Likewise, one can go through each of the 11 policy fields and see that the initial policy changes have tended in a direction of increasing the rights of the have not's. Those increases have in turn stimulated benefits for the total society, regardless whether one is talking about consumer rights, free speech, criminal justice, equal treatment, government reform, world peace-trade, poverty, education, environment, or health.

STREAMS OF RELEVANT IDEAS AND LITERATURE

There are a number of relevant ideas and literature that have played important parts in the development of the concept of achieving super-optimum solutions. One stream of ideas relates to the use of computers to facilitate systematic, evaluative, and explanatory reasoning. Some of that key literature includes Patrick Humphreys and Ayleen Wisudha, *Methods and Tools for Structuring and Analyzing Decision Problems* (London: London School of Economics and Political Science, 1987); Saul Gass et al. (eds.), *Impacts of Microcomputers on Operations Research* (Amsterdam: North-Holland, 1986); and S. Nagel, *Evaluation Analysis with Microcomputers* (Greenwich, CT: JAI Press, 1989).

The second stream of inspiration has come from people in the field of mediation and alternative dispute resolution. Some of that key literature includes Lawrence Susskind and Jeffrey Cruikshank, *Breaking the Impasse: Consensual Approaches to Resolving Disputes* (New York: Basic Books, 1987); Stephen Goldberg, Eric Green, and Frank Sander (eds.), *Dispute Resolution* (Boston: Little, Brown, 1984); and S. Nagel and M. Mills, "Microcomputers, P/G%, and Dispute Resolution," 2 *Ohio State Journal on Dispute Resolution* 187-223 (1987).

The third stream of inspiration has come from people who are expansionist thinkers. This includes the conservative economist Arthur Laffer and the liberal economist Robert Reich. They both have in common a belief that policy problems can be resolved by expanding the total pie of resources or other things of value available to be distributed to the disputants. The expansion can come from well-placed subsidies and tax breaks with strings attached to increase national productivity. That kind of thinking can apply to disputes involving blacks-whites, rich-poor, males-females, North-South, urban-rural, and other categories of societal disputants. Some of that key literature includes Ira Magaziner and Robert Reich, *Minding America's Business: The Decline and Rise of the American Economy* (New York: Harcourt, Brace, 1982); and Paul Roberts, *The Supply Side Revolution* (Cambridge, Mass: Harvard University Press, 1984).

Bibliography

Agranoff, Robert. The New Style in Election Campaigns. Boston: Holbrook Press, 1972.

Alberts, David. A Plan for Measuring the Performance of Social Programs: The Application of Operations Research Methodology. New York: Praeger, 1970.

American Bar Association. Minimum Standards for Criminal Justice. Chicago, Il.: Institute of Judicial Administration, a series from 1967 on.

ABA. Standards Relating to Trial Courts. Chicago, Il.: ABA, 1976.

Anderson, James. Public Policy-Making. New York: Holt, Rinehart and Winston, 1979.

Arens, Richard and Harold Lasswell. In Defense of the Public Order: The Emerging Field of Sanction Law. New York: Columbia University Press, 1961.

Aron, Nan. Liberty and Justice for All: Public Interest Law in the 1980s and Beyond. Denver, Co.: Westview, 1989.

Assoc. Bar. N.Y.C. Impartial Medical Testimony. New York: Macmillan, 1956.

Baird, Bruce.   Introduction to Decision Analysis.   Belmont, Ca.:   Duxbury, 1978.

Barnes, David.   Statistics as Proof: Fundamentals of Quantitative Evidence. Boston: Little, Brown, 1983.

Baumol, William.   Economic Theory and Operations Analysis.   Englewood Cliffs, N.J.: Prentice-Hall, 1965.

Becker, Gary and William Landes, eds.   Essays in the Economics of Crime and Punishment.   New York: Columbia University Press, 1974.

Beltrami, Edward.   Models for Public Systems Analysis.   New York: Academic Press, 1977.

Black, Guy. The Application of Systems Analysis to Government Operations. New York: Praeger, 1968.

Blalock, Hubert.   Causal Inferences in Nonexperimental Research.   Chapel Hill: Univ. of North Carolina Press, 1964.

Blalock, Hubert. Causal Models in the Social Sciences. Chicago, Il.: Aldine, 1972.

Blalock, Hubert. Social Statistics. New York: McGraw Hill, 1960.

Blalock, Hubert. Social Statistics. New York: McGraw-Hill, 1973.

Borko, H. Computer Applications in the Behavioral Sciences. Englewood Cliffs, N.J.: Prentice-Hall, 1962.

Brewer, Garry and Peter deLeon.   The Foundations of Policy Analysis. Homewood, Ill.: Dorsey, 1983.

Buros, O., ed.   Mental Measurements Yearbook.   Highland Park, N.J.: Gryphon Press, 1938-59.

Burris, R., et al. Teaching Law with Computers: A Collection of Essays. Boulder, CO: Westview, 1979.

Cairns, H. The Theory of Legal Science. Chapel Hill, NC: University of North Carolina, 1941.

Carley, Michael. Rational Techniques in Policy Analysis. London: Heinemann, 1980.

Carr, R. The Supreme Court and Judical Review. New York: Rinehart, 1942.

Caterall, James, ed. Economic Evaluation of Public Programs. San Francisco, Ca.: Jossey-Bass, 1985.

Channels, Noreen. Social Science Methods in the Legal Process. New York: Rowman and Allanheld, 1985.

Cherns, Albert. Using the Social Science and Social Problem Solving. London: Routledge and Kegan Paul, 1979.

Churchman, West, Russell Ackoff and Arnoff. Introduction to Operations Research. New York: Wiley, 1957.

Cohen, Jacob and Patricia Cohen. Applied Multiple Regression/Correlation Analysis for the Behavioral Sciences. Hillsdale, N.J.: Erlbaum, 1975.

Conway, R., et al. Theory of Scheduling. Reading, Mass.: Addison Wesley, 1967.

Cooper, George, et al. Law and Poverty: Cases and Materials. St. Paul, Minn.: West, 1973.

Davis, Floyd, et al. Society and the Law: New Meanings for an Old Profession. New York: Free Press of Glencoe, 1962.

Dean, H. Judicial Review and Democracy. New York: Random House, 1966.

Dorfman, R. Measuring Benefits of Government Investments. Washington, D.C.: Brookings, 1964.

Draper, N.R. and H. Smith. Applied Regression Analysis. New York: Wiley, 1966.

Dror, Yehezkel. Public Policy-making Reexamined. New Brunswick, N.J.: Transaction Books, 1983.

Dubois, Philip, ed. The Analysis of Judicial Reform. Lexington, Mass.:

Lexington-Heath, 1982.

Dunn, William, ed.   Values, Ethics, and the Practice of Policy Analysis. Lexington, Mass.: Lexington-Heath, 1983.

Dunn, William. Public Policy Analysis. Englewood Cliff, N.J.: Prentice-Hall, 1981.

Dutta, M. Econometric Methods. Cincinnati, Oh.: South-Western, 1975.

Easton, Allan. Complex Managerial Decisions Involving Multiple Objectives. New York: Wiley, 1973.

Easton, David. The Analysis of Political Structure. London, Routledge, 1990.

Edwards, Allen. An Introduction to Linear Regression and Correlation. San Francisco, Ca.: Freeman, 1976.

Erikson, W. and O. Hall.   Computer Models for Management Science. Reading, Mass.: Addison Wesley, 1986.

Evan, ed. Law and Sociology. New York: Free Press of Glencoe, 1962.

Evan, William.   Social Structure and Law: Theoretical and Empirical Perspectives. Beverly Hills, Ca.: Sage, 1990.

Eyestone, Robert. From Social Issues to Public Policy. New York: Wiley, 1978.

Fleishman, Joel and Bruce Payne. Ethical Dilemmas and the Education of Policy-Makers. Hastings-on-Hudson, N.Y.: Hastings Center, 1981.

Frank, J. Courts on Trial: Myth and Reality in American Justice. Princeton, N.J.: Princeton University Press, 1950.

Freed, D. and P. Wald.   Bail in the United States.   Washington, D.C.: Government Printing Office, 1964.

Friedland, Edward.   Introduction to Concepts of Rationality in Political Science. Morristown, N.J.: General Learning Press, 1974.

Friedman, B. Punched Card Primer. Chicago, Il.: Public Administration Science, 1965.

Friedman, L. and S. Macaulay, eds. Law and the Behavioral Sciences. Indianapolis, IN: Bobbs-Merrill, 1969.

Friendly, A. and R. Goldfarb. Crime and Publicity. New York: Twentieth Century Fund, 1967.

Frohock, Fred. Public Policy: Scope and Logic. Englewood Cliffs, N.J.: Prentice-Hall, 1979.

Gass, Saul, et al., eds. Impacts of Microcomputers on Operations Research. Amsterdam: North-Holland, 1986.

Gillmore, D.M. Free Press and Fair Trial. Washington, D.C.: Public Affairs Press, 1966.

Glaser, D. The Effectiveness of a Prison and Parole System. Indianapolis: Bobbs-Merrill, 1964.

Glaser, Edward, Harold Abelson, and Kathalee Garrison. Putting Knowledge to Use: Facilitating the Diffusion of Knowledge and the Implementation of Planned Change. San Francisco, Ca.: Jossey-Bass, 1983.

Gohagan, John. Quantitative Analysis for Public Policy. Hightstown, N.J.: McGraw-Hill, 1980.

Goldberg, Stephen, Eric Green and Frank Sander, eds. Dispute Resolution. Boston, Mass.: Little, Brown, 1984.

Goldfarb, R. Ransom: A Critique of the American Bail System. New York: Harper & Row, 1965.

Goode, W. and P. Hatt. Methods in Social Research. New York: McGraw Hill, 1952.

Gottfredson, Don and Michael Tonry, eds. Prediction and Classification: Criminal Justice Decision Making. Chicago, Il.: University of Chicago Press, 1987.

Gramlich, Edward. Benefit-Cost Analysis of Government Programs. Englewood Cliffs, N.J.: Prentice-Hall, 1981.

Greenberger, et al. Models in the Policy Process. New York: Russell Sage,

1976.

Gregg, Phillip, ed. Problems of Theory in Policy Analysis. Lexington, Mass.: Lexington-Heath, 1976.

Guilford, J. Fundamental Statistics in Psychology and Education. New York: McGraw Hill, 1956.

Guilford, J. Psychometric Methods. New York: McGraw Hill, 1954.

Handler, Joel. Social Movements and the Legal System: A Theory of Law Reform and Social Change. New York: Academic Press, 1978.

Harris, Clifford. The Break-Even Handbook. Englewood Cliff, N.J.: Prentice-Hall, 1978.

Haynes, E. The Selection and Tenure of Judges. New York: National Conference of Judicial Councils, 1944.

Helly, Walter. Urban Systems Models. New York: Academic Press, 1975.

Himmelblau, David. Applied Nonlinear Programming. Hightstown, N.J.: McGraw-Hill, 1973.

Hoaglin, David, et al. Data for Decisions: Information Strategies for Policymakers. Cambridge, Mass.: Abt, 1982.

Hoebel, E. Law of Primitive Man. Cambridge, Mass.: Harvard University Press, 1954.

Hoos, Ida. Systems Analysis in Public Policy: A Critique. Berkeley, Ca.: University of California Press, 1972.

Horowitz, Irving and James Katz. Social Science and Public Policy in the United States. New York: Praeger, 1975.

Humphreys, Patrick and Ayleen Wisudha. Methods and Tools for Structuring and Analyzing Decision Problems. London: London School of Economics and Political Science, 1987.

Humphreys, P. and J. Vecsenyi, eds. High Level Decision Support: Lessons from Case Studies. Amsterdam: North Holland, 1986.

Hunting and Neuwirth. Who Sues in New York City. New York: Joint Committee on Court Calendar Congestion, 1962.

Jacob, Herbert, ed. The Potential for Reform of Criminal Justice. Beverly Hills, Ca.: Sage, 1974.

James, Dorothy, ed. Analyzying Poverty Policy. Lexington, Mass.: Lexington-Heath, 1975.

James, H. Crisis in the Courts. New York: McKay, 1968.

Johnson, David and Paul Mode. Improving Law Firm Productivity by Encouraging Lawyers' Use of Personal Computers. New York: Harcourt Brace Jovanovich, 1985.

Joiner, C. Civil Justice and the Jury. Englewood Cliffs, N.J.: Prentice-Hall, 1962.

Jones, Charles. An Introduction to the Study of Public Policy. N. Scituate, Mass.: Duxbury, 1977.

Jones, H., ed. Legal Method: Cases and Text Materials. Mineola, N.Y.: Foundation Press, 1980.

Jones, H. The Courts, the Public, and the Law Explosion. Englewood Cliffs, N.J.: Prentice Hall, 1965.

Kalven, H. and H. Zeisel. The American Jury. Boston, Mass.: Litte Brown, 1966.

Kaplan, Martin, ed. The Impact of Social Psychology on Procedural Justice. Springfield, Il.: Charles Thomas, 1986.

Kaplan, Martin and Steven Schwartz, eds. Human Judgement and Decision Process. New York: Academic Press, 1975.

Kassourf, Sheen. Normative Decision Making. Englewood Cliff, N.J.: Prentice-Hall, 1970.

Katsh, Ethan, ed. Taking Sides: Clashing Views on Controversial Legal Issues. Guilford, Conn.: Dushkin, 1991.

Kempin, F. Legal History: Law and Social Change. Englewood Cliffs, N.J.:

Prentice-Hall, 1963.

Kerr, N. and R. Bray, eds. The Psychology of the Courtroom. New York: Academic Press, 1982.

Klein, Fannie, ed. The Improvement of the Administration of Justice. Chicago, Il.: American Bar Association, 1981.

Kotler, Philip. Marketing Decision Making: A Model Building Approach. New York: Holt, 1971.

Laidlaw, Charles. Linear Programming for Urban Development Plan Evaluation. New York: Praeger, 1972.

Larson, Arthur. The International Rule of Law: A Report to the Commmittee on Research for Peace. New York: Institute for International Order, 1961.

Lasswell, Harold. A Pre-View of Policy Sciences. New York: Elsevier, 1971.

Lee, Sange. Linear Optimizing for Management. Princeton, N.J.: Petrocelli/Charter, 1976.

Lee, Wayne. Decision Theory and Human Behavior. New York: Wiley, 1971.

Lerner, Daniel and Harold Lasswell, eds. Policy Sciences. Palo Alto, Ca.: Stanford, 1951.

Lewis, Don. Quantitative Methods in Psychology. Iowa City: Univ. of Iowa Press, 1966.

Leys, Wayne. Ethics for Policy Decisions: The Art of Asking Deliberative Questions. Englewood Cliffs, N.J.: Prentice-Hall, 1952.

Lindblom, Charles and David Cohen. Usable Knowledge: Social Science and Social Problem Solving. New Haven, Conn.: Yale, 1979.

Lindblom, Charles. The Policy-Making Process. New Haven, Conn.: Yale, 1980.

Lindzey, G., ed. Handbook of Social Psychology. Reading, Mass.:

Addison-Wesley, 1954.

Lipson, Leon and Stanton Wheeler, eds. Law and the Social Sciences. New York: Russell Sage Foundation, 1986.

Llewelleyn, K. The Common Law Tradition: Deciding Appeals. Boston: Little Brown, 1960.

Llewellyn, Robert. Linear Programming. New York: Holt, 1963.

Loh, Wallace, ed. Social Research in the Judicial Process: Cases, Readings, and Text. New York: Russell Sage Foundation, 1984.

MacIver, R. Social Causation. New York: Harper, 1964.

Mack, Ruth. Planning on Uncertainty: Decision Making in Business and Government Administration. New York: Wiley, 1971.

MacRae, Duncan and James Wilde. Policy Analysis for Public Decisions. N. Scituate, Mass.: Duxbury, 1979.

Magaziner, Ira and Robert Reich. Minding America's Business: The Decline and Rise of the American Economy. New York: Harcourt, Brace, 1982.

Mason, M. An Introduction to Using Computers in the Law. St. Paul, Minn: West Publishing, 1984.

Matlack, William. Statistics for Public Policy and Management. N. Scituate, Mass.: Duxbury, 1980.

May, Judith and Aaron Wildavsky, eds. The Policy Circle. Beverly Hills, Ca.: Sage, 1978.

McCarty, D.G. Psychology and the Law. Englewood Cliffs, N.J.: Prentice Hall, 1960.

McCormick, T. and R. Francis. Methods of Research in the Behavioral Sciences. New York: Harper, 1958

McGaw, Dickinson and George Satson. Political Social Inquiry. New York: Wiley, 1976.

McKean, Roland. Efficiency in Government through Systems Analysis. New York: Wiley, 1958.

McKenna, Christopher. Quantitative Methods for Public Decision Making. Hightstown, N.J.: McGraw-Hill, 1980.

McMillan, Claude, Jr. Mathematical Programming: An Introduction to the Design and Application of Optimal Decision Machines. New York: Wiley, 1970.

McPheters, Lee and William Stronge, eds. The Economics of Crime and Law Enforcement. Springfield, Ill.: Thomas, 1976.

McRae, Duncan. The Social Function of Social Science. New Haven, Conn.: Yale, 1976.

Miller, David and Martin Starr. Executive Decisions and Operations Research. Englewood Cliffs, N.J.: Prentice-Hall, 1960.

Mishan, Ezra. Cost-Benefit Analysis. New York: Praeger, 1976.

Mitra, Gautam, ed. Computer Assisted Decision Making: Expert Systems, Decision Analysis, Mathematical Programming. Amsterdam: North Holland, 1986.

Moore, Carl. Profitable Applications of the Break-Even System. Englewood Cliffs, N.J.: Prentice-Hall, 1971.

Mueller, et al. Statistical Reasoning in Sociology. Boston, Mass.: Houghton Mifflin, 1970.

Myrdal, Gunner. An American Dilemma. New York: Harper, 1944.

Nachmias, David and Chava Nachmias. Research Methods in the Social Sciences. New York: St. Martin's, 1981.

Nagel, S. Causation, Prediction, and Legal Analysis. Westport, Conn.: Quorum Books, 1986.

Nagel, S. Comparing Elected and Appointed Judicial Systems. Beverly Hills, Ca.: Sage American Politics Series, 1973.

Nagel, S., ed. Basic Literature in Policy Studies: A Comprehensive

Bibliography. Greenwich, Conn.: JAI Press, 1984.

Nagel, S., ed. Encyclopedia of Policy Studies. New York: Marcel Dekker, 1983.

Nagel, S. Evaluation Analysis with Microcomputers. Greenwich, Conn.: JAI Press, 1988.

Nagel, S. Improving the Legal Process: Effects of Alternatives. Lexington, Mass.: Lexington-Heath, 1975.

Nagel, S. Law, Policy, and Optimizing Analysis. Westport, Conn.: Quorum Books, 1986.

Nagel, S. Microcomputers as Decision Aids in Law Practice. Westport, Conn.: Greenwood-Quorum, 1987

Nagel, S. Minimizing Costs and Maximizing Benefits in Providing Legal Services to the Poor. Beverly Hills, Ca.: Sage, 1973.

Nagel, S. Policy Evaluation: Making Optimum Decisions. New York: Praeger, 1982.

Nagel, S. Public Policy: Goals, Means, and Methods. New York: St. Martin's, 1984.

Nagel, S. The Legal Process from a Behavioral Perspective. Homewood, Ill: Dorsey, 1969.

Nagel, S. Using Personal Computers for Decision-Making in Law Practice. Philadelphia: American Law Institute, 1986.

Nagel, S., John Long, and Miriam Mills. Evaluation Analysis with Microcomputers. Greenwich, Conn.: JAI Press, 1989.

Nagel, S. and M. Neef. Decision Theory and the Legal Process. Lexington, Mass.: Lexington-Heath, 1979.

Nagel, S. and M. Neef. Legal Policy Analysis: Finding an Optimum Level or Mix. Lexington, Mass.: Lexington-Heath, 1977.

Nagel, S. and M. Neef. Policy Analysis: In Social Science Research. Beverly Hills, Calif.: Sage, 1979.

Nagel, S. and M. Neef. The Application of Mixed Strategies: Civil Rights and Other Multiple-Activity Policies. Beverly Hills, Ca.: Sage, 1976.

Nathan, Richard. Social Science in Government: Uses and Misuses. New York: Basic Books, 1988.

Orfield, Gary. Must We Bus? Washington, D.C.: Brookings, 1978.

Parsons, T., et al., eds. Theories of Society. New York: Free Press of Glencoe, 1961.

Parten, M. Surveys, Polls, and Samples--Practical Procedures. New York: Harper, 1950.

Patton, Carl and David Sawicki. Basic Methods of Policy Analysis and Planning. Englewood Cliffs, N.J.: Prentice Hall, 1986.

Payne, S. The Art of Asking Questions. Princeton, N.J.: Princeton University Press, 1951.

Posner, Richard. Economic Analysis of Law. Boston, Mass.: Little, Brown, 1977.

Quade, Edward and Grace Carter. Analysis for Public Decisions. Amsterdam: North-Holland, 1989.

Quade, Edward and Hugh Miser, eds. Handbook of Systems Analysis. New York: Elsevier, 1984.

Quade, Edward. Analysis for Public Decisions. Amsterdam: North Holland, 1982.

Quade, Edward. Analysis for Public Decisions. New York: Elsevier, 1975.

Rasmusson, T., ed. System Science and Jurisprudence. Lansing, Mich.: Spartan Press, 1986.

Remer, D. Computer Power for Your Law Office. Berkeley, Ca.: Sybex, 1983.

Richardson, Jacques, ed. Models of Reality: Shaping Thought and Action. Mt. Airy, Md.: Lomond Books, 1984.

Richmond, Samuel. Operations Research for Management Decisions. New York: Ronald Press, 1968.

Roberts, Paul. The Supply Side Revolution. Cambridge, Mass.: Harvard University Press, 1984.

Rossi, Peter, Howard Freeman and Sonia Wright. Evaluation: A Systematic Approach. Beverly Hills, Calif.: Sage, 1979.

Sales, B., ed. The Trial Process. New York: Plenum Press, 1981.

Samuelson, Paul. Economics: An Introductory Analysis. Hightstown, N.J.: McGraw-Hill, 1980.

Sassone, Peter and William Schaefer. Cost-Benefit Analysis: A Handbook. New York: Academic Press, 1978.

Sawaragi, Yoshikazu, ed. Multiple-Criteria Decision Making. Berlin: Springer-Verlag, 1987.

Sayre, W. and Kaufman, H. Governing New York. New York: Russell Sage Foundation, 1960.

Schattschneider, E.E., et al. A Guide to the Study of Public Affairs. New York: Dryden, 1952.

Schubert, G., ed. Judicial Behavior: A Reader in Theory and Research. Chicago, Il.: Rand McNally, 1964.

Scioli, Frank and Thomas Cook, eds. Methodologies for Analyzing Public Policies. Lexington, Mass.: Lexington-Heath, 1975.

Sellin, J. The Death Penalty. Philadelphia: American Law Institute, 1959.

Selltiz, C., et al. Research Methods in Social Relations. New York: Society for Psychological Study of Social Sciences,1959.

Shoup, Donald and Stephen Mehay. Program Budgeting for Urban Policy Services. New York: Praeger, 1971.

Siegal, S. Non-Parametric Statistics for the Behavioral Sciences. New York: McGraw Hill, 1956.

Sigler, Jay and Benjamin Beede. The Legal Sources of Public Policy. Lexington, Mass.: Lexington-Heath, 1977.

Silverstein, L. Defense of the Poor. Boston: Litte Brown, 1966.

Silverstein, T. Defense of the Poor in Criminal Cases in American State Courts: A Preliminary Summary. Chicago, Il.: ABA, 1964.

Simon, Herbert. Reason in Human Affairs. Palo Alto, Ca.: Stanford, 1983.

Skolnick, J. Justice without Trial: Law Enforcement in a Democratic Society. New York: John Wiley, 1967.

Statsky, W. and J. Wernet. Case Analysis and Fundamentals of Legal Writing. St. Paul, Minn.: West, 1977.

Stinchcombe, Arthur. Constructing Social Theories. New York: Harcourt, 1968.

Stokey, Edith and Richard Zeckhauser. A Primer for Policy Analysis. New York: Norton, 1978.

Susskind, Lawrence and Jeffrey Cruikshank.   Breaking the Impasse: Consensual Approaches to Resolving Disputes. New York: Basic Books, 1987.

Talarico, Susette, ed. Criminal Justice Research: Approaches, Problems, and Policy. Cincinatti, Oh.: Anderson, 1980.

Tappan, P. Crime, Justice, and Correction. New York: McGraw-Hill, 1960.

Thode, W., et al., eds.   Introduction to the Study of Law: Cases and Materials. Mineola, N.Y.: Foundation, 1970.

Thompson, Mark. Benefit-Cost Analysis for Program Evaluation. Beverly Hills, Calif.: Sage, 1980.

Thompson, Mark. Decision Analysis for Porgram Evaluation. Cambridge, Mass.: Ballinger, 1982.

Tufte, Edward. Data Analysis for Politics and Policy. Englewood Cliffs, N.J.: Prentice-Hall, 1974.

Tullock, Gordon. The Logic of the Law. New York: Basic Books, 1971.

Tullock, Gordon. Trials on Trial: The Pure Theory of Legal Procedure. New York, Columbia University Press, 1980.

Vanderbilt, A. Minimum Standards of Judical Administration. New York: National Conference of Judical Councils, 1949.

Varner, W. Computing with Desk Calculators. New York: Rinehart, 1957.

Vinson, Donald and Philip Anthony. Social Science Research Methods for Litigation. New York: Michie, 1985.

Wahlke, et al. The Legislative System: Explorations in Legislative Behavior. New York: Wiley, 1962.

Wald, P. Law and Poverty. Washington, D.C.: Government Printing Office, 1965.

Walker, H. and J. Lev. Statistical Inference. New York: Holt, 1953.

Watson, R. and R. Downing. The Politics of the Bench and the Bar: Judicial Selection Under the Missouri Non-partisan Court Plan. New York: John Wiley, 1969.

Weiss, Carol, ed. Using Social Research in Public Policy Making. Lexington, Mass.: Lexington-Heath, 1977.

White, Michael, et al. Managing Public Systems: Analytic Techniques for Public Administration. Belmont, Calif.: Duxbury, 1980.

Wilson, James Q., ed. Crime and Public Policy. New Brunswick, N.J.: Transaction, 1983.

Wilson, O.W. Police Administration. New York: McGraw Hill, 1963.

Wright, Burton, et al. Criminal Justice and the Social Sciences. Philadelphia: Saunders, 1978.

Young, R., ed. Approaches to the Study of Politics. Evanston, Ill.: Northwestern University Press, 1958.

Yuker, H. A Guide to Statistical Calculations. New York: Putnam, 1958.

Zeisel, Hans. Say It With Figures. New York: Harper and Row, 1968.

Zeisel, H., H. Kalven and B. Bucholz. Delay in the Court. Boston: Little Brown, 1959.

Names Index

Subject Index